W9-AAR-853

WASHINGTON

OFF THE BEATEN PATH ®

WITHDRAWN

OFF THE BEATEN PATH® SERIES

TENTH EDITION

WASHINGTON

OFF THE BEATEN PATH®

DISCOVER YOUR FUN

REVISED BY MEGAN HILL

Globe
Pequot

Guilford, Connecticut

All the information in this guidebook is subject to change. We recommend that you call ahead to obtain current information before traveling.

Globe Pequot

An imprint of The Rowman & Littlefield Publishing Group, Inc.
4501 Forbes Blvd., Ste. 200
Lanham, MD 20706
www.rowman.com

Distributed by NATIONAL BOOK NETWORK

British Library Cataloguing in Publication Information available

Library of Congress Cataloging-in-Publication Data available

ISBN 978-1-4930-3763-6 (paperback)
ISBN 978-1-4930-3764-3 (e-book)

∞™ The paper used in this publication meets the minimum requirements of American National Standard for Information Sciences—Permanence of Paper for Printed Library Materials, ANSI/NISO Z39.48-1992

Printed in the United States of America

Contents

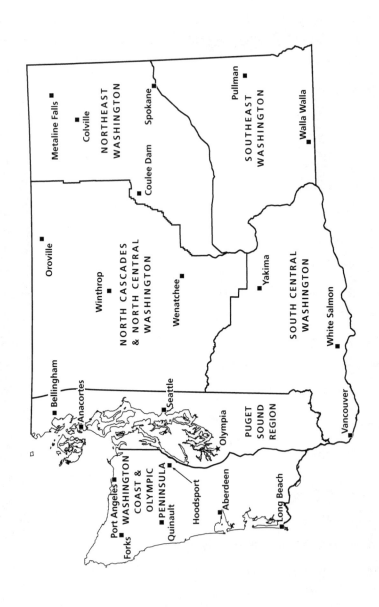

Metaline Falls

Colville

NORTHEAST
WASHINGTON

Spokane

Pullman

SOUTHEAST
WASHINGTON

Walla Walla

Coulee Dam

Oroville

Winthrop

NORTH CASCADES
& NORTH CENTRAL
WASHINGTON

Wenatchee

Yakima

SOUTH CENTRAL
WASHINGTON

White Salmon

Bellingham

Anacortes

Seattle

Olympia

PUGET
SOUND
REGION

Vancouver

Port Angeles

WASHINGTON
COAST &
OLYMPIC
PENINSULA

Forks

Quinault

Hoodsport

Aberdeen

Long Beach

About the Reviser

Megan Hill is a Seattle-based travel writer. When she's not writing, you can find her enjoying the beauty of the Pacific Northwest via hiking trail or sailboat.

Acknowledgments

Our many thanks to the dozens of folks who were very helpful in updating the information in this tenth and latest edition. No one knows an area as well as the local residents do: the restaurants, cafes, bakeries, and coffee shop owners; museum and park staff and volunteers; shopkeepers and innkeepers; visitor information centers' staff and volunteers; regional history gurus; and the men and women on the street who gave us information and opinions. Our special thanks to the book's writers over the years, including Myrna Oakley, Sharon Wootton, Maggie Savage, and Chloe Ërnst.

Introduction

The Space Needle, Mount Rainier, Seattle, and the Olympic Mountains are well-known tourist destinations in Washington, but the real fun begins when you explore off the beaten path. Washington's attractions are diverse and scattered across the state, mixed in with dense evergreen forests, fertile farmlands, and foggy islands as well as secluded windblown beaches, rivers, small-town cafes, and tiny hamlets, particularly in the southeast and northeast corners. Because of our interest in historic hotels and local cuisine eateries, readers will find these subjects expanded on in this, the tenth edition of *Washington Off the Beaten Path*. We've also added more websites for your easy reference.

Using This Guide to Plan Great Trips

Although it sometimes seems that there are only two seasons in Washington—the rainy season and the dry season—we do have four to consider when planning your trips. The busiest times for most destinations west of the Cascade Mountains, particularly around Puget Sound waters and the San Juan Islands, will be during June, July, and August. Major freeways and all ferries will carry more traffic, and lines at ferry terminals will be considerably longer. If you want less traffic and fewer crowds, plan to travel midweek or during the shoulder seasons, April and May or September and October. Autumn in the Northwest is usually sunny and mild, with fall colors especially fine in October.

If you enjoy snow and winter sports, plan treks to the Cascade Mountains from late November through February. Be prepared with all-weather tires, snow tires, or even chains for some alpine roads, layers of warm clothing, emergency kits, and plenty of snacks and beverages. To start your winter research you'll find helpful telephone numbers and websites in the Skiing Washington sidebar in the "Mountain Passes, Valleys & Canyons" section of the North Cascades & North Central Washington chapter.

The eastern two-thirds of the Evergreen State offer crisp, cold winters and hot, dry summers. Travel early spring and fall for some of the best weather east of the Cascade Mountains. Eastern Washington also offers fewer crowds, quieter byways, and many pleasant, undiscovered destinations. You'll encounter friendly locals who are glad to help travelers with directions. **Note:** Plan for long distances between services in the eastern regions—gas up often and load up on picnic foods, snacks, beverages, and ice for the cooler.

To help plan your accommodations, within each chapter we've offered lodging suggestions including telephone numbers and, usually, a website. Nearly all establishments are smoke-free, and many do not allow pets. Call ahead to ask specific questions and to make reservations. See Places to Eat at the end of each chapter for cafes, coffee shops, and casual restaurants in selected towns and cities. You will also find dining suggestions within each chapter.

A Few More Ideas

We suggest maintaining a flexible schedule. Allow plenty of time to stop for unexpected sights. Even with the best research, a place or attraction may be closed or hours or telephone numbers changed. If this occurs, stop at the nearest visitor information center or chamber of commerce (often the same) where staff and volunteers can offer current contact details and suggestions. Often these centers are open on weekdays as well as weekends during summer months. Additionally, locals around town are usually willing to offer travelers information, ideas, and directions.

If you're traveling with youngsters, encourage them to write notes to new folks they meet and to collect information on historic sites, attractions, geology, natural history, and whatever else tickles their fancies. In this way you can help them become savvy travelers who appreciate making new friends and who care for preserving towns and cities as well as respecting the great outdoors.

Travel Styles & Interests

Is your family the rugged outdoors type? Do you want four-season recreation information? Go to the chapter on North Cascades & North Central Washington. For assistance with serious backcountry and wilderness trip planning, contact the Outdoor Recreation Information Center in the REI flagship store in Seattle (206-470-4060). National park or forest service rangers are there 10 a.m. to 6 p.m. daily at 222 Yale Ave. North. Or perhaps you and your family are water-loving types, fond of salt water, surf sounds, and watching the tides change. Go to the chapters on the Washington Coast & Olympic Peninsula and Puget Sound Region.

If you have a hankerin' to pull on Levi's, boots, and a wide-brimmed hat or you want to see a rodeo or ride a horse, browse Northeast Washington, Southeast Washington, and the Okanogan Valley region in the North Cascades & North Central Washington chapter. If you want to explore the routes taken by the Lewis and Clark expedition go to the chapters on the Washington Coast & Olympic Peninsula, South Central Washington, and Southeast Washington.

A Final Word

May your travels in the Pacific Northwest be filled with great adventures, much serendipity, many outstanding vistas, and new friends from the diverse cultures that live and work in this vast region of waters, islands, mountains, rolling farmlands, deep gorges, and high deserts.

Fast Facts about Washington

- **Population:** 7.1 million according to a 2015 census estimate

- **Area:** 66,456 square miles

- **Capital:** Olympia, located in Thurston County south of Seattle at the southernmost tip of Puget Sound

- **Number of counties:** 39

- **County names, from west to east:** Wahkiakum, Pacific, Grays Harbor, Jefferson, Clallam, Mason, Thurston, Lewis, Cowlitz, Clark, Skamania, Pierce, King, Kitsap, Snohomish, Island, San Juan, Skagit, Whatcom, Okanogan, Chelan, Kittitas, Yakima, Klickitat, Benton, Grant, Douglas, Ferry, Lincoln, Adams, Franklin, Walla Walla, Columbia, Garfield, Asotin, Whitman, Spokane, Stevens, Pend Oreille

- **Highest point:** Mount Rainier (14,411 feet), located southeast of Tacoma

- **Largest county:** Okanogan; 5,268 square miles

- **Least populated county:** Garfield; 2,266 people

- **Major body of water:** Puget Sound, which carves deep into the northwest section of the state from the Strait of Juan de Fuca south to Olympia

- **Major rivers:** Columbia River east of the Cascade mountain range flows south and west to the Pacific Ocean; Snake River flows west from the Idaho border and empties into the Columbia River at the Tri-Cities; and the Skagit River flows west from the Cascades to Puget Sound.

- **Largest natural lake:** Fifty-five-mile-long Lake Chelan in central Washington, fed by streams from the North Cascades at Stehekin and east to the town of Chelan.

- **Nickname:** Evergreen State

- **State bird:** Willow goldfinch

- **State fish:** steelhead trout

- **State flower:** coastal rhododendron

- **State gem/rock:** petrified wood

- **State tree:** Western hemlock

- **State folk song:** "Roll on Columbia, Roll On"

- **State song:** "Washington, My Home"

- **State dance:** square dance

- **State grass:** bluebunch wheatgrass

- **State insect:** green darner dragonfly

- **State fossil:** Columbian mammoth

- **State fruit:** apple

- **State vegetable:** Walla Walla sweet onion

- **State marine mammal:** orca

- **State amphibian:** Pacific chorus frog

Washington Coast & Olympic Peninsula

Washington's Pacific Ocean coastline is a stretch of contrasts from the Strait of Juan de Fuca in the north to the mouth of the Columbia River in the south. The Olympic Peninsula's ocean shoreline is rugged, with steep cliffs and rocky formations sculpted by wave and wind. Farther south are gentle, sandy beaches lined with summer cottages and tourist communities. Grays Harbor and Willapa Bay break up the coastline and create extensive wetlands that are important wildlife habitats, especially during bird migrations. The Olympic Peninsula rain forest has the highest annual rainfall on the continental US, yet the Dungeness Valley on the Strait of Juan de Fuca—near the community of Sequim—has the lowest precipitation on the coast north of Los Angeles.

The snow-covered peaks of the Olympic Mountains provide a stunning backdrop to beaches, forests, and valleys in the region. Most of the Olympic Peninsula is thickly forested and includes some of the world's largest trees. Many local families have been loggers, fishermen, or mill workers for three or four generations, although logging is now a shadow of its former self. Several small Indian reservations are on the Olympic Peninsula including, those of the Makah, the Jamestown S'Klallam,

WASHINGTON COAST & OLYMPIC PENINSULA

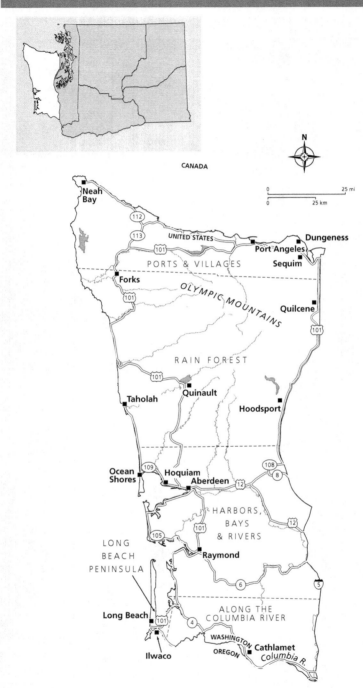

CANADA

N

0   25 mi
0   25 km

Neah
Bay

112

113   UNITED STATES

101   Dungeness

Port Angeles

PORTS & VILLAGES   Sequim

Forks

101   OLYMPIC MOUNTAINS

Quilcene

101

RAIN FOREST

101

Quinault

Taholah

Hoodsport

108

Ocean   109   Hoquiam   8
Shores   Aberdeen   12

HARBORS,
BAYS
& RIVERS   12

105

LONG
BEACH   101
PENINSULA   Raymond

6   5

Long Beach   101

ALONG THE
COLUMBIA RIVER

4

WASHINGTON   Cathlamet

Ilwaco   OREGON   Columbia R.

the Lower Elwha, the Quileute, the Hoh, the Quinault, the Shoalwater, and the Skokomish.

Outdoor activities include hiking, bicycling, kite-flying, kayaking, fishing, birding, and beachcombing. Bring along rain gear and good walking shoes or boots so that you and the kids can take advantage of the trails and beaches that are accessible most of the year.

Ports & Villages

Fifteen miles west and north of **Olympia** on US 101, as you enter the Hood Canal area, the craggy Olympic Mountains will come into view on the northern horizon. The first stop, 20 miles from Olympia, is the timber town of **Shelton,** dominated by a lumber mill that sprawls along the waterfront; its entire complex can be seen from the hilltop viewpoint adjacent to the huge sawmill wheel, a monument to the forestry industry. The Shelton-Mason County Chamber of Commerce (800-576-2021; sheltonchamber.com) is at 215 W. Railroad Ave. The visitor center (360-427-8168) is across the street in the red caboose at 230 W. Railroad Ave. Nearby, you can order a juicy hamburger at **Ritz Drive-In** (325 S. 1st St.; 360-427-9294) or for quick snacks and great coffee and espresso, check out **Urraco Coffee Company** (628 W. Cota St.; 360-462-5282; urracocoffee.com) and **Riverside Espresso** (332 S. 1st St.; 360-426-3300).

At the corner of Railroad Avenue and 5th Street, the **Mason County Historical Society Museum** (360-426-1020; masoncountyhistoricalsociety.org) offers exhibits of the region's logging and frontier past. Located in a library building constructed in 1914, the museum features family photographs, pioneer tools and artifacts, and a 19th-century schoolroom. The museum is open from 11 a.m. to 5 p.m. Tues through Fri and 11 a.m. to 4 p.m. Sat. Stroll down Railroad Avenue and Cota Street to get a feel for the town and its antiques and secondhand shops.

From Shelton continue north on US 101 along the salty tidal waters of Hood Canal, passing through the waterside communities of Hoodsport, Lilliwaup, Brinnon, and Quilcene on your way to Port Townsend, Sequim, and Port Angeles in the northern section of the Olympic Peninsula. A scenic spot that may entice an overnight stay is the **Glen Ayr Resort** (25381 N. US 101; 360-877-9522; glenayr.com) about 1 mile north of Hoodsport. Glen Ayr is part RV park, part motel, part 1-bedroom suites, and a 2-bedroom town house. The Hoodsport Visitors Center (150 N. Cushman Rd.; 360-877-2021) can offer a wealth of information on Hood Canal attractions, recreation, lodging, and dining. Or continue north on winding US 101 for 3 miles and check out waterside RV sites at **Rest-a-While RV Park** (360-877-9474; restawhile.com). It was homesteaded in 1889 and turned into a resort in the early 1900s. For more upscale accommodations, try the veritable ***Alderbrook Resort and Spa*** (360-898-2200; alderbrookresort.com), which faces the Hood Canal at 10 E. Alderbrook Ridge Dr. in Union. The on-site restaurant harvests resort-grown oysters right off the pier, and an indoor pool looks out over the fjord.

Oysters have the run of things in Lilliwaup. Sample the Hood Canal's wares at the ***Hama Hama Oyster Saloon*** (35846 US 101; 360-877-5811; hamahamaoysters.com), where you can dine on freshly harvested oysters and clams right on the water. If you stay at ***Mike's Beach Resort*** (38470 US-101; 360-877-5324; mikesbeachresort.com), you can harvest your own oysters with the help of the proprietors, who also run a commercial shellfish farm here. Accommodations include rustic cabins glamping tents, and RVs.

The towering peaks of the Olympic Mountains shelter the northernmost Dungeness Valley from the copious rainfall of the rest of the peninsula, making it the "banana belt" of the Northwest Coast. ***Sequim,*** which is so arid it is home to an endemic species of cactus, is the commercial center of the valley and

WASHINGTON COAST'S TOP ATTRACTIONS

Cape Disappointment State Park
Mouth of the Columbia River

Columbia Pacific Heritage Museum
Ilwaco

Dungeness National Wildlife Refuge
Sequim

Feiro Marine Life Center
Port Angeles

Grays Harbor Historical Seaport
Aberdeen

Hoh Rain Forest
Forks

Hurricane Ridge
Port Angeles

Lake Quinault Resort
Lake Quinault

Leadbetter Point State Park
Oysterville

Lewis and Clark Interpretive Center
Ilwaco

Makah Museum
Neah Bay

Northwest Carriage Museum
Raymond

Pacific County Historical Museum
South Bend

Tokeland Hotel
Tokeland

Westport Maritime Museum
Westport

Whale-watching
Westport

World Kite Museum & Hall of Fame
Long Beach

a good base from which to explore this scenic region. For an overnight stay close to the water, check out *Juan de Fuca Cottages* (182 Marine Dr.; 360-683-4433; juandefuca.com) where there are 6 cozy cottages with kitchens and wide-angle views of the strait, as well as 4 beach house rooms, lodge rooms, and 3 off-site vacation rentals. Or call *Dungeness Bay Cottages* (140 Marine Dr.; 360-683-3013; dungenessbaycottages.com) and ask about its 6 comfy units with great water views and a private beach. For a more historical stay, try one of the 6 cabooses from the golden age of rail at the *Red Caboose Getaway* at 24 Old Coyote Way (360-683-7350; redcaboosegetaway.com). A stay includes a queen-size feather bed and a Jacuzzi for two in some rooms. Look forward to a gourmet breakfast on a white linen tablecloth with crystal glassware in a 1937 Zephyr dining car.

rainshadow

It might rain 140 inches in the *Hoh Rain Forest* on the Olympic Peninsula's west side, but Sequim's average rainfall is 17 inches, the driest Pacific Coast climate north of Los Angeles. It's in the rain shadow of the Olympic Mountains on the peninsula's northeast corner. The mountains block most of the rain.

Just west of the city limits at the end of Hendrickson Road is the *Dungeness River Railroad Bridge Park,* a scenic spot with nature trails to the river and an Audubon center near the parking lot (dungenessrivercenter.org). On another excursion take Taylor Cut-off Road south from US 101 toward the mountains to reach *Lost Mountain Lavender* (1541 Taylor Cutoff Rd.; 360-681-2782; lostmountainlavender.com), a 3-acre farm with more than 120 varieties of lavender.

Find a delightful place to eat lunch at *Purple Haze Lavender Farm* (180 Bell Bottom Ln.; 360-582-1131; purplehazelavender.com) where you can inspect a colorful display garden, collect a bouquet from the U-pick field of organic lavender plants, and browse a nice selection of lavender products during the summer season. Lavender lovers can also stop at *Jardin du Soleil Lavender Farm* (3932 Sequim–Dungeness Way; 360-582-1185; jardindusoleil .com).

To sample another bounty of the region, swing by the weathered, century-old barn of *Olympic Cellars Winery* at 255410 US 101 (360-452-0160; olympic cellars.com). Three women started the winery in 1979, which has since grown into a gift shop and tasting room that's open daily year-round.

To explore the historic community of *Dungeness,* head north from US 101 on Sequim–Dungeness Way from downtown Sequim. Dungeness is old by Washington standards, named in 1792 by British explorer Captain George Vancouver. Charles Seal established the Dungeness Trading Company in the

Lavender Town USA

Sequim's rich soil, low rainfall, and warm temperatures have spawned a booming agricultural industry. Waves of lavender plants from pale violet to deep purple grow on farms in the Dungeness Valley. To see and sniff hundreds of varieties such as Provence, Grosso, and Munstead, plan to attend the annual Lavender Festival the third weekend of July. Enjoy activities that include farm tours, a street fair, great food, art shows, and live music. See lavenderfestival.com for details, then enjoy visiting lavender farms and finding lavender plants for your gardens while stocking up on lavender soaps, bath oils, and lotions appealing to your senses.

CreekSide Lavender Farm
(888) 881-6055
lavenderconnection.com

Jardin du Soleil Lavender
(360) 582-1185
jardindusoleil.com

Lost Mountain Lavender
(360) 681-2782
lostmountainlavender.com

Martha Lane Lavender
(360) 582-9355
marthalanelavender.com

Olympic Lavender Company
(855) 683-4475
olympiclavendercompany.com

Purple Haze Lavender Farm
(360) 582-1131
purplehazelavender.com

Sequim Lavender Growers Association
(360) 681-3035
lavendergrowers.org

Sunshine Herb & Lavender Farm
(360) 683-6453
sunshinelavender.com

late 1800s and built a large country farmhouse with the proceeds in 1886. For a delightful place to stay in Dungeness, try Williams Manor Bed and Breakfast (4043 Sequim Dungeness Way; 360-460-3763; williamsmanor-sequim.com), a historic two-bedroom home that sleeps up to six people. Your stay includes homemade quiche, fruit, croissants, juice, preserves, and coffee for a do-it-yourself breakfast. In the downtown Sequim area, try **Oak Table Cafe** at the corner of 3rd and Bell Streets (360-204-5198; oaktablecafe.com) for waist-bulging breakfasts. Other options include **Alder Wood Bistro** for wood-fired coastal cuisine (139 W. Alder St.; 360-683-4321; alderwoodbistro.com), **Dockside Grill** (360-683-7510; docksidegrill-sequim.com) at John Wayne Marina (yes, that John Wayne!), and **Seven Cedars Casino** at 270756 US 101 (360-683-7777; 7cedarsresort.com).

A fun place to visit near Dungeness is the **Olympic Game Farm** at 1423 Ward Rd. (800-778-4295; olygamefarm.com). Year-round drive-through tours will put you in the company of four-legged stars. Walt Disney Studios has employed farm residents, including grizzlies and wolves, in more than 80 wild-life productions. Many animals you'll see are endangered species. Enjoy Bengal tigers, African lions, zebras, timber wolves, and a small herd of bison, which are so habituated to human presence they'll walk right up to your car. There's also a coffee and ice cream stop, Hardy's Market, at the farm.

The ***Dungeness National Wildlife Refuge,*** located west of the game farm, offers an exhilarating immersion in nature in the spring and fall when thousands of migrating waterfowl stop here. From the parking lot, take an easy quarter-mile walk to a viewpoint overlooking ***Dungeness Spit,*** one of the nation's largest natural sand hooks. For slightly hardier walkers, follow all or part of the 11-mile round-trip trail through the forest, down the beach, out to New Dungeness Lighthouse, and back. Allow enough time to walk the whole distance and come back during low tide (it takes about 5 hours), or just meander a section. There's a $3 per family fee for refuge exploration. Watch out for harbor seals bobbing about as they fish and frolic offshore. The last half-mile of the spit beyond the ***New Dungeness Lighthouse*** and the south shore is closed to ensure protection of the seals. The lighthouse and foghorn, built in 1857 and automated in 1976, are the oldest north of the Columbia River.

See Washington by Following the Flocks

Dancing sandhill cranes can inspire superlatives, the cry of an eagle a shiver, the hoot of an owl an ear tuned to an answering call, a songbird a smile. This year, go where the birds are: Join experienced birders and listen to expert presenters at one of the Washington birding festivals, then explore the area on your own.

BirdFest & Bluegrass
Oct, Ridgefield
ridgefieldfriends.org

Grays Harbor Shorebird Festival
May, Hoquiam
shorebirdfestival.com

Leavenworth Bird Festival
May, Leavenworth
leavenworthspringbirdfest.com

Olympic Peninsula BirdFest
Apr, Sequim
olympicbirdfest.org

Othello Sandhill Crane Festival
Mar, Othello
othellosandhillcranefestival.org

Port Susan Snow Goose & Birding Festival
Feb, Camano Island and Stanwood
snowgoosefest.org

Puget Sound Bird Fest
Sept, Edmonds
pugetsoundbirdfest.org

Upper Skagit Bald Eagle Festival
Dec, Rockport
skagiteagle.org

There was a keeper on-site until 1994, but now the lighthouse provides basic accommodations to tourists (or "temporary keepers") on a weekly basis. For information about exploring, touring the lighthouse, or becoming a lighthouse keeper, call (360) 683-6638 or check newdungenesslighthouse.com.

The best way to go through the Dungeness Valley between Sequim and Port Angeles is on the **Old Olympic Highway.** This pleasant, less-traveled route through green farmlands offers great views of the mountains rising to the south. Those yearning for luxurious lodgings and a 5-course gourmet breakfast featuring locally grown fare could stay at **Domaine Madeleine Bed & Breakfast Inn** (146 Wildflower Ln.; 360-457-4174; domainemadeleine.com), a contemporary, solar-powered home on a bluff above the Strait of Juan de Fuca. Four of the five guest rooms have whirlpool tubs. Guests can wander 2.5 acres of gardens spread over 10 acres of grounds or cozy up in the living room near the huge basalt fireplace. Each room also has a fireplace and panoramic views. The inn is about 9.5 miles west of Sequim and 2 miles off the Old Olympic Highway.

For a different and adventuresome perspective, drive about 5 miles east of downtown Port Angeles and turn right on Deer Park Road for a narrow, winding 16-mile drive over the forest-covered slopes of Blue Mountain to Deer Park in **Olympic National Park** (nps.gov/olym). Since the last half is graveled and also the steepest section, don't bring RVs or trailers. You'll find an alpine campground, a summer-only ranger station, and scenic hikes that provide views of the interior Olympics, Dungeness Valley, Port Angeles, and the Strait of Juan de Fuca.

A less adventurous but still stunning ride is to take paved Hurricane Ridge Road uphill for 17 miles out of Port Angeles to **Hurricane Ridge** and several easier trails, wildflowers in early summer, and great views of Olympic peaks. Please don't feed the deer in the parking lot! If there's a question about snow conditions, call (360) 565-3131. During the summer park rangers lead nature walks, and campfire programs are given nightly in the Heart o' the Hills Campground amphitheater located about 5 miles away from July 1 through Labor Day. On winter weekends, there are guided snowshoe hikes. The panoramic views on the way down are of the strait and its Canadian islands to the north. The visitor center is a good place to start. It has a museum, deli, and gift shop. Restrooms are open year-round. For more information stop by the Olympic National Park Visitor Center in Port Angeles at 3002 Mount Angeles Rd. (360-565-3130).

Port Angeles (portangeles.org), the largest city on the Olympic Peninsula, is dominated by its busy waterfront. This deepwater harbor is a port of call for international shipping, a base for ocean fishing, a major Coast Guard station, and terminus for **Black Ball's Coho ferry** for walk-on passengers and vehicles (360-457-4491; cohoferry.com). The ferry makes daily trips to Victoria, British Columbia, a city with a British flavor tucked at the southern tip of Vancouver Island.

The City Pier, 1 block east of the ferry terminal, is a good starting point for your explorations. You'll find a small park, a viewing tower, a berth for the 110-foot Coast Guard cutter *Cuttyhunk,* a public marine laboratory, and plenty of nearby restaurants and shops. The **Feiro Marine Life Center** (360-417-6254) on the City Pier is the place to see and touch some of the remarkable sea creatures that live on Washington's coast. Watch the graceful movements of an octopus, stroke a stuffed sea lion, and handle a variety of marine life in the touch-tanks. Volunteers answer questions and tell visitors about the Northwest region's marine ecology. The laboratory is open for a small admission fee; call for hours or go to feiromarinelifecenter.org.

To explore along the lively Port Angeles waterfront, pick up a walking-tour brochure at the visitor center (located next to the City Pier). The **Olympic Discovery Trail,** which follows the harbor shore east along Hollywood Beach to Sequim, is ideal for walking or bicycling. You can also bicycle west to **Ediz Hook,** the natural sand spit that forms the Port Angeles harbor. Bikes are available for rent at **Sound Bikes and Kayaks** at 120 E. Front St. (360-457-1240; soundbikeskayaks.com). Not into biking today? Pop into **Captain T's** at 114 E. Front St. (360-452-6549; captaints.com) for railroad-related T-shirts or **Pacific Rim Hobby** (138 W. Railroad Ave.; 360-457-0794; olypen.com/prhobby), for more railroad souvenirs.

For good eats in Port Angeles, try a local breakfast favorite, **First Street Haven Cafe** (107 E. 1st St.; 360-457-0352), or Barhop Brewing and Artisan Pizza for reliable pies and beer facing the newly rebuilt Port Angeles waterfront, just steps from the ferry terminal. (124 W. Railroad Ave.; 360-797-1818). For an upscale evening meal, dine on *Twilight*-famous mushroom ravioli at **Bella Italia** (118 E. 1st St.; 360-457-5442; bellaitaliapa.com) or slow-roasted short ribs at **LD's Woodfire Grill** (929 W. 8th St.; 360-452-0400; ldswoodfire grill.com).

The downtown has benefited from a recent face-lift. For information on activities such as art walks, outdoor sculptures, an underground tour, a 5-acre outdoor gallery, and events, check out portangelesdowntown.com.

If you enjoy being in the heart of things, consider the European-style accommodations at **Port Angeles Downtown Hotel** at 101½ E. Front St. (360-565-1125; portangelesdowntownhotel.com) where the bargain-priced rooms each have a sink and share a bathroom down the hall. Or contact the innkeepers at **Five SeaSuns Bed & Breakfast** at 1006 S. Lincoln St. (360-452-8248;

seasuns.com). Guests find sumptuous accommodations and grounds that feature a pond, an elegant pergola, and garden beds and planters overflowing with colorful flowers.

There is still much to see on the north end of the Olympic Peninsula. Stop at the **Elwha Ranger Station** (3911 Olympic Hot Springs Rd.; 360-452-9191) for information on hiking trails, or take a raft trip down the scenic Elwha River. Contact **Adventures through Kayaking** in Port Angeles (888-900-3015; atkayaking.com) to ask about kayaking on Lake Aldwell or sea kayaking Freshwater Bay.

Continuing west of Port Angeles, follow US 101 inland or take Highway 112 along the coastline. If you opt for the inland route, you'll find **Lake Crescent** set in the forest. The lake is 12 miles long and more than a mile wide. Much of the area around the lake is part of **Olympic National Park.** A right turn onto E. Beach Road at Lake Crescent's eastern edge takes you along a scenic, winding lakeside road to **Log Cabin Resort** at 3183 E. Beach Rd. (360-928-3325; olympicnationalparks.com). Established in 1895 on the lake's isolated north shore, the "sunny side of the lake," its simple lodge rooms, rustic cabins dating to the 1920s (with no plumbing), RV sites, camping spots, a general store, and deli restaurant provide a secluded, friendly atmosphere. It's a favorite for family vacations, and some folks return generation after generation. Hike among giant old-growth cedars and firs on forest trails. Take the 4-mile **Spruce Division Railroad Trail,** originally a railroad grade built during World War I to help extract spruce logs for airplane production.

The Storm King visitor information center is located on the lake's south shore, just off US 101, in a log cabin built in 1905. From the cabin a nearly 1-mile trail follows a level, gravel path through the forest and ends with an uphill climb through the rain forest to 90-foot **Marymere Falls. Lake Crescent Lodge** at 416 Lake Crescent Rd. (360-928-3211; lakecrescentlodge.com), just west of the visitor center, is a classic old resort that has changed little since it was built on the lakeshore in 1916. While staying here in 1937, President Franklin Roosevelt decided to create Olympic National Park to preserve this area's beauty for future generations. Visitors enjoy lodge rooms or cottages, boating, fishing, and nature hikes. Reservations are recommended for the resort's restaurant; watch the sunset over

olympic
discoverytrail

The partially completed **Olympic Discovery Trail,** a nonmotorized multiple-use path, will one day stretch 126 miles from Port Townsend to La Push on the Pacific Coast.

Quick Guide to Victoria and Vancouver Island, British Columbia

Getting to Victoria from Port Angeles is easy. Park at the Port Angeles ferry terminal and take your car aboard the *M.V. Coho ferry* for its 90-minute cruise across the Strait of Juan de Fuca (360-457-4491; ferrytovictoria.com).

Or hop aboard as a foot passenger and enjoy the easy walking in Victoria's scenic *Inner Harbor area* to see the ivy-covered Empress Hotel, stately Parliament buildings and landscaped grounds that sparkle with thousands of lights after dark, the don't-miss Royal BC Museum, and harbor activities from Inner Harbor walkways. Sample a plethora of cafes, coffeehouses, boutiques, and teahouses. For information contact *Tourism Victoria Visitor Information Centre* at 812 Wharf St. (250-953-2033) and *Tourism British Columbia* (800-435-5622; hellobc.com).

Other places to explore near Victoria include spectacular *Butchart Gardens* north of Victoria (plan late spring and summer visits during midweek to avoid the crowds); *Brentwood Bay and Saanich Inlet* (try Seahorses Cafe, 250-544-1565, near Mill Bay ferry landing); *Sooke* (good hiking, eateries, and shops); and *Port Alberni* (fishing and forestry village). Drive north to the seaside community of *Sidney.* For simple eats on the waterfront at Port Sidney Marina, try *Rumrunner Pub* at 9881 Seaport Place (250-656-5643), *Boondocks Cafe & Pub* at 9732 1st St. (250-656-4088), or *Fish on Fifth Cafe* at 9812 5th St. (250-656-4022; fishon5th.com). For overnight lodging check *Best Western Emerald Isle Inn* (2306 Beacon Ave.; 800-315-3377; bwemeraldisle.com).

From Sidney you can visit the San Juan Islands via international ferry sailing on *Washington State Ferries* (wsdot.wa.gov/ferries). Check with San Juan Islands Visitor Bureau (888-468-3701; visitsanjuans.com).

For border crossing requirements, go to the *US–Canadian Border Crossing* website at cbp.gov or call (703) 526-4200 or (877) 227-5511.

the lake while savoring a fine dinner. The Roosevelt Dining Room also serves breakfast and lunch.

You'll find forested campgrounds, boat rentals, and groceries at Fairholm on the western edge of Lake Crescent. Farther west on US 101, a 12-mile drive south on Sol Duc Road takes you to *Sol Duc Hot Springs Resort* (360-327-3583; visitsolduc.com). *Sol duc* means "sparkling water" in the Quileute language. Visitors have been flocking to these mineral waters since a magnificent spa was built at the site in 1912 (which, sadly, burned in 1916). The resort, open Apr through Oct, offers 3 large outdoor hot mineral pools, a freshwater heated swimming pool, dining, massage therapy, a gift shop, groceries, RV hookups, and cabins. Camping, hiking trails, and naturalist programs are available at nearby *Sol Duc Campground.*

An alternative route is to leave US 101 at the junction west of Port Angeles and take Highway 112, a National Scenic Byway, for close-up views of the Olympic Peninsula's rugged northern coastline. Ten miles west of Port Angeles, turn on Camp Hayden Road to reach **Salt Creek Recreation Area,** a marine sanctuary with tidal pools full of waving sea anemones, gooseneck barnacles, coal-black mussels, and colorful starfish, as well as kelp beds and small rocky islands. The adjacent Clallam County Park offers campsites, showers, and a beach. Continuing west on Highway 112, you may see a gray whale spouting or a pod of orcas or a California sea lion. Watch for crowds of harbor seals relaxing on the small offshore islands. A great place to take a break is at 4-acre **Pillar Point County Park** (360-417-2291). Try beachcombing along a beautiful estuary, admire the views and birding opportunities, and have a picnic. Look for crabs on the mudflats during low tide.

onebeak
twobeak

Every year bird-watchers gather at Salt Creek Recreation Area west of Port Angeles to count migrating turkey vultures. The kettle of vultures stages at the southern tip of Vancouver Island before flying across the Strait of Juan de Fuca in groups as large as 400 birds on their way to California and Central America.

Clallam Bay and **Sekiu** are two fishing villages along the Strait of Juan de Fuca, just the right size for finding a seafood-oriented meal, poking about the marinas, renting a boat, or catching a fishing charter. Contact the **Clallam Bay-Sekiu Chamber of Commerce** (360-963-2339; clallambay.com) for more information. The website has a few dining and lodging options, most of them low-key.

Continue west to **Neah Bay** or take the turnoff on Hoko-Ozette Road, just past the fishing village of Sekiu on Clallam Bay, to **Lake Ozette,** one of the largest natural bodies of freshwater in Washington State. The 9-mile loop trail from the lake to Cape Alava and over the ocean beach to Sandpoint makes a very long day hike, or pack for an overnighter at secluded oceanside campsites. The Ozette Ranger Station (360-963-2725) at the lake can provide tide tables and other important information. The park offers interpretive programs in the summer as well as a pleasant 15-site campground at the lake's north end.

Or contact **Lost Resort** at 20860 Hoko-Ozette Rd. (800-950-2899; lostresort .net) in Clallam Bay, about a quarter-mile from the ranger station. It offers a campground, cabins, and a store. For more upscale accommodations in Clallam Bay, contact **Winter Summer Inn** overlooking the Strait of Juan de Fuca at 16651 Hwy. 112 (360-963-2264; wintersummerinn.com), open year-round.

For an easy day hike from Ozette, walk along the 3-mile boardwalk over coastal wetlands to Cape Alava, the site of an ancient Makah Indian fishing village that was buried by a mud slide 500 years ago and partially excavated in the 1970s and early 1980s. The well-preserved contents of the village, exposed by tidal action in 1970, are housed at the *Makah Museum* (360-645-2711; makah.com), which is part of the Makah Cultural and Research Center in Neah Bay on the *Makah Indian Reservation,* about 70 miles west of Port Angeles. Owned and operated by the Makah Tribe, this first-class museum tells the story of people who lived a rigorous life hunting whales, seals, and fish. It's open daily 10 a.m. to 5 p.m.

Neah Bay holds its *Makah Days* celebration the last weekend in August, featuring traditional salmon bakes along with dancing, singing, and canoe races. There are several modest motels and RV parks.

Follow signs to the Makah Air Force Station west of Neah Bay and take the right-hand fork to reach the three-quarters-of-a-mile trail to *Cape Flattery,* improved by the Makahs to include better footing, some wooden walkways, and fences. This gem is the northwesternmost point of the US mainland and includes several observation decks and picnic tables. At the end and high above the ocean, experience great views of Tatoosh Island, a half-mile-long volcanic outcropping that was once a favorite Makah retreat, and now home to the century-and-a-half-old Cape Flattery Light and nesting seabirds. From here you may see gray whales during their spring and fall migrations. Cape Flattery is well known for its high winds, extremely high rainfall, and incredibly clean air. Scientists from the University of Washington have declared it to be the purest anywhere they've tested.

To reach additional scenic ocean beaches, take the south fork at the Air Force Station. *Hobuck and Sooes Beaches* are on the outer coast a few miles south of Neah Bay. *Hobuck Beach Resort* at 2726 Makah Passage has tidy cabins with kitchenettes and a large campground area for tents and RVs

Olympic National Park

Olympic National Park was designated as a World Heritage Site by UNESCO in 1981. It contains one of the world's largest stands of virgin temperate rain forest and the largest wild herd of Roosevelt elk in the US. The park hosts more than 1,450 types of plants, more than 300 species of birds, and more than 60 species of mammals. At least 13 kinds of plants and 7 kinds of animals are found only on the Olympic Peninsula, including the Olympic marmot and snow mole; Flett's violet, Piper's bellflower, and Olympic Mountain daisy; and Beardslee and Crescenti trout.

Byways off the Beaten Path

The *Cape Flattery Tribal Scenic Byway* that runs 12 miles from Neah Bay to Cape Flattery is the first Tribal Scenic Byway in the state. Drive the byway, designated in 2002, as part of a 36-mile loop route that starts at the Makah Cultural and Resource Center. Highlights include the Makah National Salmon Hatchery, Neah Bay and marina, Olympic Coast National Marine Sanctuary, Shi Shi Beach, Tatoosh Island and lighthouse, and the Cape Flattery Trail, which leads to the northwesternmost point on the US mainland.

The state has seven nationally designated routes: two *All-American Roads, Chinook Pass Scenic Byway (SR 410)* and *International Selkirk Loop (SR 31, 20)*; and five National Scenic Byways: *Mountains to Sound Greenway (I-90), Strait of Juan de Fuca Highway (SR 112), Coulee Corridor (SR 17, 155), Stevens Pass Greenway (US 2),* and *White Pass (US 12).* There are also dozens of state-designated byways and scenic drives.

For more information or to obtain a Washington State Scenic Byways Map, call (800) 544-1800.

(360-645-2339; hobuckbeachresort.com). From Makah Bay south the beaches are mostly undisturbed by humans, but even pristine wilderness beaches like *Shi Shi Beach,* accessible via a 3-mile hiking trail, are popular come summer. Remember, a reservation operates by tribal rules and fees. Check makah.com or call (360) 645-2201 for specifics.

Rain Forest

When you're ready to continue your peninsula journey, return on Highway 112 and take the turnoff south on Burnt Mountain Road, located 6 miles south of Clallam Bay, which connects to US 101 at Sappho. A third of a mile farther west you can take Pavel Road 2 miles to the *Sol Duc Salmon Hatchery* and a small interpretive center with colorful dioramas illustrating the life cycle of the salmon and the challenges facing fisheries industries. Just north of *Forks,* La Push Road connects US 101 with *Rialto Beach, Mora Campground* (part of Olympic National Park), and the Quileute community of *La Push.*

A short distance from the beach is *Manitou Lodge* at 813 Kilmer Rd. in Forks (360-374-6295; manitoulodge.com). Take advantage of its proximity to rain forests, rivers, and unspoiled beaches. To spend a night closer to the ocean, try *Quileute Oceanside Resort* at 330 Ocean Dr. (800-487-1267; quileuteoceanside.com) in La Push, a Quileute tribal enterprise. Guests enjoy ocean views and access to miles of sandy and rocky beaches.

Back on US 101, explore Forks, historically a logging town although logging is down to a shadow of its former self. The **Forks Timber Museum** (360-374-9663) south of town next to the visitor information center offers a comprehensive introduction to the history, economy, and culture of logging. Photographs, old logging equipment, and dioramas give a glimpse of what life was like in old logging camps and pioneer homes and how simple tools and hard work were employed to fell, transport, and saw timber into commercial lumber. The old-fashioned **Fourth of July** celebration in Forks highlights traditional logging skill competitions. For more information contact the Forks Chamber of Commerce at (360) 374-2531 or forkswa.com.

For good eats along US 101 in Forks and to meet local folks, try Pacific Pizza, which serves specialties like a basil pesto pizza and meatball sandwich (870 S. Forks Ave.; 360-374-2626) or the espresso bar at **Forks Outfitters** (950 S. Forks Ave.; 360-374-6161; forksoutfitters.com) at the south end of town. **Sully's Burgers** (220 N. Forks Ave.; 360-374-5075) has capitalized on its *Twilight* fame with the Bella Burger on its menu of milk shakes, pizzas, and sandwiches.

For a stay in Forks call the **Miller Tree Inn Bed & Breakfast** (360-374-6806; millertreeinn.com), a 1916 homestead on a parklike, 1-acre property at 654 E. Division St. At **Misty Valley Inn Bed & Breakfast** (194894 US 101 N; 360-374-9389; mistyvalleyinn.com), enjoy pastoral views and gourmet breakfasts. For a cozy cottage in town, contact **Shady Nook Cottage** (81 Ash Ave.; 360-374-5497; shadynookcottage.com) or **Mill Creek Inn** (1061 S. Forks Ave.; 360-374-5873; forksbnb.com). Unless you are camping or driving a self-contained RV, be sure to arrange your summer overnight accommodations well ahead of visiting the Forks–Neah Bay area.

Twelve miles south of Forks, Upper Hoh Road follows the Hoh River Valley 18 miles east into one of the thickest parts of the rain forest. At the end of the road are the Olympic National Park's **Hoh Rain Forest Visitor Center** (360-374-6925; nps.gov/olym), campground, and eye-opening nature trails. More than 140 inches of rain fall here annually, creating a lush multilayered environment highlighted with every shade of green imaginable. Even a quick excursion through the Hall of Mosses Trail or along the Spruce Nature Trail offers an opportunity to experience the grandeur of the old-growth hemlock/spruce forests that once covered much of western Washington. To reach more secluded areas, walk a few miles toward the Blue

rainydays

Forks, on the far north section of the Olympic Peninsula, is the westernmost incorporated town in the mainland US. It's also one of the rainiest: On average, Forks sees 210 days a year of measureable precipitation.

Glacier. Backpackers can take longer hikes along the Hoh River Trail to camp-sites such as the summer ranger station at Olympus (9 miles from the visitor center) or Glacier Meadows (an additional 8 miles).

Located next to the Hoh River, about 7 miles from Highway 101, the **Hoh Valley Cabins** at Elk Meadows (360-374-5111; hoh-valley-cabins-at-elk -meadows.washington-state.net) offers well-appointed accommodations suit-able for groups and families. Nearby, **Rainforest Paddlers** can set you up with guided river rafting and estuary kayaking trips and rentals at 4883 Upper Hoh Rd. (360-374-5254; rainforestpaddlers.com). The **Rain Forest Hostel** (360-374-2270; rainforesthostel.com), located 23 miles south of Forks on US 101, offers basic accommodations at a minimal price; reservations are required. It's a popular base for young adult travelers exploring the Olympic Peninsula, so part of the fun is meeting visitors from around the world.

US 101 curves west to follow the cliffs above **Ruby and Kalaloch** (pro-nounced CLAY-lock) **Beaches,** offering magnificent views of the Pacific Ocean. It's a rugged coastline punctured with sea stacks and rock pillars where waves leap, foam, and crash against rocks, driftwood, and offshore islands. At night you'll see flashes from the lighthouse, which has provided a warning to coastal mariners since it was built in 1891 on distant Destruction Island.

Olympic National Park's only oceanfront lodging is the **Kalaloch Lodge** (866-662-9928; thekalalochlodge.com) south of Forks at 157151 US 101. It's rus-tic, cedar-shingled, and perched on a bluff looking across a wide beach to the Pacific Ocean; the much-in-demand bluff cabins have views. Make reservations many months in advance, or consider this as a winter storm-watching destina-tion. Bring your raincoat. Kalaloch gets more than 150 inches of rain a year.

At Queets the highway turns inland to **Lake Quinault,** one of the dens-est parts of the rain forest. To experience this lush green place with its giant cedar, hemlock, and spruce, stay at **Lochaerie Resort Cabins** at 638 N. Shore Rd., Amanda Park (360-288-2215; lochaerie.com), located 4 miles east of US 101 on the lake's north shore. The 6 rustic cabins with kitchens have changed little since they were built on the cliffs above the lake in the 1920s and 1930s. Information about day hikes can be obtained from the **Quinault Ranger Sta-tion** on S. Shore Road (360-288-2525).

Locals suggest dining at **Salmon House Restaurant** at **Rain Forest Resort Village** (516 S. Shore Rd.; 360-288-2535; rainforestresort.com). Rain Forest Resort also offers lake-view cabins.

On the south side of the lake about 2 miles east of the highway at 345 S. Shore Rd. sits **Lake Quinault Lodge** (360-288-2900; visitlakequinault.com), a 92-room waterfront resort built in 1926. Guests can rent boats and canoes, soak in the pool, and enjoy gourmet cuisine in the Roosevelt Dining Room. For more rustic accommodations ask about the 1923 **Boathouse Annex** where pets are allowed. There are no TVs or telephones in the rooms.

If you'd like to explore the Quinault Valley rain forest and scenic Lake Quinault from the sunny side of the lake and stay in a more intimate lodging, contact the folks at the newer **Lake Quinault Resort** (314 N. Shore Rd.; 360-288-2362; quinaultrainforest.com/Lake-Quinault-Lodging/lake-quinault-resort .html). In this quiet spot you can relax in your Adirondack chair amid a flotilla of flowers and savor views of the lake, which can be seen from all the guest rooms. Choose from units with kitchenettes or town-house suites.

This section of the Olympic Peninsula also can be reached from Olympia by heading west on US 12 to Aberdeen and then north on US 101 for about 40 miles to Quinault and Amanda Park.

Harbors, Bays & Rivers

The twin port cities of **Hoquiam** and **Aberdeen** on Grays Harbor are hard-working communities where logging, fishing, and shipping are nearly every-body's business. Accommodations here are mostly humble motels and chain hotels. A comfortable option is **Abel House Bed & Breakfast** at 117 Fleet St. S in nearby Montesano (360-249-6002).

Downtown Hoquiam has a waterfront park where you can watch work and pleasure boats on the river. Or climb the viewing tower at the end of 28th Street on Grays Harbor to see the oceangoing cargo ships. Continue west past Hoquiam to follow the coast north on Highway 109 through a number of small communities. Along the way you'll find windswept beaches, art galleries, antiques, gift shops, and resorts. For more information on places to stay in the area, contact Grays Harbor Tourism, (800) 621-9625 or visitgraysharbor.com.

Elwha Ecosystem

Nine miles west of Port Angeles, you can turn south on Olympic Hot Springs Road to explore the scenic *Elwha River Valley.* The Elwha ecosystem was the most pro-ductive salmon stream system on the Olympic Peninsula until two dams were built; they were torn down in 2012 and 2014 in what constitutes the largest dam removal project in US history. Since then, ecosystem restoration has been remarkable, with free-flowing sediment rebuilding beaches at the river's mouth, plants and trees taking root on once-drowned shoreline, and a surging number of salmon returning to their historic spawning grounds above where the dams had been.

Aberdeen is the hometown of legendary Nirvana frontman Kurt Cobain. One of the few memorials to the deceased rockstar is low-key Kurt Cobain Landing, along a curve in the Wishkah River. Simple stone markers bear some of Cobain's song lyrics and fans have added graffiti under the adjacent Young Street Bridge. You can find a handful of other reminders that this was once Cobain's stomping grounds: his childhood house, at 1210 E. 1st St. (today a private home) and a 68-foot Nirvana mural on the Aberdeen Moore's Building at Wishkah and Broadway St.

Grays Harbor was a major shipbuilding center during the days of sail when locally milled lumber was in great demand for hulls, masts, and spars. Three- and four-masted schooners, wooden steamships, and tugboats were constructed along the bay, and they crowded the harbor's docks. At the **Grays Harbor Historical Seaport** (500 N. Custer St.; 360-533-9384; historicalseaport .org), absorb marine history aboard a full-scale reproduction of the *Lady Washington,* one of the ships used by explorer Robert Gray to sail into the harbor in 1792. The state's official ship was built in 1989 as part of Washington's centennial celebration and now sails regularly along the West Coast. On the organization's website, there's information about dockside tours, educational programs, adventure sail training, and the current sailing schedule. The seaport also owns the 161-foot *Hawaiian Chieftain,* available for tours. For additional information, contact the Grays Harbor Visitor Information Center (506 Duffy St.; 800-321-1924; graysharbor.org).

Explore **Ocean Shores** (20 miles from Hoquiam) and the scenic north coast area, including Ocean City, Copalis Beach, Pacific Beach, Moclips, and at the far northern end of Highway 109, Taholah. The string of oceanfront communities studs a windswept, 30-mile shore. You'll find funky cafes, cozy bookstores, and warm places to hole up for the night.

On the south shore of Grays Harbor, there's **Westport.** Maritime life and fishing ways abound in this wind-battered town, 20 miles west of Aberdeen, just off Highway 105. At the bustling marina the fishing and charter boats prepare for offshore tours or return loaded with fish and crabs. Check out the boardwalk, an ideal place to stroll and watch the waterfront activity, or climb the viewing tower for a bird's-eye view of Grays Harbor. Westport happens to be Washington State's unofficial surfing capital, with some of the most consistent breaks in the Northwest. Surfers come from all over Washington to catch the waves at Half Moon Bay, Westhaven State Park, and the Finger Jetties. If you don't mind cold water, you can rent gear and take lessons at Montesano Street's Steepwater Surfshop (360-268-5527; steepwatersurfshop.com).

Westport is home to **LOGE** at the Sands (360-268-0091; logecamps.com/ westport-wa), a motel on Montesano St. that's been restored with a vintage

TOP ANNUAL EVENTS ON THE WASHINGTON COAST & OLYMPIC PENINSULA

MARCH

Gray Whale Watching
Westport, Mar–May
(800) 345-6223

APRIL

Crab Races, Crab Feed & Crab Derby
Westport
(800) 345-6223

Grays Harbor Shorebird Festival
Hoquiam, late Apr/early May
(360) 289-5048
shorebirdfestival.com

Olympic Peninsula BirdFest
Sequim
(360) 681-4076
olympicbirdfest.org

Rainfest
Forks
(800) 443-6757

JULY

Lavender Festival
Sequim
(360) 681-3035
lavenderfestival.com

AUGUST

Clallam County Fair
Port Angeles
(360) 417-2551
clallam.net/Fair

International Kite Festival
Long Beach
(800) 451-2542
kitefestival.com

Makah Days
Neah Bay
(360) 645-2201
makah.com

OCTOBER

Cranberry Harvest Festival
Grayland
(800) 345-6223

Dungeness Crab & Seafood Festival
Westport
(360) 452-6300
crabfestival.org

Irish Music Festival
Ocean Shores
(360) 289-2300
galwaybayirishpub.com

OysterFest:
West Coast Shucking Championships
& Seafood Festival
Shelton
(800) 576-2021
oysterfest.org

beach theme. The café serves craft beer and coffee, and there are bicycles, surfboards, paddleboards and kayaks for rent, plus wetsuits. In addition to hotel rooms, there are also spots for tents and campers, and there's live music at an outdoor stage some nights.

Most of the dining in Westport is low-key and divey, but you'll find a standout in *Aloha Alabama BBQ and Bakery* (360-268-7299; alohaalabama

.com) at the downtown waterfront. As the name suggests, the menu melds Southern and island influences. The cocktails are a win, too.

The colonial-revival structure located at 2201 Westhaven Dr. was built in 1939 to house the Coast Guard's Lifeboat Station at Grays Harbor but now houses the **Westport Maritime Museum** (360-268-0078; westportmaritime museum.com). Tour the **Grays Harbor Lighthouse** at nearby Point Chehalis or see the lighthouse from a roadside viewing platform. The 107-foot-tall structure is more than a hundred years old, and its automated light, at 123 feet above the water, ranks as the highest light on the Washington coast. But shifting sands have set the lighthouse about 3,000-feet inland rather than on the coast.

For a long look at the Pacific just before you turn in for the night, choose an ocean-view room out of the 104 accommodations available at **Chateau Westport** (710 Hancock; 350-268-9101; chateauwestport.com). Enjoy a continental breakfast and a morning swim in a heated pool before heading to the beach.

March and April are peak times to catch sight of gray whale families migrating from their breeding lagoons in Baja California, to the krill-rich waters of the Bering Sea. To find out about whale-watching cruises, contact the Westport–Grayland Chamber of Commerce (2985 S. Montesano St.; 800-345-6223; westportgrayland-chamber.org).

Continue south from Westport on the coastal route. Drive along Highway 105 through the cranberry bogs of Grayland. The route joins again with US 101 after 30 miles in Raymond. Passing oceanfront parks like Grayland Beach State Park and South Beach State Park, Highway 105 wraps in along the east shore of Willapa Bay. This long, shallow bay is rich with wildlife and shellfish. En route to Raymond, you can sample this bivalve bounty by passing the Shoalwater Indian Reservation turnoff and stopping at the **Tokeland Hotel & Restaurant** (2964 Kindred Ave.; 360-267-7006; tokelandhotel.com). The hotel's dining room offers a panoramic view of Willapa Bay as well as hearty, Southern-influenced food that uses local products whenever possible. Owners Heather Earnhardt

Cranberry Coast

The semicircle of Aberdeen, Westport, and Raymond includes the Cranberry Coast Scenic Byway which focuses on the historical tribal culture of the Shoalwater Bay Native Americans and the community industries built around harvesting salmon, oysters, clams, timber, and cranberries. Inhabited by Native Americans and hardy settlers, this area's flavor of history is in the salt sea air and the uses of the lands and water including the rich natural resources of Willapa Bay.

A Coffin Goes West

Willie Keil, a 19-year-old anxious to lead his father's commune's wagon train west to Washington Territory in 1855, died of malaria just before departure, but his father kept his son's dream alive. Willie, in a lead-lined coffin filled with 100-proof whiskey and placed in a black-draped wagon/hearse, led the way. When stopped by Indians, Dad opened the coffin, and after they took a quick look, a potentially hostile encounter was avoided. Willie's marked grave is along Highway 6 about 6 miles east of Raymond.

and Zac Young raise chickens, bees, rabbits, and miniature pigs on the property and manage a lovely garden. Established in 1889 as the Kindred Inn, this is the oldest operating hotel in Washington State, offering simple but satisfying accommodations. But as with many coastal properties, there is concern over the ever-encroaching bay waters reclaiming land along the shoreline.

Raymond, just south of the junction of US 101 and Highway 105, is on the Willapa River. The old *Dennis Company* building at Blake and 5th Streets offers a glimpse of the region's history in an 85-foot-long mural depicting shipping and logging activity in 1905. Pop into *Ugly Ed's & Deb's New & Used Furniture* (100 3rd St.; 360-942-2345), 3 blocks from Dennis Company, for antiques, garage-sale-type items, and collectibles. Then visit the *Northwest Carriage Museum* (314 Alder St.; 360-942-4150; nwcarriagemuseum.org), open daily, year round, except Thanksgiving and Christmas day. Inspect 28 horse-drawn carriages, buggies, and sleighs dating from the late 1800s. In summer, browse for goodies like handmade quilts and local produce at the *Willapa Bay Public Market* (312 Alder St.). The 5-mile-long Willapa River Trail is part of a long-term 57-mile project called the Willapa Hills State Trail. It runs along the western part of Highway 6 in Raymond and on US 101 as it follows the river to South Bend.

Continuing on US 101, the roadsides are dotted with steel sculptures (loggers, Native Americans, bears, shorebirds) on the *Raymond Wildlife-Heritage Sculpture Corridor.* Then pass through the picturesque village of *South Bend,* also on the Willapa River. The town's shoreline is worth a leisurely stroll to view the fishing docks, piles of empty oyster shells, and oyster- and crab-processing plants. *Summerhouse* (931 Cole Ave.; 360-942-2843; willapaharbor.org/member/summerhouse), has a comfy guesthouse and 2 full RV hookups. The *Pacific County Historical Museum* (1008 W. Robert Bush Dr.; 360-875-5224; pacificcohistory.org), offers glimpses of the area's colorful past. The museum is open daily 12 p.m. to 3 p.m. Walk up the hill past some of the town's stately old houses for great views of the Willapa River and the Willapa Hills, and visit one of Washington's finest county courthouses on the corner of Memorial and Cowlitz Streets. Open during business hours, this elegant 1910 building sports an impressive art-glass dome and historical scenes painted in the 1940s.

sundaythieves

An economically collapsing Oysterville was the Pacific County seat. An illegal election handed that honor over to South Bend; in case an appeal was upheld (it was), 85 men crossed the Willapa Bay on a Sunday in 1893 and stole the records from Oysterville. They later sent a bill for services to the commissioners. It wasn't paid. The county seat remained South Bend.

The highway follows Willapa Bay's southeastern shore past South Bend, by rich wetland scenery, feasting grounds for migrating black brant geese. The estuary environment supports a mind-boggling array of life-forms, from mud-dwelling clams, shrimps, and oysters to the millions of marine birds that consume them. After crossing the Naselle River, see **Long Island** to the west, part of **Willapa National Wildlife Refuge** (360-484-3482; fws.gov/willapa). The island supports a coastal rain forest that includes a stand of old-growth cedars as well as mammal and shorebird populations. But you'll need a kayak or boat to reach the island and its trail and campsites.

Long Beach Peninsula

The Long Beach Peninsula is an inviting place to explore for day or weekend rambles. The roar of the surf is never far off, the air is washed clean by ocean winds, and there are activities galore. The larger beachside communities are popular tourist destinations, but you don't have to go far to find lesser-known treasures and quiet walking trails.

Enjoy a public art treasure hunt by searching for the numerous historical murals that grace the exteriors of many buildings in Ilwaco, Seaview, and Long Beach. A list of paintings in the **Centennial Murals Tour** is available from the **Long Beach Peninsula Visitors Bureau** (intersection of Hwys. 101 and 103, Seaview; 800-451-2542; funbeach.com).

Ilwaco is a fishing community at the peninsula's south end. The town's harbor is a great place to browse and see charter boats heading out to fish for salmon, sturgeon, bottom fish, or tuna. In the harbor area are canneries for fish and crab processing, fresh-fish markets, gift shops, and eateries. For gourmet food served up with Northwest wines and microbrews, the locals suggest **OleBob's Seafood Market and Gallery** (151 Howerton Way; 360-642-4332;

olebobs.com) with a combination of a fresh seafood market, gallery, and cafe. It's open for lunch Thurs to Mon. *Roots* (111 First Ave. N; 360-642-7668) is a go-to for coffee, smoothies, salads, acai bowls, and breakfast sandwiches. Between 1889 and 1930 the Ilwaco Railroad and Navigation Company transported goods and people up and down the peninsula, first by coach along the beach, then by narrow-gauge railway. We recommend stopping at the *Columbia Pacific Heritage Museum* (formerly the Ilwaco Heritage Museum). It's housed in the old telephone utilities building at 115 SE Lake St. (360-642-3446; columbiapacificheritagemuseum.com). There's a scale model of the 1890s narrow-gauge railway that ran along the beach between Ilwaco and tiny Nahcotta about 12 miles to the north, near present-day *Ocean Park.* Often referred to as the Clamshell Railway, it operated on a schedule governed by tides. The old railway depot is on display in the museum's courtyard. Have a seat on an original Clamshell Railway car. The museum is open year-round from 10 a.m. to 4 p.m. Tues through Sat. The first outdoor mural produced on the peninsula, a 1920s railway scene, is on the north side of the Doupe Brothers Hardware Store at Ilwaco's only traffic light. *Bailey's Bakery and Cafe* (26910 Sandridge Rd.; 360-665-4449; baileysbakerycafe.com) in Nahcotta is worth the slight detour off the main drag. This local favorite sells homemade scones, cookies, pastries, and sandwiches perfect for taking to the beach. At *Streetside Tacos* (1910 Bay Ave.; 360-244-5949) creative twists on the classic taco include a spicy Korean-inspired option.

Two and a half miles southwest of Ilwaco, off US 101, *Cape Disappointment State Park* (360-642-3078; parks.wa.gov) offers beaches, forest trails, campsites, and two historic lighthouses. Although it's easy to snare a spot in the winter without a reservation, all sites must be reserved in the summer. Call Washington State Parks for reservations, (888) 226-7688, or visit parks.wa.gov.

Waikiki Beach, a sheltered cove well-supplied with driftwood and smooth sand near the park entrance, is a great place to watch the Columbia River's busy shipping activities as well as a powerful storm's waves break high off the lighthouse cliff. For more dramatic views, hike along the trail to the *North Head Lighthouse.* The *Lewis and Clark Interpretive Center*

Sleep with History

Looking for unusual places to sleep? Washington offers US Forest Service fire lookouts (long on views, short on square footage), lighthouse keepers' residences at Cape Disappointment State Park, and the Victorian-furnished houses of Officer's Row at Fort Worden State Park in Port Townsend.

Storm Watching 101

When powerful winter storms batter Washington's ocean coast, it's time to pick a spot and enjoy the show. The trick is to be smart by wearing layers of warm clothing topped by raincoats, boots, gloves, and headgear. Then you can laugh in the face of 10-foot-high waves pounding cliffs and sand, 60 mph winds, and high-velocity spray. What you can't be casual about are huge driftwood logs being tossed about like toothpicks or rolling at the water's edge. People have been killed when swept out to sea by an extra-large rogue wave or struck by a log. Five good storm-watching spots along the Washington coastline are Waikiki Beach at Cape Disappointment State Park (Ilwaco), Kalaloch, Ocean Shores, Ruby Beach, and Westport. For more information on the safest locations, call the Long Beach Peninsula Visitors Bureau, (800) 451-2542, or Westport–Grayland Visitor Information Center, (800) 345-6223.

(360-642-3029) offers views of the Columbia River. A stroll through the center takes you on Lewis and Clark's heroic journey from Camp Du Bois in Wood River, Illinois, to the Pacific Ocean.

Now head north on US 101 to **Seaview** for meandering back roads that offer pleasant views of quaint cottages, many established during the late 19th century as summer retreats. The **Shelburne Country Inn B&B** at 4415 Pacific Hwy. (360-642-2442; shelburnehotelwa.com) was built in 1896 and restored in the 1970s. Along with antiques, homemade quilts, and a bountiful herb garden, the inn features hearty country breakfasts, lunches, and dinners in the restaurant. The Shelburne also provides breakfast for the **China Beach Retreat** (222 Robert Gray Dr.; 360-777-3312; chinabeachretreat.com), an early 1900s waterfront cabin; the Audubon Cottage is on the China Beach grounds. Nearby, the **Depot Restaurant** (1208 38th Place; 360-642-7880; depotrestaurantdining .com) operates in Seaview's original Clamshell Railway Depot.

Long Beach, the largest town on the Long Beach Peninsula, has a wooden boardwalk stretching a half-mile along the beach from Bolstad Avenue providing easy access to the roaring surf, rustling dune grass, and wide, sandy beach. Subtle lighting along the way makes the boardwalk ideal for a romantic evening stroll. From here you can see the array of multicolored kites that folks of all ages fly on the beach in late August during the **Washington State International Kite Festival** (and any time the wind's right). **Discovery Trail,** an 8-mile walk through the dunes, parallels the boardwalk for part of its journey from Long Beach to Ilwaco.

The hip **Adrift Hotel** (409 Sid Snyder Dr.; 800-561-2456; adrifthotel.com) sports ocean views, modern stylings, and complimentary bicycles. Worth dining at whether you're staying here or elsewhere is the hotel's **Pickled Fish** restaurant (360-642-2344; pickledfishrestaurant.com), on the top floor of the hotel. Locally-caught fish meets craft beer and cocktails here. The owners also operate the slightly more upscale *Inn at Discovery Coast* (360-642-5265; innatdiscoverycoast.com), practically next door and also on the beach and the Shelburne in Seaview.

Be sure to stop at the *World Kite Museum & Hall of Fame* (303 SW Sid Snyder Dr.; 360-642-4020; worldkitemuseum.com) in Long Beach, which features displays from delicate butterfly and dragon kites to huge fighting kites and videos. The museum's impressive collection numbers more than 1,500 kites representing cultures around the world. You can visit Wed through Sun, 11 a.m. to 5 p.m. from May 1 to June 15; daily 11 a.m. to 5 p.m. June 16 through Sept 15; and 11 a.m. to 5 p.m. Fri through Tues, Sept 16 through April 30. Good places to grab a bite to eat on the Long Beach Peninsula include the *Berry Patch* (1513 Bay Ave., Ocean Park; 360-665-5551); *Captain Bob's Chowder* (409 Pacific Ave., Long Beach; 360-642-2082; captainbobschowder.com); and *Cottage Bakery & Deli* (118 Pacific Hwy., Long Beach; 360-642-4441).

Continuing north from Long Beach, travelers can find access to the beach at Cranberry Road, Loomis Beach, Ocean Park, and Pacific Pines State Park; or a walk on sandy paths lined with wild strawberry plants. The beaches are great spots for quiet seaside picnics. If you like being closer to the action, check out *Boardwalk Cottages* at 800 Boulevard Ave. in Long Beach (360-642-2305; boardwalkcottages.com) or the *Seaview Motel & Cottages* (3728 Pacific Way; 360-642-8008; seaviewmotelandcottages.com). To bed down in the former digs of the lighthouse keepers, located just inland from North Head Lighthouse and

Lewis and Clark Corps of Discovery

On November 7, 1805, William Clark wrote in his journal: "Great joy in camp we are in view of the Ocian. . . ." For the record, the party was still some 20 miles from the Pacific Ocean, but they finally arrived at the mouth of the Columbia River on November 20 and set up Station Camp. Although Clark scouted up the Long Beach Peninsula some 9 miles for a possible winter headquarters site, the party backtracked upriver and, on the advice of Clatsop Indians about food sources, started crossing to the Oregon side of the river on November 26. By December 7 the whole party was hunkered down at the *Fort Clatsop* site and began building their winter quarters. Now the *Lewis and Clark National Historical Park* can be found near Astoria, which was also established as a trading site at the mouth of the Columbia River in 1811. For more information, check *Discovering Lewis & Clark,* a multimedia site incorporating the entire route (lewis-clark.org) or *Lewis and Clark Trail Heritage Foundation* (lewisandclark.org).

Cape Disappointment State Park, reserve at (888) 226-7688. For information on other cottages, motels, and beachside RV parks, contact the **Long Beach Peninsula Visitors Bureau** (800-451-2542; funbeach.com).

Romantics can contact innkeepers Susie Goldsmith and Bill Verner at **Boreas Bed & Breakfast Inn,** also close to the ocean at 607 N. Ocean Beach Blvd. in Long Beach (360-642-8069; boreasinn.com). There's a whirlpool spa in an enclosed cedar-and-glass gazebo. Breakfast is a lively event, with guests gathering on the main level for such tasty treats as roasted Washington pears stuffed with pecans, peach kuchen baked in custard, and a three-mushroom frittata sautéed with sherry. Another pleasant place to stay is the 1929 **Moby Dick Hotel, Restaurant and Oyster Farm** (25814 Sandridge Rd., Nahcotta; 360-665-4543; mobydickhotel.com).

The tiny town of **Nahcotta** has been the center of the peninsula's oyster industry. Native oysters, a tribal staple for centuries, were wiped out by the 1920s through overharvesting, disease, and freezing weather. The introduction of Japanese oysters and new cultivation techniques has made this Willapa Bay area one of the top oyster-growing places in the world. Pop over to **Oysterville Sea Farms** at 1st and Clark Streets in Oysterville (360-665-6585; willabay .com) to see the oyster-shucking process and to shop for fresh oysters and cranberry goodies.

Visit the **Willapa Bay Oyster House Interpretive Center** at 273rd Place in a replica of an oyster station house on Nahcotta's breakwater. The center (360-665-4547; portofpeninsula.org/oysterhouse.html) exhibits 150 years of oyster-growing and is open from 11 a.m. to 4 p.m. on Fri, weekends, and holidays Memorial Day through Labor Day. The walls are covered with old photographs, memorabilia, oyster-harvesting tools, maps, and a 20-foot mural of Willapa Bay. From here continue north on Sandridge Road to **Oysterville,** established in 1854 to house oyster workers and families. Every building in town is listed on the National Historic Register. You can see the local church, a one-room schoolhouse, the general store, and early 1900s houses as you stroll through this extremely quiet bayside village.

Marine Trails

Four marine trails offer paddlers not only routes but camping sites accessible to non-motorized craft: the 140-mile **Cascadia Marine Trail** in Puget Sound, **Willapa Bay Water Trail, Lakes-to-Lock Water Trail** in Seattle, and the 146-mile **Lower Columbia River Water Trail** between Washington and Oregon. For maps and information visit wwta.org/trails and columbiawatertrail.org.

Three miles north of Oysterville, take the tree-lined Stackpole Road to **Leadbetter Point State Park** at the far end of the peninsula with its 28-mile-long continuous ribbon of beaches. A favorite place for bird--watchers, Leadbetter Point's tidal flats overflow with migrating shorebirds and geese in April and May. Four trails lead walkers and birders through park or refuge with Willapa Bay on the east and the Pacific Ocean on the west.

Along the Columbia River

From Ilwaco head east to little **Chinook** on US 101 along the Columbia River. It was one of the most prosperous communities in Washington during the 1880s when fishing traps lined the river and tons of fish were processed in waterfront canneries. The traps were banned in 1935, but the port of Chinook is still a major fishing center in the area where you can see many old homes built in the late 1800s.

Passing the Astoria-Megler Bridge to Oregon, which links across the river mouth, and traveling north on Highway 401 and east on Highway 4, the landscape is mostly forestlands along the Columbia River. Pass the communities of **Naselle, Rosburg, Grays River, Skamokawa,** and **Cathlamet.** Stop for a photo opportunity in Grays River at the state's oldest remaining covered bridge used by the public. The 1905 wooden bridge stretches across the Grays River and is a 1-minute drive off Highway 4 on Covered Bridge Road, a few miles west of Rosburg; call or visit the Wahkiakum County Chamber of Commerce (360-795-9996; cathlametchamber.com) for directions.

Plan to stop at the **Julia Butler Hansen National Wildlife Refuge** (46 Steamboat Slough Rd.; 360-795-3915; fws.gov/jbh) near Cathlamet and drive through its more than 6,000 acres of diked floodplain covered with thick grass and woodland habitat for birds and land animals. There are also trails for walking or bicycling. The refuge was created to protect the endangered Columbia white-tailed deer.

Travelers can find lodgings at **Skamokawa Resort** (1391 W. Hwy. 4; 360-795-0726; skamokawaresort.com). The light and airy guest rooms are situated in the historic Skamokawa General Store building, constructed on a wide deck that extends about 40 feet over the north bank of the Columbia River. From your lofty perch on the second floor, enjoy views of one of the main sections of the **Lower Columbia River Water Trail** (columbiawatertrail.org) and to the adjacent **Julia Butler Hanson and Lewis and Clark National Wildlife Refuges.** Ask the innkeepers about kayak rentals, instruction, and guide services.

The **Inn at Crippen Creek** (15 Oatfield Rd.; 360-795-0585; crippencreek .com) in Skamokawa offers 2 rooms on a secluded 14-acre valley setting with a

Female Force

Julia Butler Hansen, who had a national wildlife refuge named after her, won all 21 elections in her 43-year political career at three levels. As a congressional representative, she was the first woman to chair a subcommittee of the House Appropriations Committee and was an expert on the US highway system. Her Cathlamet home at 35 Butler St., built in 1860, is the county's oldest building and the town's main attraction.

meandering creek. A little more inland in the Willapa Hills is the *Inn at Lucky Mud* (44 Old Chestnut Dr.; 360-795-8770; luckymud.com). Ask your musician hosts to tell you the story behind the B&B's name; if you're lucky, they'll sing and play for you at breakfast. For eateries in the Skamokawa area, try the *Grays River Cafe* (3745 State Route 4; 360-465-2999) or *Duffy's Irish Pub* (3779 State Route 4 West; 360-465-2898), both located in Grays River.

The town of Cathlamet sits above the Columbia River, well situated for watching the parade of river traffic and enjoying views of the rural farmland of *Puget Island.* The 7-mile-long island is perfect for an easy bicycle ride, and from the south end you can board the last remaining passenger ferry on the Lower Columbia River to the Oregon side, connecting you to Westport on Highway 30, running east to Portland or west to Astoria.

For local accommodations, you could call the innkeepers at the *Bradley House Inn,* 61 Main St. in Cathlamet (360-269-6737). Bed down in comfort in this gracious 1907 Eastlake home built by an early lumber baron. Enjoy a stay at the Italian-style *Villa at Little Cape Horn* (48 Little Cape Horn Rd.; 360-578-9100; villalittlecapehorn.com) a few miles east of Cathlamet. The 4-bedroom lodging sits above the Columbia River with magnificent views and a private 2-mile beach.

Cathlamet offers good eats with friendly service at *Sharon's Pizza & More* (140 3rd St.; 360-795-3311; sharonspizza.com). The *Wahkiakum County Historical Museum* (65 River St.; 360-795-3954), which has been collecting community histories for more than half a century, offers artifacts of work and daily life from when the town was young.

Places to Stay on the Washington Coast

ABERDEEN

Abel House Bed & Breakfast
117 Fleet St. South
Montesano
(360) 249-6002

AMANDA PARK

Lake Quinault Lodge
345 S. Shore Rd.
(360) 288-2900
lakequinault.com

Lake Quinault Resort
314 N. Shore Rd.
(360) 288-2362
quinaultrainforest.com/
Lake-Quinault-Lodging/
lake-quinault-resort.html

Lochaerie Resort Cabins
638 N. Shore Rd.
(360) 288-2215
lochaerie.com

CATHLAMET

Bradley House Inn
61 Main St.
(360) 269-6737
bradleyhousebb.com

DUNGENESS

Williams Manor Bed and Breakfast
4043 Sequim Dungeness Way
(360) 460-3763
williamsmanor-sequim.com

FORKS AND HOH RAIN FOREST

Hoh Valley Cabins at Elk Meadows
5843 Upper Hoh Rd.
(360) 374-5111
hoh-valley-cabins-at-elk
-meadows.washington-
state.net

Kalaloch Lodge
157151 Hwy. 101
(866) 662-9928
visitkalaloch.com

Manitou Lodge
813 Kilmer Rd.
(360) 374-6295
manitoulodge.com

Mill Creek Inn
1061 S. Forks Ave.
(360) 374-5873
forksbnb.com

Miller Tree Inn Bed & Breakfast
654 E. Division St.
(360) 374-6806
millertreeinn.com

Misty Valley Inn Bed & Breakfast
194894 US 101 North
(360) 374-9389
mistyvalleyinn.com

Rain Forest Hostel
Hwy. 101 between mile markers 169 and 170
(360) 374-2270
rainforesthostel.com

Shady Nook Cottage
81 Ash Ave.
(360) 374-5497
shadynookcottage.com

HOOD CANAL

Alderbrook Resort & Spa
10 E. Alderbrook Ridge Dr.
(360) 898-2200
alderbrookresort.com

Glen Ayr Hood Canal Waterfront Resort
25381 N. Hwy. 101
(360) 877-9522
glenayr.com

Rest-a-While RV Park
Hwy. 101
(360) 877-9474
restawhile.com

LA PUSH

Quileute Oceanside Resort
330 Ocean Dr.
(800) 487-1267
quileuteoceanside.com

LILLIWAUP

Mike's Beach Resort
38470 US-101
(360) 877-5324
mikesbeachresort.com

LONG BEACH

Adrift Hotel
409 Sid Snyder Dr.
(800) 561-2456
adrifthotel.com

Boardwalk Cottages
800 Boulevard Ave.
(360) 642-2305
boardwalkcottages.com

Boreas Bed & Breakfast Inn
607 North Blvd.
(360) 642-8069
boreasinn.com

Inn at Discovery Coast
421 11th St. SW
(360)642-5265
innatdiscoverycoast.com

NAHCOTTA

Moby Dick Hotel,
Restaurant and Oyster
Farm
25814 Sandridge Rd.
(360) 665-4543
mobydickhotel.com

NEAH BAY/CLALLAM BAY

Hobuck Beach Resort
2726 Makah Passage
(360) 645-2339
hobuckbeachresort.com

Lost Resort
20860 Hoko-Ozette Rd.
(800) 950-2899
lostresort.net

Winter Summer Inn
16651 Hwy. 112
(360) 963-2264
wintersummerinn.com

OCEAN SHORES

The Canterbury Inn
643 Ocean Shores Blvd.
NW
(360) 289-3317
canterburyinn.com

PORT ANGELES

Five SeaSuns Bed &
Breakfast
1006 S. Lincoln St.
(360) 452-8248
seasuns.com

Lake Crescent Lodge
416 Lake Crescent Rd.
(360) 928-3211
lakecrescentlodge.com

Log Cabin Resort
3183 E. Beach Rd.
(888) 896-3818
olympicnationalparks.com

Port Angeles Downtown
Hotel
101½ E. Front St.
(360) 565-1125
portangelesdowntownhotel
.com

Sol Duc Hot Springs
Resort
12076 Sol Duc Rd.
(360) 327-3583
visitsolduc.com

RAYMOND

Summerhouse
931 Cole Ave.
(360) 942-2843
willapaharbor.org/member/
summerhouse

SEAVIEW/ILWACO

China Beach Retreat
222 Robert Gray Dr.
(360) 777-3312
chinabeachretreat.com

Seaview Motel &
Cottages
3728 Pacific Way
(360) 642-8008
seaviewmotelandcottages
.com

Shelburne Country Inn
B&B
4415 Pacific Hwy.
(360) 642-2442
shelburnehotelwa.com

SEQUIM

Domaine Madeleine Bed
& Breakfast Inn
146 Wildflower Ln.
(360) 457-4174
domainemadeleine.com

Dungeness Bay Cottages
140 Marine Dr.
(360) 683-3013
dungenessbaycottages
.com

Juan de Fuca Cottages
182 Marine Dr.
(360) 683-4433
juandefuca.com

Red Caboose Getaway
24 Old Coyote Way
(360) 683-7350
redcaboosegetaway.com

ALSO WORTH SEEING

The Cranberry Museum & Farm
Long Beach
cranberrymuseum.com

Moclips
Hwy. 109, north of Ocean Shores
visitmoclips.com

SELECTED INFORMATION CENTERS & OTHER HELPFUL WEBSITES

Forks
(360) 374-2531
forkswa.com

Grays Harbor County
(800) 321-1924
graysharbor.org

Hood Canal
(360) 877-2021
explorehoodcanal.com

Lewis and Clark
lewisandclarkwa.com

Long Beach Peninsula
(800) 451-2542
funbeach.com

Olympic National Forest
fs.usda.gov/olympic

Olympic National Park
nps.gov/olym

Olympic Peninsula
(800) 942-4042
olympicpeninsula.org

Port Angeles
(360) 452-2363
portangeles.org

Sequim
(800) 737-8462
visitsunnysequim.com

Shelton-Mason County
(800) 576-2021
explorehoodcanal.com

Westport/Grayland
(800) 345-6223
westportgrayland-chamber.org

SKAMOKAWA

Inn at Lucky Mud
44 Old Chestnut Dr.
(360) 795-8770
luckymud.com

Skamokawa Resort
1391 W. Hwy. 4
(360) 795-0726
skamokawaresort.com

TOKELAND

Tokeland Hotel & Restaurant
2964 Kindred Ave.
(360) 267-7006
tokelandhotel.com

WESTPORT

Chateau Westport
710 Hancock
(360) 268-9101
chateauwestport.com

Loge at the Sands
1416 S. Montesano St.
(360) 268-0091
logecamps.com/
westport-wa

Places to Eat on the Washington Coast

ABERDEEN

Billy's Bar and Grill
322 E. Heron St.
(360) 533-7144

CATHLAMET

Sharon's Pizza & More
140 3rd St.
(360) 795-3311
sharonspizza.com

FORKS

Creekside Restaurant at Kalaloch Lodge
157151 US 101
(360) 962-2271

Pacific Pizza
870 S. Forks Ave.
(360) 374-2626

Sully's Drive-in
220 N. Forks Ave.
(360) 374-5075

ILWACO

OleBob's Seafood Market and Gallery
151 Howerton Way
(360) 642-4332
olebobs.com

Roots
111 First Ave. N
(360) 642-7668

LILLIWAUP

Hama Hama Oyster Saloon
35846 US-101
(360) 877-5811
hamahamaoysters.com

LONG BEACH

Captain Bob's Chowder
409 Pacific Ave.
(360) 642-2082
captainbobschowder.com

Cottage Bakery & Deli
118 Pacific Hwy.
(360) 642-4441

Pickled Fish
409 Sid Snyder Dr.
(360) 642-2344
pickledfishrestaurant.com

NAHCOTTA

Bailey's Bakery and Cafe
26910 Sandridge Rd.
(360) 665-4449
baileysbakerycafe.com

Streetside Tacos
1910 Bay Ave.
(360) 244-5949

OCEAN PARK

Berry Patch
1513 Bay Ave.
(360) 665-5551

PORT ANGELES

Barhop Brewing and Artisan Pizza
124 W. Railroad Ave.
(360) 797-1818

Bella Italia
118 E. 1st St.
(360) 457-5442
bellaitaliapa.com

First Street Haven Cafe
107 E. 1st St.
(360) 457-0352

LD's Woodfire Grill
929 W. 8th St.
(360) 452-0400
ldswoodfiregrill.com

SEQUIM

Alder Wood Bistro
139 W. Alder St.
(360) 683-4321
alderwoodbistro.com

Dockside Grill
John Wayne Marina
(360) 683-7510
docksidegrill-sequim.com

Oak Table Cafe
3rd and Bell Streets
(360) 204-5198
oaktablecafe.com

SHELTON

Ritz Drive-In
325 S. 1st St.
(360) 427-9294

Riverside Espresso
332 S. 1st St.
(360) 426-3300

Urraco Coffee Company
628 W. Cota St.
(360) 462-5282
urracocoffee.com

WESTPORT

Aloha Alabama BBQ and Bakery
2309 Westhaven Dr.
(360) 268-7299
alohaalabama.com

Puget Sound Region

You could spend your whole life exploring the Puget Sound region and still need more time. Its inland waterways, cut out by glaciers, offer travelers thousands of miles of shoreline, waterfront communities, and dozens of islands. The region's moist maritime climate supports lush forests and farms. A dynamic economy based on high tech, natural resources, agriculture, and industry has attracted a diverse culture.

Although population explosions have brought communities off I-405 east of Seattle onto the beaten path, *Bellevue,* Redmond, Kirkland, and Woodinville also have their share of offerings. Plan an hour or more to enjoy the splendid *Bellevue Botanical Gardens* at 12001 Main St., Bellevue (425-452-2750; bellevuebotanical.org). Stroll along and through a lush perennial border garden, a summer dahlia display, a rhododendron glen, a meditative Japanese garden, an alpine rock garden, and a loop trail through the reserve.

To the east, 6 miles north of Fall City on Highway 203, *Remlinger Farms* has more than 200 acres of fruits, vegetables, and berries, as well as a farm-animal petting zoo for children, picnic tables, a farm-fresh produce store, restaurant, and bakery. Remlinger Farms offers a Ripe 'n Ready Report of

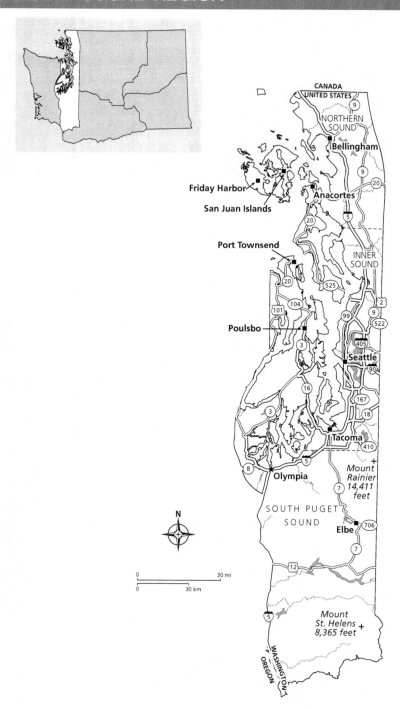

For Wine Aficionados

The grand duchess of wineries in the Seattle area is the elegant **Chateau Ste. Michelle** at 14111 NE 145th in Woodinville. Tall Douglas fir, colorful rhododendrons, and lush beds of annuals and perennials greet visitors entering the gates. Folks can enjoy shady picnic areas, the gift shop, seasonal events, and a tour of the wine-making process. The winery's extremely popular summer concert series attracts top names and large crowds who sit on the lawn. For information, call (425) 488-1133 or check out ste-michelle.com. Wine aficionados also have other options:

Alexandria Nicole Cellars
14810 145th Ave. NE
Woodinville
(425) 487-9463
alexandrianicolecellars.com

DeLille Cellars
14208 Redmond-Woodinville Rd. NE
Woodinville
(425) 489-0544
delillecellars.com

Novelty Hill Januik
14710 Redmond-Woodinville Rd. NE
Woodinville
(425) 481-5502
noveltyhilljanuik.com

WT Vintners
19495 144th Ave. NE, Ste. B210
Woodinville
wtvintners.com

For additional information check the website: woodinvillewinecountry.com.

in-season produce by calling (425) 333-4135 or browsing the farm's website, remlingerfarms.com. The farm is located half a mile off Hwy. 203 on NE 32nd St., just south of Carnation.

Farther east is the picturesque **Snoqualmie Valley,** surrounded by the foothills of the Cascade mountain range. The Snoqualmie River, flowing through the valley, creates the spectacular 270-foot Snoqualmie Falls between Snoqualmie and Fall City. Above the falls are a public overlook and the posh **Salish Lodge & Spa** (6501 Railroad Ave.; 425-888-2556; salishlodge.com).

The **Northwest Railway Museum** (38625 SE King St., Snoqualmie; 425-888-3030; trainmuseum.org) is open daily. Scenic rides on a diesel-electric train are offered on Sat and Sun, Apr through Oct as well as many holidays, leaving from the restored Victorian train station to the nearby community of North Bend and then to the top of Snoqualmie Falls and back.

For toothsome treats, be sure to stop by **Snoqualmie Falls Candy Shoppe** (8102 Railroad Ave. Southeast; 425-888-0439; snofallcandyshoppe.com) for delicious fudge, taffy, peanut brittle, and caramel corn as well as a great selection of ice cream. You could also stop at **Gilman Village** in nearby **Issaquah** to sample chocolate confections at **Boehm's Candies** (255 NE Gilman Blvd.; 425-392-6652; boehmscandies.com). For a cozy place to spend the night, call the **Roaring River Bed & Breakfast** (46715 SE 129th St., North Bend; 425-888-4834; theroaringriver.com), which offers 1 cabin and 4 rooms with private entrances, sitting areas, and decks overlooking the bubbling Middle Fork of the Snoqualmie River. For extra privacy, the hosts deliver a hot breakfast directly to the room, often with French toast, eggs, sausage, and fruit.

South Puget Sound

Using a generous definition of **South Puget Sound,** let's go southeast from The Sound toward picturesque **Mount Rainier,** a dominant feature seen from the lower sound and a stunning up close backdrop to many interesting places in the area around Mount Rainier National Park.

The steam-powered **Mount Rainier Scenic Railroad** excursion train takes riders on a slow jaunt from Mineral Lake near the southwest entrance to the park. On this 1.5-hour round-trip, you'll pass through thick evergreen forests, cross bubbling mountain streams, and enjoy spectacular views of the sleeping volcano's summit. Passengers can sit in an open carriage or relax in a closed, heated car. Trains leave at Fri, Sat, and Sun from Memorial Day through the end of Sept, with special event trains for the fall foliage and Halloween and Christmas holidays. For further information call (888) 783-2611 or check mtrainierrailroad.com.

In the nearby **Elbe** railyard, about 10 miles from the national park entrance, two classic dining cars of the **Mount Rainier Railroad Dining Company** are permanently parked on the tracks—a 1922 Southern Pacific and a 1910 Great Northern, offering a railroad dining car experience. A lounge named the Side Track Room is located in a late-1930s Chicago, Burlington, and Quincy coach. The dining cars are open daily for breakfast, lunch, and dinner. Call (360) 569-2505 or visit rrdiner.com for reservations.

Eight miles farther east on Highway 706 is **Ashford,** a small community of artists, outdoor enthusiasts, and old-timers who appreciate living at the entrance to **Mount Rainier National Park** (nps.gov/mora). On your way from Elbe, look for **Dan Klennert's Ex-Nihilo** outdoor sculpture park (danielklennert.com) on the right-hand side of

ultimatesummit

Each year between 9,000 and 11,000 climbers try to reach the top of 14,411-foot Mount Rainier, which has the most glaciers (25) of any US mainland mountain. Only about half reach the summit; some die trying. The park's climbing rangers are the go-to folks for information: (360) 569-6641.

the road. Travelers are welcome to walk among large metal sculptures, such as elk, a skeleton on a Harley-Davidson motorcycle, a larger-than-life bicycle, and a 17-foot-tall giraffe named Aspen Zoe. Klennert's work was featured in the Disney movie *America's Heart and Soul.*

Ashford is Rainier-climbing central, home to **Rainier Mountaineering Inc.** (30027 Hwy. 706 E; 888-892-5462; rmiguides.com). RMI has guided thousands of climbers to the summit since 1969. **International Mountain Guides** (31111 Hwy. 706 E; 360-569-2609; mountainguides.com) also works out of Ashford. Peter and Erika Whittaker's **Whittaker Mountaineering** (30027 Hwy. 706 E; 800-238-5756; whittakermountaineering.com) sells and rents climbing gear. The adjacent **Base Camp Grill** (360-569-2727; basecampgrill.com) is open in the summer. Grab a bite and let the kids work off some energy on the nearby not-too-high climbing wall.

Also here is **Whittaker's Historic Bunkhouse Motel** and **Whittaker's Cafe** (30205 Hwy. 706 East; 360-569-2439; whittakersbunkhouse.com). Win and Sarah were the force behind creating the annual **Rainier Independent Film Festival** (rainier.film) at three venues in the Ashford Valley. On the east edge of Ashford, stop at **Ashford Creek Pottery** (30510 Hwy. 706; 360-569-1000; ashfordcreekgallery.com). The charming studio offers functional stoneware enlivened with irises and also displays pottery by local artists.

The **Mountain Meadows Inn** (28912 Hwy. 706 East; 360-569-0507; mountainmeadows-inn.com) is a comfortable bed-and-breakfast. It was the home of the superintendent of National Mill in 1910, once the biggest lumber mill west of the Mississippi River. Guests wake to a hearty, gourmet country breakfast. Wildlife is often visible from the generous front porch or on a stroll on forest trails.

Another favorite lodging and eatery in these parts is **Alexander's Lodge at Mount Rainier** (37515 Hwy. 706 East; 360-569-2300; alexanderslodge.com), just 3 miles east of Ashford. Luminaries such as Theodore Roosevelt and William Howard Taft have bunked down at this 12-room 1912 homestead. The panfried trout comes from its own glacier-fed pond; the baked salmon and beef tenderloin are served with roasted potatoes; and there's homemade blackberry pie for dessert.

Before heading up to the mountain, consider being pampered at **Stormking Spa and Cabins** (37311 Hwy. 706; 360-569-2964; stormkingspa.com) or **Wellspring Spa and Retreat** (54922 Kernahan Rd.; 360-569-2514; wellspring spa.com) where licensed massage therapist Sunny Thompson has created a mountain paradise of saunas, waterfalls, hot tubs, comfortable rooms, cozy log cabins, and a tree house. The outdoor hot tubs overlook landscaped gardens with terraced waterfalls and cooing doves.

Seattle Tours

Seattle's Space Needle, Seattle Center, Pike Place Market, and other landmarks are definitely not off the beaten path, so if you've been there, done that, opt for tours that will take you behind the scenes instead.

Although Seattle is not known for its crime, it does have a dark side. *Private Eye Tours* (206-365-3739; privateeyetours.com) explores the unusual, macabre, and sometimes just strange side of the city—if you're brave enough. Choose between the Queen Anne and Capitol Hill Mystery and Murder tours (a mass murder, an axman, brothels, Jimi Hendrix, serial killer Ted Bundy) or the two ghost tours (phantoms and poltergeists, a mortuary, a gambling den, a poor farm, a castle, a haunted theater, a notorious rooming house).

Even the famous *Pike Place Market* (pikeplacemarket.org) can be home to a different type of visit. If tourists go on their own, the sights, sounds, smells, and crowds may be a little overwhelming and confusing. But at least three companies offer 2- to 3-hour walking food tours that include the culinary landmark, jaunts best taken early in a multiday stay to introduce you to bakeries or restaurants worth a return visit. It's a chance to experience Pike Place Market like a local and learn a few tips, perhaps how to pick the best fish or where the best local hangouts are. Not to mention you get to nibble your way through the tour.

Show Me Seattle (206-633-2489; showmeseattle.com) covers the market and adjacent Belltown with its lunch tours. Guides share stories about area history, chefs' backgrounds, ethnic eateries, nightlife, and restaurant specialties, including Pacific Rim–inspired cuisine and award-winning chowder. *Savor Seattle Tours* (206-209-5485; savorseattletours.com) is a food-and-cultural adventure with cherry-inspired treats, Russian piroshky pastries, artisan-made cheeses, and clam chowder.

Bill Speidel's Underground Tour (206-682-4646; undergroundtour.com) is worth the admission just to hear the guide's wildly entertaining spiel at the start of the tour inside a

Other accommodations close to Ashford include **Nisqually Lodge** (31609 Hwy. 706 East; 360-569-8804; whitepasstravel.com/nisqually) for comfy lodge-style rooms and **Mounthaven Resort** (38210 Hwy. 706 East; 360-569-2594; mounthaven.com) for cabins and RV spaces.

On the far north side of Mount Rainier, **Alta Crystal Resort** (68317 State Rte. 410 E; 360-663-2500; altacrystalresort.com) offers cabins and chalets at the Crystal Mountain Ski Area, a short walk from summer hiking and mountain biking trails through old-growth trees within the Mount Baker–Snoqualmie National Forest. In 2011, the resort opened the Mount Rainier Gondola for summertime sightseeing. It travels up the ski hill in less than 10 minutes, and the views are worth the trip: see five of Washington's volcanic peaks from the summit, where there is a restaurant.

For a complete list of area lodging, go to visitrainier.com.

1890s saloon. The tour takes groups under the streets and sidewalks into former downtown Seattle with plenty of humorous commentary.

For an Asian cultural tour, take a trip with *Chinatown Discovery* (206-623-5124; seattle chinatowntour.com) through the fragrances, foods, languages, and history of the International District. While you're there, make time for an extended stroll through the *Wing Luke Museum of the Asian Pacific American Experience* (206-623-5124; wingluke .org), transformed in 2008 to more than eight times its original size in a 1910 building financed by Chinese immigrants. Parts of the museum, like the Yick Fung Company store, are accessible only through daily guided tours. Or follow the long journey told in the *Northwest African American Museum* (206-518-6000; naamnw.org), also opened in 2008. Tragedy and triumph, creativity and context, history and tales of new immigrants are part of the mix.

Specialty tours are also abundant. *Fifth Avenue Theatre* (206-625-1418; 5thavenue.org) has a free 20-minute guided tour that covers the building's past and ornate architecture. *CenturyLink Field* (centurylinkfield.com), home of the Seahawks, and *Safeco Field* (seattle.mariners.mlb.com), home of the Mariners, offer tours. Or join an architecture tour put on by the *Seattle Architecture Foundation* (seattlearchitecture.org).

If you want more traditional tours, take a look at *Tours Northwest* (888-293-1404; tours northwest.com), a 50-mile ride by popular attractions, including the salmon ladder at the Ballard Locks and the sports stadiums.

Let's Tour Seattle (206-632-1447; letstourseattle.com) has 3- and 4-hour whirlwind tours stuffed with sights, history, and humor as you roll by floating homes, the Fremont troll, Washington Park Arboretum, and many other notable locations. *Seattle Free Walking Tours* (425-770-6928; seattlewalkingtours.com) offers easy to moderate on-foot excursions that can cover Bill Boeing to Bill Gates. Among several options, *Gray Line of Seattle* (800-426-7532; grayline.com) offers a hop-on, hop-off double-decker bus.

Mount Rainier National Park celebrated its centennial anniversary in 1999; its jewel, Mount Rainier, rises to an elevation of 14,411 feet above sea level—although until high-tech GPS measurements in the 1980s, the height was listed (and often still is) at 14,410 feet. Because of its elevation, ice, and snow, weather-related changes can happen here almost without warning, and scientists say that the mountain can—one day—erupt again. But for now you can enjoy two scenic drives that lead to panoramic locations. The first, **Paradise,** is reached from Ashford or Packwood and is accessible based on weather conditions; the second, **Sunrise,** is reached from the east side near the Chinook Pass highway only from June until late September or early October. Sunrise is the more winding drive, but the rewards are many, including wonderful wildflower meadows with environmentally sensitive paths and trails among the native flora. There's a visitor center and day lodge.

American Camp, English Camp
San Juan Island National Historical Park
San Juan Island
nps.gov

Bloedel Reserve Gardens
Bainbridge Island
bloedelreserve.org

Center for Wooden Boats
Seattle
cwb.org

Ebey's Landing
Whidbey Island
nps.gov/ebla

Fort Worden State Park
Port Townsend
parks.wa.gov/fortworden

Hovander Homestead Park
Ferndale

Island County Historical Museum
Coupeville
wp.islandhistory.org

Pacific Northwest Quilt & Fiber Arts Museum
La Conner
qfamuseum.org

Langley Whale Center
Langley
orcanetwork.org

Lynden Pioneer Museum
Lynden
lyndenpioneermuseum.com

Mason County Historical Society Museum
Shelton
masoncountyhistoricalsociety.org

Meerkerk Rhododendron Gardens
Whidbey Island
meerkerkgardens.org

Mount Rainier National Park
Ashford
nps.gov/mora

Mount Rainier Scenic Railroad
Elbe
mtrainierrailroad.com

Museum of Glass
Tacoma
museumofglass.org

Peace Arch International Park
Blaine
peacearchpark.org

Pioneer Farm Museum
Eatonville
pioneerfarmmuseum.org

Port Townsend Marine Science Center
Port Townsend
ptmsc.org

Sidney Art Gallery
Port Orchard
sidneymuseumandarts.com

Skagit Valley Tulip Festival
Mount Vernon
tulipfestival.org

SPARK Museum of Electrical Invention
Bellingham
sparkmuseum.org

Suquamish Museum
Suquamish
suquamishmuseum.org

Wolf Haven International
Tenino
wolfhaven.org

Paradise is more of a year-round destination with late spring wildflowers, summer hiking, and winter snowshoeing and tubing. The grand Paradise Inn stays open mid-May to early Oct, but you can also stop in for brunch or shopping. Nearby, find a visitor center with excellent exhibits about the mountain. Both Paradise and Sunrise are more than 5,000 feet in elevation, so travelers should take warm sweaters and jackets on this trek.

flyingsaucers

On June 24, 1947, a pilot saw nine unusual-looking aircraft flying very fast by Mount Rainier. Kenneth Arnold made what is considered the first modern UFO sighting. The term flying saucers came out of his description: "flying like a saucer." The alleged UFO crash in Roswell, New Mexico, was reported later that same year.

There are three developed campgrounds in Mount Rainier National Park; check the websites nps.gov/mora and visitrainier.com for information about camping, hiking, horse camping, and backpacking in the park. Additional information can be obtained from park headquarters in Ashford (360-569-2211). During winter, cross-country skiers can contact the **Mount Tahoma Trails Association** about skiing hut-to-hut on some 50 miles of logging road trails; check skimtta.com or, on winter season weekends, call (360) 569-2451, the Mount Tahoma Ski Trail office.

Good places to grab a bite to eat include **Copper Creek Inn Restaurant** in Ashford (35707 SR 706 East; 360-569-2799; coppercreekinn.com); **National Park Inn Restaurant** in nearby Longmire (360-569-2275; mtrainierguestservices .com); and **Scaleburgers** (54109 Mountain Hwy., Elbe; 360-569-2247). Located in a weigh-station building built in 1939, Scaleburgers has been serving juicy hamburgers since 1987.

In the lowlands near Eatonville, you can enter a time warp at the **Pioneer Farm Museum** (7716 Ohop Valley Rd.; 360-832-6300; pioneerfarmmuseum .org). One-and-a-half-hour tours are run from 11:15 a.m. to 4 p.m. daily in summer and on weekends during spring and fall. The museum gift shop, housed in an 1887 trading post cabin, brims with old-fashioned treats.

North of Eatonville is **Northwest Trek** (11610 Trek Dr. E; 360-832-6117; nwtrek.org), an unusual park where a variety of wildlife live in a woodland setting, wildlife that you can see up close—really close. By taking the 50-minute tram tour through 435 acres of forest, wetland, and meadow, you'll be (sometimes extremely) close to free-roaming bison, elk, moose, caribou, and bighorn sheep. Seen from walking trails in another area of the park will be captive cougar, lynx, bobcat, bear, and other animals. There are more than 200 North American animals in the park. It is open at 9:30 a.m. daily from mid-Mar through late Sept

Old & New Blend on Mount Rainer

Mount Rainier National Park has two historic inns as well as the Henry M. Jackson Visitor Center at Paradise that opened in 2008. The 121-room *Paradise Inn,* which took six months to build in 1916 and two years and $22.5 million to renovate in a manner that kept that warm cozy feeling inside, reopened in 2008. A German carpenter designed and built much of the decorative woodwork on the interior, and most of that, as well as furniture and other items, was stored during renovation (including the rocks, all numbered, of each fireplace). So if you've been to the inn before, don't worry: the woodwork is still there, the rustic piano has a new soundboard, and the 14-foot grandfather clock carved by carpenter Hans Fraehnke sits in the same corner. The inn, at a 5,400-foot elevation, is closed from late fall to late spring, although the Paradise area is accessible year-round, weather-willing and if plows are able to keep ahead of the snowfall.

The 25-room *National Park Inn* at Longmire (elevation 2,761 feet), near the Nisqually entrance to the park, was renovated in 1990 and is on the Register of Historic Places. The rustic inn has a stupendous backdrop on a clear day—stand on the north porch and let your jaw drop at the sight of Mount Rainier, right there. It can be particularly beautiful at sunset. The inn is complemented by a good restaurant, the Longmire Museum, a general store in a 1911 cabin, and a gift shop. It's open year-round so take advantage of off-season rates and bring your cross-country skis and snowshoes.

You can book either through Mount Rainier Guest Services at (360) 569-2275 or online mtrainierguestservices.com.

The star of the park, of course, is Mount Rainier. To folks who live within sight, it's called The Mountain, as in, "The Mountain is out today!" It has the most major glaciers (25) of any mountain in the mainland US; the Carbon Glacier is the lowest-elevation glacier in the contiguous US; and the Emmons Glacier is the largest by area at 4.3 square miles. Its last major eruption was about 2,500 years ago, but there was a minor blowing off of steam and ash in the 1800s. Geologists say that the eruption that created the Osceola Mudflow (about 1,600 vertical feet of the peak slid away) sent mud roaring across the landscape to where Tacoma and south Seattle now sit. Seattle is about 50 miles from Mount Rainier.

but closes at various hours depending on the season. Open weekends in early Mar and Oct through Dec. Admission is $11 to $23 and includes the tram tour.

To the northwest of the park is *Olympia,* the state capital and former home of the now-shuttered Olympia Brewery plant. Many visitors tour only the capitol building, then move on, but there are many lesser-known sights worth experiencing. Start with a sidewalk tour of downtown as described in the brochure "Olympia's Historic Downtown: A Walking Tour," which highlights outstanding historic buildings, homes, and parks. This brochure is available from the *Olympia-Lacey-Tumwater Visitor & Convention Bureau*

(103 Sid Snyder Ave. SW; 877-704-7500; experienceolympia.com), open 9 a.m. to 5 p.m. weekdays, and until 3 p.m. on weekends.

icecream youscream

The world's first soft-serve ice cream machine was used in an Olympia Dairy Queen.

Families with young children will want to stop at Olympia's **Hands On Children's Museum** (414 Jefferson St. NE; 360-956-0818; hocm.org). This creative place offers a diverse collection of interactive exhibits for kids 10 years old and younger. Kids also love **Tumwater Falls Park** at Deschutes Way & C Street, Tumwater (360-943-2550; olytumfoundation.org). It's free, open during daylight hours, and the perfect park for a family picnic with a scenic waterfall, walking trails, and a salmon ladder.

East of Olympia, the **Lacey Museum** (829 Lacey St. SE; 360-438-0209) showcases the area's history from Oregon Trail days to the present. Housed in a 1926 building that served as a private residence, 1940s fire station, and Lacey's first city hall, the museum features exhibits, artifacts, and old photos. It's free and open Thurs and Fri 11 a.m. to 3 p.m.; Sat 10 a.m. to 4 p.m.

For a bite to eat, hit the **222 Market** (222 Capitol Way N), a refurbished historic building housing a creperie, ice cream shop, Mexican restaurant, bakery, and bistro. The standout of the bunch is **Chelsea Farms Oyster Bar** (360-915-7784; 222market.com), a restaurant offshoot of a nearby oyster farm. The menu here skews upscale and includes excellent raw oysters, cocktails, brunch, and dinner options.

Stroll along the **Percival Landing** boardwalk on Olympia's waterfront to see boats and ships and occasionally view the playful antics of a seal. The

The Venerable Capitol

Olympia's Legislative Building, completed in 1928, was the last domed capitol built in the US. Forty-two steps lead to the entrance, symbolizing that Washington was the 42nd state to join the Union. The granite for the steps and foundation was quarried in the Washington town of Index, and the sandstone of its face is from the foothills of Mount Rainier. The dome weighs more than 30 million pounds and sits 287 feet above the ground. The dome's 5-ton Angels of Mercy chandelier was designed by Louis Comfort Tiffany. A Visitor Information Center at 14th and Capitol Way offers more information. The building is open 7 a.m. to 5:30 p.m. weekdays and 11 a.m. to 4 p.m. weekends. Guided tours are available on the hour, from 10 a.m. to 3 p.m. daily during the week and 11 a.m. to 3 p.m. weekends. For tour information, call (360) 902-8880 or visit ga.wa.gov/visitor.

Mound Mystery

Many theories try to explain the **Mima Mounds,** fairly evenly spaced 5- to 8-foot-tall mounds of rock and dirt 10 to 70 feet in diameter on the Mima Prairie south of Olympia. Theories include that they were formed during the post–Ice Age thaw when the ground fractured and melted and the mounds were what was left or by Ice Age pocket gophers; earthquakes; American Indians as raised beds for growing vegetables; fish nests when the area was underwater; and Paul Bunyan and his workers walking off a job leaving dirt-filled wheelbarrows which rotted, leaving the mounds behind.

boardwalk begins on 4th Avenue behind Bayview Market. A viewing tower at the landing's north end offers great vistas of the port, the city and, on a clear day, the Olympic Mountains. Also at Percival Landing is the *Sand Man* (tugsandman.org), Olympia's grand old tugboat launched there in 1910, a tireless workhorse until 1987 and now open to the public from 10 a.m. to 4 p.m. Sat and Sun. Step aboard to relive Puget Sound maritime history as volunteer docents tell the tales.

You'll find several places to eat, including the **Olympia Farmers' Market,** located at the north end of Capitol Way. The spacious, covered market is open from 10 a.m. to 3 p.m. Thurs through Sun, year-round.

To absorb the atmosphere of Olympia's past, enjoy a meal at the historic **McMenamins Spar Cafe** (114 E. 4th Ave.; 360-357-6444; mcmenamins.com). The Spar retains many details from its early days: chairs have a clip on the back to hold the patron's hat; sports scores are announced on a chalkboard; and the walls are decorated with old logging photos. With the McMenamins' ownership, hand-crafted ales are now brewed on-site using the Spar's legendary artesian water.

Enjoy other eateries and coffee shops in the Olympia area, including **Budd Bay Cafe** (525 Columbia St. NW; 360-357-6963; buddbaycafe.com) and **Wagner's European Bakery & Cafe** (1013 Capitol Way; 360-357-7268; wagnersoly .com). Whether you drink beer or not, the pubhouse at **Three Magnets Brewing Company** (600 Franklin St. SE #105; 360-972-2481; threemagnetsbrewing .com) is worth a visit. It specializes in playful twists on classic bar food, and then some. There are great options here for vegetarians, too.

For lodgings near downtown, call the innkeepers at **Swantown Inn Bed & Breakfast** (1431 11th Ave. SE; 360-753-9123; swantowninn.com), a 4-bedroom 1893 Queen Anne/Eastlake Victorian mansion. A sumptuous 3-course gourmet breakfast is served in the grand dining room, or you can have a boxed continental breakfast to take on the road. In 2008, Swantown added a day spa.

From the ***Puget View Cottage*** (7924 61st Ave. NE; 360-413-9474), a few miles northeast of Olympia on Puget Sound, guests enjoy wide water views of Nisqually Reach, Anderson Island, and Longbranch Peninsula. By prior arrangement, you can be dropped off by floatplane. Walk the nearby beaches and trails of ***Tolmie State Park*** and watch for marine wildlife. The Nisqually River, which flows from glaciers on Mount Rainier, empties into Puget Sound at the nearby ***Nisqually National Wildlife Refuge,*** where visitors may see more than 200 bird species, including migratory waterfowl, and many small mammals. Enjoy walking on 7 miles of trails with observation blinds, including the 1-mile Twin Barn Loop to the Nature Shop with its exhibits and marsh views. The center is open 9 a.m. to 4 p.m. Wed through Sun. For information, contact the refuge office at 100 Brown Farm Rd. NE, Lacey (360-753-9467; fws .gov/nisqually) from 7:30 a.m. to 4 p.m. weekdays.

Splendid nature trails are found a few miles south of Olympia at ***Mima Mounds Natural Area Preserve,*** an unanswered "whodunit" of uniformly spaced giant mounds. An interpretive center is built into one of these geological wonders. An observation deck, a barrier-free interpretive path, and hiking trails are set among the riot of colorful wildflowers and native grasses that bloom in spring and summer. For directions, go to southsoundprairies.org.

TOP ANNUAL EVENTS IN THE PUGET SOUND REGION

APRIL

Skagit Valley Tulip Festival
Mount Vernon area
(360) 428-5959
tulipfestival.org

MAY

Northwest Folklife Festival
Seattle, Memorial Day weekend
(206) 684-7300
nwfolklife.org

AUGUST

Washington State Fair
Puyallup
Aug–Sept
thefair.com

Bumbershoot
Seattle, Labor Day weekend
(206) 701-1482 (tickets)
bumbershoot.org

OCTOBER

OysterFest & Seafood Festival
Shelton
(800) 576-2021
oysterfest.org

A few miles east of Mima Mounds is **Wolf Haven International** at 3111 Offut Lake Rd. SE, Tenino (360-264-4695; wolfhaven.org). The only way to see the wolves is to go on one of the 45-minute tours offered on the hour. Wolf Haven is a privately owned refuge for abandoned wolves and other feral animals that can't be returned to the wild. Volunteers describe wolf biology and lore as well as the personalities of individual wolves living at the sanctuary. Camera lenses more than 200 mm are not allowed although there are separate photography tours for a fee. Campfire songfests and howl-ins happen some Friday and Saturday nights in summer starting at 6 p.m.

Nearby, visit **Lattin's Country Cider Mill & Farm** (9402 Rich Rd. SE; 360-491-7328; lattinscider.com) and purchase freshly made cider, homemade pies, jams, and syrups as well as seasonal fruits and vegetables. Stop by on weekends to sample homemade doughnuts. For lodging, call **Blueberry Hill Farm Guest House Bed & Breakfast,** 12125 Blueberry Hill Ln. in nearby Yelm (360-458-4726; blueberryhillfarmguesthouse.com). The innkeeper makes Grandma's Gourmet Berry Jam and also serves guests delicious farm-style breakfasts (at a nominal charge per person).

South of Wolf Haven on Highway 99 is the town of **Tenino,** a community famous around the turn of the 20th century for its sandstone quarries. The scenic **Tenino City Park** was built around one of the abandoned quarries. Water cascades down moss- and vine-covered sandstone walls into a pond, now used each summer as the community's public swimming pool.

Tenino was a railroad town named, some say, after the Number 10-9-0 engine that pulled local trains, but railroad records don't support the theory. Another is that the term comes from a native word meaning "meeting place." The 1914 **Tenino Depot Museum** (399 Park Ave. West; 360-264-4321; ci.tenino .wa.us/Train_Depot_Museum), adjacent to the city park, is one of many local sandstone buildings. Museum exhibits illustrate techniques used in the old quarries to transform raw stone into everything from bricks to flowerpots, as well as railroad lore and local history. The museum is open noon to 4 p.m. weekends. For more information about the town, visit the Tenino Chamber website at teninochamberofcommerce.com.

Steilacoom, 20 miles northeast of Olympia via I-5, is a small town perched on a bluff overlooking the southernmost part of Puget Sound and nearby Anderson Island. Its history is rich with stories of fast ships, quick business deals, and slow trains. Washington Territory's first incorporated town was established in 1854 by Maine sea captain Lafayette Balch. During the late 19th century, it was an important seaport, county seat, and commercial center.

To learn more about the town, visit the **Steilacoom Historical Museum** (253-584-4133; steilacoomhistorical.org) at the corner of Rainier and Main

Streets, the **Wagon Shop** on Main below the museum, and the **Nathaniel Orr Home,** adjacent to the museum on Rainier Street. The museum buildings offer glimpses of the town's history, and docents are often available to explain and demonstrate old-time skills. Call for current times.

Stroll through the downtown National Historic District, with more than 30 buildings on the historic register. Ask for a walking tour map at the museum; guides are also available.

For a historic site that takes visitors back to the days of early American settlement, take in the nearby **Fort Steilacoom Museum** on the grounds of Western State Hospital (9601 Steilacoom Blvd.; historicfortsteilacoom.org). Four officers' quarters are all that is left of the original 26 wood-frame structures. They interpret the early military history of that area. It's open 1 to 4 p.m. Sun from Memorial Day through Labor Day, and otherwise only the first Sun of the month.

Then, for a comfortable overnight stay in this historic village, contact **Above the Sound Bed & Breakfast** (806 Birch St.; 253-589-1441; abovethe sound.com), just a short walk away from the 20-minute ferry ride to Anderson Island. Or try the **Inn at Saltar's Point** (68 Jackson St.; 253-588-4522; innat saltarspoint.com), a modern (2007) B&B a few blocks from downtown. For a treat, try the upscale farm-to-table fare at **De la Terre** (1606 Lafayette St.; 253-584-0258; restaurantdelaterre.com).

From downtown, hop on the **Pierce County Ferry** (253-588-1950; co .pierce.wa.us/ferry) to **Anderson Island** at the Steilacoom Landing Facility, 56 Union Ave. Anderson Island is only about 4 miles from end to end, but there are plenty of little nooks to explore. At the center of the island, you'll find the **Johnson Farm,** which was operated by the Johnson family from 1912 to 1975 and is now maintained by the Anderson Island Historical Society (andersonislandhs .org) as a display of the labors and comforts of traditional rural life. Tools and artifacts are on display, including the wheelhouse of the ferry *Tahoma,* which plied the Anderson Island route for decades. The farm, always open during daylight hours, has summer weekend tours.

Anderson Marine Park, on the southwest shore, is a delightful and secluded place (andersonislandparks.org). Take the gravel nature trail through the woods and down to Carlson's Cove. Well-marked signs point out the diverse plant life and bird activity in the evergreen forest. Short stretches of the trail are marked "skid road," "corduroy," and "puncheon." These terms, which describe the shape of the logs under your feet in the muddier parts of the walk, demonstrate historic road surfacing techniques to show how logging roads were once built. The last stretch includes a steep descent to a small dock floating in the sheltered cove rich with intertidal life. Beware of the poison oak beyond the marked path along the shore and be sure to wear good walking shoes.

Ken and Annie Burg offer families the fun and comfort of their large log home, *Inn at Burg's Landing Bed & Breakfast* (8808 Villa Beach Rd.; 253-884-9185; burgslandingbb.com), near the Anderson Island ferry dock. From the inn's large decks, you can watch the boat traffic on Puget Sound with a backdrop of Mount Rainier and the Cascades on blue-sky days or collect seashells on the private beach. Ken Burg, who grew up on Anderson Island and attended its one-room school, can tell stories of island life "back in the good old days." Annie guarantees that no guest goes hungry for breakfast.

Back on the mainland, take time to stop at the *DuPont Historical Museum* (207 Barksdale Ave.; 253-964-2399; dupontmuseum.com), near I-5 exit 119. In 1906, the DuPont Company bought nearly 5 square miles of land to manufacture black powder and explosives. Tar-paper shacks housed the construction crew, but those shacks soon morphed into a company town, initially comprising 58 permanent homes built for the employees.

It had its own school, newspaper, post office, church, butcher shop, hotel, and clubhouse. Eventually DuPont moved on, sold the houses to the former employees, and donated parkland and the infrastructure to the town. In 1976, Weyerhaeuser Company bought all 3,200 acres of the property for the planned community of Northwest Landing. In 1987, the company town area, known as The Village, was placed on the National Register of Historic Places. The museum preserves pieces of the town's history, legacy, and artifacts.

For an overnight, the easily accessible *Liberty Inn* at 1400 Wilmington Dr. (253-912-8777; bestwestern.com) is between I-5 and the museum. Weather willing, Mount Rainier dominates the view behind the inn. All rooms are smoke-free and the complimentary breakfast options are many.

Inner Sound

Historically the home of the Puyallup and Nisqually Indian tribes, the *Tacoma* area did not see people of European descent until 1833 when the British Hudson's Bay Company established a fur-trading post, Fort Nisqually. In the early 1850s the first permanent settlers, mainly lumbermen, arrived. But they fled during the Indian War of 1855–56. In 1864, Job Carr arrived and called the spot Eureka. More people followed and built sawmills along the Commencement Bay waterfront, which soon bustled with cargo ships and workers of many nationalities, including American, English, Scottish, Irish, Hawaiian, Native American, and Chinese. Back then the old Whiskey Row area sported saloons, brothels, and gambling houses. By the early 1870s the fledgling town had successfully courted the Northern Pacific Railroad to designate Tacoma its western terminus. The transcontinental railroad was completed in 1887, thus linking

Tacoma to the rest of the country, and the city's population soared from some 1,098 in 1880 to 36,006 by 1890.

Today a 21st-century renaissance continues to transform Tacoma. Several historic neighborhoods, downtown hotels and museums, shops, and places to eat offer a variety of excursions. A Museum District has emerged along the Thea Foss Waterway, where visitors can find its stunning centerpiece, the **Museum of Glass** (1801 Dock St.; 253-284-4750; museumofglass .com). Its impressive tilted 90-foot-tall cone wrapped in shimmering stainless steel is reminiscent of the sawmill woodburners of the mid-1800s and symbolizes the city's transformation from an industrial to a cultural enclave. Indoors you can see artisans creating with molten glass in the Hot Shop Amphitheater and enjoy rotating exhibits in the gallery spaces, as

gallopinggertie

Washington has bragging rights to the most dramatic failure in US bridge history. The third-longest suspension bridge in the world lasted less than 5 months in 1940. It behaved like a roller coaster when poor design met moderate winds. The 5,939-foot-long Tacoma Narrows Bridge's center span bucked, twisted, and tumbled into the water below, taking with it vehicles and one spaniel.

well as browse the museum store, which sells some of the Hot Shop creations. For good eats with views of the waterway, try **Social Bar and Grill** (1715 Dock St. E; 253-301-3835; thesocialbarandgrill.com).

The **Washington State History Museum** (1911 Pacific Ave.; 253-272-3500; washingtonhistory.org) is connected to the Museum of Glass by the spectacular Chihuly Bridge of Glass, a 500-foot pedestrian walkway over I-705 that showcases the work of internationally respected glass artist and Tacoma native Dale Chihuly. Next door is historic Union Station, also displaying Chihuly glass in its rotunda. The **Tacoma Art Museum** (253-272-4258; tacomaartmuseum .org) is just 1 block away at 1701 Pacific Ave. Another unusual museum is the **Karpeles Manuscript Library Museum** (407 S. G St.; 253-383-2575; rain .org/~karpeles).

Downtown Tacoma's historic **Broadway Theater District** and, adjacent to it, Antiques Row on Broadway and St. Helens Avenues between 7th and 9th Streets, offer the restored 1918 Pantages and Rialto Theaters and the contemporary Theatre on the Square.

Venture a little outside Tacoma to the **Pacific Bonsai Museum** (2515 S. 336th St.; 253-353-7345; pacificbonsaimuseum.org) in Federal Way. A worthwhile diversion, this free outdoor park boasts a stunning collection of more than 100 bonsai trees from China, Japan, Canada, Korea, Taiwan, and America. These artfully sculpted miniatures usher in fall with changing leaves and spring

Vintage Automobiles Galore

The city of Tacoma, a true museum district, added another major exhibition space in 2012. *America's Car Museum* (877-902-8490; americascarmuseum.org) show-cases the huge vintage automobile collection of Tacoma collector Harold LeMay in a 165,000-square-foot museum and 3.5-acre show field. Needing all that space, the museum is located southeast of downtown, near the Tacoma Dome at 2702 E. D St. It's open daily 10 a.m. to 5 p.m.

with flowers. In winter, when they're bare, you can fully appreciate the intricate, twisting shapes of their branches.

From here head north to the Stadium District, named for the imposing 1906 chateau-like fortress that began as an elegant hotel but now houses Stadium High School. Continue to **Old Town** to see the **Job Carr Cabin Museum** (2350 N. 30th St.; 253-627-5405; jobcarrmuseum.org), a replica of the 1865 home of Tacoma's first mayor, public notary, and postmaster. At the far northern tip of the city, **Point Defiance Park** (5400 N. Pearl St.; 253-591-5337; pdza .org) offers a zoo and aquarium (gardens, saltwater beaches, and trails). The **Fort Nisqually Living History Museum** (253-404-3970; fortnisqually.org) has docents in period garb reenacting life at this Hudson's Bay Company fur trading post circa 1855. You can also find a flock of antiques shops along N. Pearl Street en route to the park.

For entertaining eating, try **Dirty Oscar's Annex** (2309 6th Ave.; 253-572-0588; dirtyoscarsannex.com) for top-notch tacos, burgers and sandwiches; **Indo Street Eatery** (110 N. Tacoma Ave.; 253-503-3527; indostreeteatery .com) for excellent Asian fare; **Red Wagon** (2315 N. Pearl St.; 253-212-3705; redwagonburgers.com) for over-the-top burgers; and **The Chili Parlor** (5640 S. Tacoma Way; 253-472-6829) for well-done throwback food including—you guessed it—chili.

Pearl Street ends to the north at Point Defiance, where a ferry leaves every hour until late evening for **Vashon Island,** one of the largest of Puget Sound's islands. When you ferry over to visit, stop at the **Heron Art Center** (19704 Vashon Hwy.; 206-463-5131; vashonalliedarts.org) to get a feel for the thriving island arts community.

Next, call ahead to see if artists are working at the **Brian Brenno Blown Glass Studio & Gallery** (9850 SW 148th St.; 206-567-5423; brianbrenno blownglass.com). During studio tours, you can check out fantastical creations at the gallery like life-size glass hats. Don't miss visiting the **Country Store and Gardens** (20211 Vashon Hwy. SW; 206-463-3655; countrystoreandfarm

.com) and its Ceiling Museum of antique kitchen appliances and kitchenware as well, and browse the natural foods, preserves, and garden goodies plus the 10-acre nursery. Head down to ***Point Robinson*** at the southeast tip of the island, called Maury Island, connected to Vashon Island by an isthmus created by the Army Corps of Engineers, to see the working lighthouse. It's open noon to 5 p.m. on weekends, from mid-May to mid-Sept. The rest of the year, call the president of the Keepers of Point Robinson (206-463-6672) well ahead if

Estates, Mansions, Villas & Castles

A number of Pacific Northwest timber, ship, and industrial barons of the late 1800s and early 1900s exhibited a tendency to the immense, ornate, and showy when it came to building their houses. Many of these palatial homes eventually fell into disrepair; some were razed, but a number of fine structures have recently been renovated. Here are five among the top-drawer variety, four of them open as bed-and-breakfast inns and one as a splendid estate garden, also open to the public. Each offers a fascinating history.

Branch Colonial House Bed & Breakfast Inn
2420 N. 21st St.
Tacoma
(253) 752-3565
branchcolonialhouse.com
6,000 square feet
Ca. 1904 home restored by Robin Korobkin

Chinaberry Hill Grand Victorian Inn and Cottage
302 Tacoma Ave. North
Tacoma
(253) 272-1282
chinaberryhill.com
6,000 square feet
Ca. 1889 home restored by Cecil and Yarrow Wayman

Lakewold Gardens Estate
12317 Gravelly Lake Dr. Southwest
Tacoma
(253) 584-4106
lakewoldgardens.org
Ten-acre estate gardens developed in 1938 by owners George Corydon and

Eulalie Wagner. Gardens and a 1907 Georgian-style manor house now kept up by Friends of Lakewold; splendid gardens and gift shop open to the public.

Thornewood Castle Inn and Gardens
8601 N. Thorne Ln. Southwest
Lakewood
Also shown by appointment
(253) 584-4393
thornewoodcastle.com
This 27,000-square-foot inn includes a bed-and-breakfast and private residence. Note that the property does not allow walk-up guests.
Ca. 1911, renovation ongoing by Wayne and Deanna Robinson

The Villa Bed & Breakfast Inn
705 N. 5th St.
Tacoma
(253) 572-1157
villabb.com
12,000 square feet
Ca. 1925 home

Other Friendly B&Bs & Inns, Tacoma–Gig Harbor–Vashon Island Area

Aloha Beachside Bed & Breakfast
8318 Hwy. 302
Gig Harbor
(888) 256-4222
alohabeachsidebb.com

Betty MacDonald Farm Bed & Breakfast
11835 99th Ave. Southwest
Vashon Island
(206) 567-4227
bettymacdonaldfarm.com

Green Cape Cod Bed & Breakfast
2711 N. Warner St.
Tacoma
(253) 752-1977
thegreencapecod.com

Waterfront Inn
9017 N. Harborview Dr.
Gig Harbor
(253) 857-0770
waterfront-inn.com

you'd like to arrange a tour. You can also rent the former lighthouse keeper's quarters through the local parks district (206-463-9602; vashonparkdistrict.org). Linger overnight on Vashon Island by arranging for cozy suites at the *Betty MacDonald Farm Bed & Breakfast* (11835 99th Ave. SW; 206-567-4227; bettymacdonaldfarm.com) where you can look across Puget Sound to see Mount Rainier. For additional lodging information browse the Visitor Information Center site, vashonchamber.com.

Vashon Island is home to an impressive range of restaurants, making it a veritable dining destination. Clustered around the Vashon town center on either side of Vashon Highway, try *May Kitchen + Bar* (206-408-7196; maykitchen .com) for some of the best Thai food in the region, period; *The Ruby Brink* (therubybrink.com), which specializes in farm-to-table food supplemented by nose-to-tail butchery and great cocktails; *Snapdragon* (206-463-1310; vashon snapdragon.com), specializing in comfort food and breakfast favorites; *Gravy* (206-463-0489; gravyvashon.com), for well-done Southern-style comfort food; and *Zombiez* (206-463-7777), a quirky spot for ice cream, burgers, and fish and chips.

Gig Harbor is a delightful fishing village nestled in a protected bay on the northwest side of the Tacoma Narrows. The harbor is crowded with both pleasure and fishing boats. Harborview Drive, which hugs the shore, is lined with shops, sidewalk cafes, and galleries, making it a great place to stroll. On a clear day, Mount Rainier looms in the distance.

Gig Harbor Yachts (3419 Harborview Dr.; 253-358-3491; gigharboryachts .com) your boating options include adorable Duffy electric boats that work well for groups, or kayaks and stand-up paddleboards that make for a more peaceful excursion.

Galleries featuring local artisans include the ***Ebb Tide Co-op Gallery*** (7809 Pioneer Way; 253-851-5293), which started in 1984 and stocks colorful woven clothing, jewelry, watercolors, wood carvings, pottery, and other arts. You'll also find great gifts at the ***Beach Basket*** (4102 Harborview Dr.; 253-858-3008), the year-round Beach Basket Christmas Shop next door. For a good selection of regional wines as well as gifts, stop by the ***Keeping Room*** (7811 Pioneer Way; 253-858-9170).

For comfortable lodgings, most of them with views of Henderson Bay, Carr Inlet, or Colvos Passage, check with the volunteers at the ***Gig Harbor Visitor Information Center*** (3125 Judson St.; 253-853-3554; gigharborguide.com).

Recommended eating spots in the Gig Harbor area include farm-focused ***Table 47*** (5268 Point Fosdick Dr. NW; 253-857-4777; t47.com); ***Tides Tavern*** (2925 Harborview Dr.; 253-858-3982; tidestavern.com); and ***Java & Clay Cafe*** (3210 Harborview Dr.; 253-851-3277; javaclaycafe.com).

From Gig Harbor you can backtrack a few miles to Tacoma via the Tacoma Narrows Bridge and rejoin I-5 heading north. For a pleasant day trip, head to the Seattle waterfront and board the ferry for a 35-minute ride to nearby ***Bainbridge Island.*** Browse the shops and boutiques along Winslow Way in the island's main town, where the ferry arrives. The must-stop goal is ***Bainbridge Arts & Crafts*** (151 Winslow Way E; 206-842-3132; theartproject.org). More than 250 artists participate in the co-op, which is open daily.

Enjoy the food at one of the several spots in downtown: try the breakfast waffles at the ***Streamliner Diner*** at 397 Winslow Way East (206-842-8595; streamlinerdiner.com) near the ferry landing or the sumptuous pastries at ***Blackbird Bakery*** at 210 Winslow Way East (206-780-1322; blackbirdbakery

Bloedel Reserve Bainbridge Island

Brimming with rich scenery and history and just a 35-minute ferry ride from Seattle, Bainbridge Island is the perfect day-trip destination. It's also the gateway for the get-away-from-it-all activities on the Kitsap and Olympic Peninsulas. One of the loveliest historic places on the island is the *Bloedel Reserve* (7571 NE Dolphin Dr.; 206-842-7631; bloedelreserve.org). Once a private estate, the 150-acre reserve offers a feast for the senses with its beautifully maintained grounds, including a bird marsh, an English landscape garden, a moss garden, a reflection pool, a Japanese garden, and woodlands. The reserve is open to the public Tues through Sun from 10 a.m. to 4 p.m.; it stays open until 7 p.m. Thurs through Sun, June to Aug; reservations are required.

.com). Make it ice-cream time at **Mora Iced Creamery** (139 Madrone Ln.; 206-855-1112; moraicecream.com), which serves delicious homemade sorbets and ice creams from stainless-steel, temperature-controlled ice-cream cabinets.

To stay overnight on the island, check with **Eagle Harbor Inn** at 291 Madison Ave. South (206-842-1446; theeagleharborinn.com), where town-house-style rooms have large patios and pretty gardens. The accommodations put you in the center of a stroll-worthy downtown, with small businesses like **Pegasus Coffee House** (131 Parfitt Way; 206-201-3606; pegasuscoffeehouse .com), located in one of the town's oldest buildings on the waterfront and a local favorite for three decades. It also has live music some Friday and Saturday nights.

Bainbridge Island is home to some of Puget Sound's best restaurants. Farmer and celebrated chef Brendan McGill takes island-grown ingredients to new heights at his restaurants in the Winslow town center, which include fine-dining **Hitchcock** (206-201-3789; hitchcockrestaurant.com) and next-door **Hitchcock Deli** (206-451-4609; hitchcockdeli.com). He also does outstanding pizzas at **Bruciato** (206-201-3462; pizzeriabruciato.com). Don't miss the baked goods at **Blackbird Bakery** (206-780-1322; blackbirdbakery.com) or the ice cream at **Mora Iced Creamery** (206-347-0721; moraicecream.com). For an

Family Excursions on the Kitsap Peninsula

Gig Harbor Yachts
3419 Harborview Dr.
Gig Harbor
(253) 358-3491
gigharboryachts.com

J. A. and Anna F. Smith Children's Park
7601 Tracyton Blvd. Northwest
Bremerton
(360) 337-5350
Creative demonstration garden

Pacific Bonsai Museum
2515 S. 336th St.
Federal Way
(253) 353-7345
pacificbonsaimuseum.org

Point Defiance Zoo & Aquarium
5400 N. Pearl St.
Tacoma
(253) 591-5337
pdza.org
Picnic and play areas, gardens

For more information:

Kitsap County Parks & Recreation
(360) 337-5350
kitsapgov.com/parks

Kitsap Peninsula Visitor Information
(800) 337-0580
visitkitsap.com

adult beverage, Winslow sports four wine tasting rooms: Eagle Harbor Wine Co., Eleven Winery, Amelia Wynn Winery, and Fletcher Bay Winery (bainbridge wineries.com). There's also the festive **Bainbridge Brewing Alehouse** (206-317-6986; bainbridgebeer.com) with beer on tap, board games, trivia nights, and live music.

For other lodging options, check bainbridgelodging.com. From Bainbridge Island you can access other Kitsap Peninsula destinations such as Poulsbo, Port Orchard, and Gig Harbor.

A ferry from Seattle takes visitors to Bremerton to explore the **Kitsap Peninsula** and the western sections of Puget Sound. Kitsap County offers about 230 miles of freshwater and saltwater shoreline, with every community on the water. When you reach Gorst, a tiny town southwest of Bremerton on the edge of Sinclair Inlet, you'll find an ex-landfill and log dump transformed into the remarkable **Elandan Gardens and Gallery** (3050 W. Hwy. 16, Bremerton; 360-373-8260; elandangardens.com). The garden's extensive bonsai collection and its gallery, which offers elegant antiques and art treasures, are open from 10 a.m. to 5 p.m. Tues through Sun from Apr to Oct.; Fri through Sun from Nov to Mar.

Port Orchard, a few miles east of Gorst on Highway 166, has a hospitable downtown ideal for window-shopping. Bay Street, the main commercial street, has old-fashioned sidewalks with a wooden canopy for comfortable strolling, rain or shine. Murals on downtown walls illustrate life during the late 19th century, when Port Orchard was a major stop for the **Mosquito Fleet,** the small steamboats that were once a common form of transportation on the Sound. At the north end of Sidney Avenue, you can catch the *Carlisle II,* one of the original fleet, which carries pedestrians and bicycles across the bay to Bremerton every half hour. A waterfront observation deck offers views of marine activities in the bay and across the water to Bremerton's naval shipyards.

To get a taste of Port Orchard's early days as well as the richness of local artistic talent, stroll a few blocks south on Sidney Avenue to the **Sidney Art Gallery** (202 Sidney Ave.), open year-round Tues through Sat, 10 a.m. to 4 p.m. and Sun 1 p.m. to 4 p.m. The first floor of this former Masonic Temple, built in 1908, features monthly exhibits highlighting the works of Northwest artists. The second floor houses the **Sidney Museum,** featuring exhibits of turn-of-the-20th-century stores and coastal scenes. More Port Orchard history can be found at the **Log Cabin Museum,** just up the hill at 416 Sidney Ave. All three are owned by the Sidney Museum and Arts Association (360-876-3693; sidneymuseumandarts.com). The 1914 Log Cabin Museum includes nine resident mannequins dressed in period costumes in historical scenes. Occasionally mannequin relations join the scenes.

For anyone into Victorian teas, the place to stop is *The Grey House Café* (1130 Bethel Ave.; 360-876-0529; thegreyhousecafe.com). It's a restaurant and tea house in a gray Victorian home.

Reflections Bed and Breakfast (3878 Reflection Ln. E; 360-871-5582), a spacious home filled with New England antiques, offers wide views of Bainbridge Island and Port Orchard Passage from each guest room and deck. One option is the Annette Room, complete with a private sitting room and soaker tub.

Poulsbo is a friendly community on the shores of *Liberty Bay.* It was settled in the 1880s by Norwegians. The Poulsbo business community has revived this heritage to create a Scandinavian-themed town. Scandinavian delights await at every turn in the town's historic district, from potato lefse (pancakes) to the painted folk art designs (rosemaling) adorning shutters and doorways. Be sure to visit *Sluys Poulsbo Bakery* (18924 Front St.; 360-779-2798) at the town's main street, which is close to the water and the marina. They serve delicious Poulsbo bread and Scandinavian pastries. It's one of three wonderful bakeries on Front Street.

There's plenty of food to tempt the palate and drinks to quench the thirst at *Cups Espresso* (18881 Front St.; 360-697-2559), the funky and fun *Poulsbohemian Coffeehouse* (19003 Front St.; 360-779-9199), *JJ's Fish House* (18881 Front St.; 360-779-6609; jjsfishhouse.com).

After browsing in the shops or learning about marine biology at the *SEA Discovery Center* (18743 Front St. NE; 360-598-4460; wp.wwu.edu/seacenter), head for *Anderson Parkway* and its large wooden gazebo (Kvelstad Pavilion), where you can relax and see the marina, the boats, Liberty Bay, and the Olympic Mountains. A 612-foot boardwalk leads from the Viking statue, along the shore, and up the forest-covered bluff. As you stroll, you may see loons or cormorants dive for fish offshore.

Berry Nice

Western Washington's climate is conducive to growing a wide array of berries, beginning in early summer with strawberries and raspberries and ending in the fall with wild blackberries and huckleberries. You'll find U-pick farms and stands throughout your journeys in the Puget Sound area. Berries are especially abundant in the Pierce, Skagit, Snohomish, Snoqualmie, and Whatcom County areas. When you're at a restaurant and the server says there's fresh berry pie, don't pass it up. You could also try the loganberry, a cross between a blackberry and a raspberry.

Paddle the Trail

If you were thinking about longer paddling distances, the *Cascadia Marine Trail* links more than 50 accessible overnight sites for human-powered craft, from comfy bed-and-breakfasts to campsites, throughout Puget Sound. The waterways stretch about 140 miles from Olympia up to the Canadian border. Kayaking visionaries foresee the day when this network of trails and campsites will take paddlers north as far as Skagway, Alaska. Trail updates are available through the Washington Water Trails Association at (206) 545-9161 or wwta.org.

Near Poulsbo's Marina, visit the tiny *Waterfront Park,* which has a boat ramp on the shore of Liberty Bay.

To find out more about the early people who first used these waters for food and travel, take Suquamish Way north off Highway 305, south of Poulsbo, to the *Suquamish Museum* (6861 NE South St., Suquamish; 360-394-8499; suquamishmuseum.org). The museum's premier exhibit, Ancient Shores–Changing Tides, introduces the history and traditional lifestyle of the Suquamish Nation. The museum is open daily from 10 a.m. to 5 p.m.

From the new museum, it's just a half-mile walk or drive down to the shoreline and *Old Man House State Park,* given to the tribe by the state. This is where Chief Sealth (better known as *Chief Seattle*) lived and died. The Old Man House was a huge plank building that once stretched along the beach. A display explains how local tribes built and used the large house. The small park is ideal for picnics and quiet reflection alongside Agate Passage. Up the hill, behind St. Peter's Church, is Chief Sealth's grave site. The new Suquamish Longhouse, the first welcoming house since the destruction of Old Man House, opened in 2009.

For a relaxing rural interlude, contact the *Manor Farm Inn* (26069 Big Valley Rd. NE, Poulsbo; 360-779-4628; manorfarminn.com), a comfortable country-style bed-and-breakfast with 6 spacious guest rooms. For other overnight stays in the area, check out the budget-friendly *Poulsbo Inn & Suites* (18680 WA-305; 360-779-3921; poulsboinn.com), which sports a pool and serves daily breakfast.

Highway 104 cuts through the center of the peninsula, before crossing the northern end of the Hood Canal on the William A. Bugge Bridge. Past Port Ludlow and Oak Bay, you can turn off to *Indian Island* and *Fort Flagler,* or continue straight toward Chimacum and *Port Townsend.* The bridge to Indian Island offers great views of the narrow strait separating this island from the mainland. The road beyond the bridge has several places to pull off to admire

The Nautical Life: Wooden Boats, Tall Ships, Schooners, Wooden Boatbuilding & Wooden Boat Festivals

Center for Wooden Boats
1010 Valley St.
Seattle
(206) 382-2628
cwb.org
Located on Lake Union, offering exhibits, programs, and classic wooden boats to rent for informal paddling excursions on the lake.

The *Lady Washington*
ladywashington.org
Tall ship makes scheduled ports of call along the West Coast from its home port of Aberdeen.

Northwest Maritime Center
431 Water St.
Port Townsend
(360) 385-3628
nwmaritime.org
Offers collaborative programs: sailing instruction, lecture series, summer workshops, boat-building projects, and historic vessel tours.

Northwest School of Wooden Boatbuilding
42 N. Water St.
Port Hadlock
(360) 385-4948
nwswb.edu
Offers classes and workshops.

Sound Experience
Port Townsend
(360) 379-0438
soundexp.org
Offers environmental sailing programs in the waters of Puget Sound aboard the historic schooner *Adventuress*.

Wooden Boat Festival
woodenboat.org
Held the first weekend after Labor Day in Port Townsend.

The Wooden Boat Foundation
431 Water St.
Port Townsend
(360) 385-3628
woodenboat.org
Center for maritime education located in the Cupola House at Point Hudson and a huge newer workshop-style building on the port.

the scenery. Turn right at the Jefferson County day-use sign and follow the gravel road to the beach to explore the pebbly tidelands, scattered with driftwood and salt marsh plants. Waterbirds are especially abundant here during their fall migration. Just above the shore you'll find the trailhead to the 4-mile South Indian Island Trail, an ideal hike through madronas and firs to a sandy beach, a narrow spit, a lagoon, and views of Mount Rainier.

The causeway from Indian Island to **Marrowstone Island** crosses lush wetlands and a lagoon between the two islands. Nearby is **Beach Cottages on Marrowstone** (10 Beach Dr., Nordland; 800-871-3077; beachcottagegetaway.com), a rustic retreat surrounded by tall grass and wild beaches. Eight cedar guest cabins encircling the meadow come with kitchens and views of Oak Bay. The caretakers recommend that guests bring boots, warm clothing, blankets, and, if possible, a canoe or kayak. Linens, towels, basic kitchen utensils, and firewood are provided.

Fort Flagler State Park covers the entire north end of Marrowstone Island, a mix of forests, former gun batteries, and coastline. The fort was used periodically for military training until it became a park in 1955. Although the campground is busy during the summer (888-226-7688 for campsite reservations; parks.wa.gov), the park is big and diverse enough to offer seclusion for those who seek it. Numerous hiking trails go through the forest to cliffs overlooking Admiralty Inlet. The **Roots of a Forest Interpretive Trail,** a short distance past the campground entrance, provides an inside look into forest ecology. There's an indoor interpretive display, open weekends, and a long beach to explore at **Marrowstone Point.**

If you don't turn off to Marrowstone Island, Oak Bay Road will lead you to the turnoff for the **Ajax Cafe** in Port Hadlock (21 Water St.; 360-385-1965; ajaxcafe.com), an unexpected delight. Along with its funky decor the much-loved cafe offers superb dinners highlighting local coastal cuisine, including scallops, salmon, duck, and beef, and the most incredible pot du crème and other delicious freshly made desserts. The public wharves, ships, and boatyards across the street add to the ambience. A sign at the dock tells of the history of a once-booming industrial site from 1878 to 1916. The cafe is open for dinner Thurs through Sat.

The rich agricultural area around **Chimacum** is home to farms and cideries like **Finnriver** (124 Center Rd.; 360-339-8478; finnriver.com), where the region's ample apples make their way into excellent cider. The farm hosts live music and sells wood-fired pizza from Dented Buoy on Saturdays, plus other events. Check the website for a full calendar.

For more farm-fresh fare, visit **Farm's Reach Café** (8972 Beaver Valley Rd.; 360-732-4200), a busy spot at where locals congregate to eat breakfast specials, pastries, and burritos. If the farm-to-table movement appeals, join it at **Resort at Port Ludlow** in nearby Port Ludlow (360-437-7000; portludlowresort.com). The romantic, waterfront spot has a locavore restaurant and a special package that gives visitors "farm bucks" to spend in the area. The restaurant's chef then crafts a multicourse, of-the-moment dinner using the ingredients you bought.

Continue north on Highways 19 and then 20 to Port Townsend for North-west history, arts events, shopping, Victorian homes, and festivals. Contact the **Port Townsend Visitor Center** (2409 Jefferson St.; 360-385-2722; enjoypt .com) for information.

Make the trip to **Finistère** (1025 Lawrence St.; 360-344-8127; restaurant finistere.com) where locavore chef Deborah Taylor gets creative with farm-sourced ingredients. Ditto the creativity at **Propolis Brewing** (2457 Jefferson St.; 360-344-2129; propolisbrewing.com) where wild-harvested ingredients make their way into Old World-inspired beers.

Port Townsend has a lively community of artists, so visitors can find many fine galleries downtown in the waterfront area as well as uptown, on the bluff. Try **Northwind Arts Center,** which showcases artists throughout the year near the Kah Tai Lagoon Nature Park, at 701 Water St. (360-379-1086; northwindarts .org).

The **Jefferson County Historical Museum** (540 Water St.; 360-385-1003; jchsmuseum.org) is located in the 1891 city hall building. The 2-story brick structure houses exhibits that describe the area's nautical, native, and Victorian history. Call for hours and ask about weekend walking tours through the town. Be sure to explore the historic neighborhoods on the hill; follow the stairs up Taylor Street or take either Quincy or Monroe Street up the hill to see many Victorian homes that once housed the cultural and financial elite of Washington Territory.

Stop to see the 75-foot wooden **Old Bell Tower** on Tyler Street on the bluff, which once summoned the volunteer fire department. At the corner of Jefferson and Taylor Streets is the 1868 **Rothschild House,** which has been preserved as it was a century ago by the historical society. Tour the house 11 a.m. to 4 p.m. daily May through Sept. Be sure to stroll through the rose garden with its fragrant varieties, some dating to the early 1800s. Call the visitor information center (360-385-2722) for the current dates of Port Townsend's favorite annual events—some of which show off the town in all its quirky glory, including **Strangebrew Fest** in January; **Victorian Heritage Days** in March; the **Rhododendron Festival** in May; the **Steampunk Festival** in June; **Jazz Port Townsend** in July; the **Wooden Boat Festival** in September; and **The Great Port Townsend Kinetic Sculpture Race** in October. Within walking distance on Jackson Street, find lovely **Chetzemoka Park** and its rose gardens, including a splendid rose arbor walkway, plantings from around the world, large glider swings, a gazebo, and views of Admiralty Inlet and the Cascade Mountains to the east. Comfortable places to stay include the report-edly haunted **Palace Hotel** (1004 Water St.; 800-962-0741; palacehotelpt.com), with its elegant, Victorian-era rooms. For another option, visit staypt.com. From the bluff walk down a series of concrete stairs to the downtown waterfront area and beautiful Haller Fountain with a special drinking fountain for your four-legged friend.

Consider stopping at the *Fountain Cafe* (920 Washington St.; 360-385-1364) for seafood and pasta specialties; *Nifty Fifties* (817 Water St.; 360-385-1931; niftyfiftyspt.com) for juicy hamburgers and old-fashioned sundaes, shakes, malts, and sodas; and *Elevated Ice Cream & Candy Shop* (631 Water St.; 360-385-1156; elevatedicecream.com), to enjoy homemade ice cream, Italian ices, and pastries, and to see local art.

While in Port Townsend, be sure to inquire about events at *Fort Worden State Park* (200 Battery Way; 360-344-4400; parks.wa.gov/fortworden). Like Fort Flagler to the east, Fort Worden was once part of the fortifications that protected Puget Sound from invasion by sea. Just a mile north of downtown, the fort is the site of *Port Townsend Marine Science Center* (532 Battery Way; 360-385-5582; ptmsc.org), which has marine and natural history exhibits as well as bird migration and Protection Island puffin cruises. The *Puget Sound Coast Artillery Museum* (360-385-0373; coastartillery.org), *Commanding Officer's Quarters Museum* (jchsmuseum.org), and *Centrum Foundation* (360-385-3102; centrum.org) are also on park grounds. Events offered by Centrum include writing, music, and dance conferences, which usually include activities open to the public. Their annual blues, jazz, and fiddle festivals sell out every year. You'll also find a rhododendron garden, nature walks, old military batteries to explore with a flashlight, and a long public beach. To stay in the park, choose from old barracks, comfortable officers' quarters, a youth hostel, or campgrounds.

Directly to the east of Port Townsend is *Whidbey Island,* accessible by the Port Townsend to Coupeville/Keystone ferry. It's the largest of the Puget Sound islands, populated for 10,000 years by native peoples and one of the first areas on the Sound to be settled by Europeans. Its extensive coastline, lush forests, and location midway between the snow-capped Olympic and Cascade mountain ranges create outstanding views. Small working farms, artist studios, and innovative home businesses are scattered among meadows, shoreline, and evergreen forests. There are several historic communities and small-scale resorts.

whidbeyisland trivia

Living on an island is not like living on the mainland. For example, when the locals leave the island they often say, "We're going shopping in America." Note from the islanders: Do not under any circumstances try to cut your automobile into the ferry line—you will incur the wrath of not only the islanders but also everyone else in line.

Whidbey Island is also accessible from the Seattle area from the south via the Mukilteo ferry, which leaves about every half hour. For information call **Washington State Ferries** at (888) 808-7977 or visit wsdot.wa.gov/ferries. The northern entry point is across the Deception Pass Bridge on Highway 20.

Highway 525, which becomes Highway 20 north of Keystone, runs down the center of the island and carries most of the through-traffic. It's also a designated Scenic Isle Way from Deception Pass to Clinton. Stop by one of the visitor centers for free guides and maps, or go to whidbeycamanoislands.com. You can also take the meandering local roads that follow the shoreline for better views and less traffic.

Langley, on Saratoga Passage, is one of our favorite communities. To get there, turn right on Langley Road off Highway 525 and follow signs into town. On the way, visit **Whidbey Island Winery** (5237 S. Langley Rd.; 360-221-2040; whidbeyislandwinery.com) and taste samples of its Port, Pinot Noir, and Siegerrebe varieties. The tasting room is closed on Tues from July to Sept; closed Mon and Tues from Oct to June.

Langley has many antiques and art galleries. For a sampling, stop at the **Brackenwood Gallery** (302 1st St.; 360-221-2978; brackenwoodgallery.com) or **Museo** (215 1st St.; 360-221-7737; museo.cc). Although a busy tourist town during summer weekends, Langley is always pleasant, with plenty of spots to sit and view the nautical scenery on Saratoga Passage. On 1st Street, cozy up to the bronze statue of a sea-gazing boy (with dog) leaning over the railing above Saratoga Passage. From here a wooden staircase leads down to the beach; stroll along a grassy walkway or descend farther to the pebbly shore below a bulkhead sculpted with images of salmon and whales. For more information on these incredible creatures, visit the **Langley Whale Center** (360-331-3543; orcanetwork.org), an educational space dedicated to local orcas and whales, with a cute gift shop.

You'll find cafes, restaurants, espresso bars, and bistros to suit every taste on 1st and 2nd Streets, including **Prima Bistro** above the Star Store at 201½ 1st St. (360-221-4060; primabistro.com). For true New York–style pizza, visit the **Village Pizzeria** at 106 1st St. (360-221-3363). The **Braeburn Restaurant** (197 2nd St.; 360-221-3211; braeburnlangley.com) is one of the locals' favorite breakfast hangouts. Also on 2nd Street is **Useless Bay Coffee Company** (121 2nd St.; 360-221-4515; uselessbaycoffee.com).

Chocolate lovers should not miss **Sweet Mona's** (221 2nd St. #16; 360-221-2728; sweetmonas.com) for European-style delicacies like thick drinking chocolate and dark salted caramels.

A little outside of the downtown Langley area, visit the noteworthy **Orchard Kitchen** (5574 Bayview Rd.; 360-321-1517; orchardkitchen.com).

Here, diners eat multi-course meals from island ingredients—some of which are grown on site, at communal tables. For more dressed-down meals, **Roaming Radish** (5417 S. Crawford Rd.; 360-331-5939; roamingradish.com) serves polished plates with craft beer inside a former airplane hangar.

For a spin on live theater, plan to attend the **Langley Mystery Weekend** sponsored by the Chamber of Commerce (360-221-6765; visitlangley.com) and held during the last full weekend of Feb. Mystery buffs meet over coffee in local cafes and coffee shops to pore over clues in order to nab the character that did the nefarious deed. It's great fun, with locals dressed in vintage garb and helping with the special effects. For an authentic walk through the past, visit the **South Whidbey Historical Society Museum** (312 2nd St.; 360-221-2101; southwhidbeyhistory.org), originally curated by renowned artist Lee Wexler.

To stay overnight in the Langley area, contact accommodations referrals for **South Whidbey** (360-221-6765; visitlangley.com). Treat yourself for a night or two at one of our favorites, the **Boatyard Inn** (200 Wharf St.; 360-221-5120; boatyardinn.com), with Saratoga Passage's in-coming tide lapping within feet of your living room. Seven 600-square-foot studios and another five 1,000-square-foot loft suites include mini-kitchens and views of the shipping lanes, Cascade Mountains, and maybe a gray whale or two. Or call the innkeepers at **Country Cottage of Langley Bed & Breakfast** (215 6th St.; 800-713-3860; acountrycottage.com) and one of the first vintage homes in the area to be remodeled for bed-and-breakfast travelers. Innkeepers Jerry and Joanne Lechner offer fine hospitality at **Eagles Nest Inn Bed & Breakfast** (4680 Saratoga Rd.; 360-221-5331; eaglesnestinn.com), a contemporary octagonal-shaped home situated with a fine view of Saratoga Passage. They've served guests more than 200,000 homemade treats from their famous cookie jar. There's also **Comforts of Whidbey** (5219 View Rd.; 360-969-2961; comfortsofwhidbey.com), a husband-and-wife-owned winery and bed and breakfast. You'll sleep in well-appointed rooms just above the gorgeous tasting room.

ferrytime

The largest ferry fleet in the US serves 24 million passengers on 23 ferries stopping at 20 ports of call in Puget Sound, the San Juan Islands, and Victoria, B.C. The 8 classes of ferries range from 152 to 460 feet long and can carry from 200 to 2,500 passengers and up to 202 vehicles.

The rhododendron, Washington's state flower, is especially prolific on Whidbey Island. If these pique your interest, you'll want to visit the very special **Meerkerk Rhododendron Gardens** (3531 Meerkerk Ln., Greenbank; 360-678-1912; meerkerkgardens.org). The rhododendron blooms are usually at their peak the last two weeks of Apr and the beginning of May, but the gardens also include a magical Japanese section and are lovely at any time. Featuring more than 800 mature rhododendron and companion plants, the landscape includes ponds, forest, and waterside nature trails.

Great dining in this area is available at **Gordon's on Blueberry Hill** (5438 S. Woodard Ave.; 360-331-7515), in Freeland and **Island Nosh** (360-341-3828; islandnosh.com) near the Clinton ferry terminal.

An integration of nature, art, spirit, and a 500-year plan has created **Earth Sanctuary** near Freeland. In 2002, Chuck Polson (author of *Secrets of Sacred Space*) and like-minded souls began restoring a 72-acre site to its old-growth glory with the maximum diversity of wildlife, birds, fungi, and plants. Earth Sanctuary is also a retreat center. A self-guided map leads you on numerous trails past ponds, a bog, medicine plant restoration area, streams, small artworks made of natural materials, and much larger structures.

A dolmen (table-shaped stone structure and surrounding 5- to 7-foot tall Montana sandstone stones) serves as a meditation room. A cottonwood stone circle may one day attract great blue herons to mature trees, and a fen stone circle is made of eight standing stones up to 7 feet high, each weighing 600 to 1,000 pounds. The stones are aligned with true north and south, the summer solstice sunrise and sunset, and the winter solstice sunset. The entry fee is $7 per person. Consider it your contribution to a remarkable vision. For information, call (360) 637-8777 or go to earthsanctuary.org.

creationof pugetsound

Puget Sound encompasses more than 2,500 square miles of water and 2,500 miles of shoreline, although sources often vary on the exact numbers. This was a glacier-carved valley about 13,000 years ago until the Puget Lobe glacier receded and an ice dam broke, after which the valley was flooded by the Pacific Ocean.

Hillsides covered with vines at the historic Whidbey's **Greenbank Farm** (off Hwy. 525 at 765 Wonn Rd.; 360-222-3797) create a pleasant setting for a picnic. Visitors are welcome to tour the farm with its art galleries, cheese and antiques shops, and trails. A wine-tasting barn offers a wide selection of Northwest wines. Pick up a homemade pie for your picnic at **Whidbey Pies Cafe** (765 Wonn Rd.; 360-678-1288; whidbeypies.com). The farm is just north of **Greenbank** and is open daily from noon to 5 p.m.

Historic **Coupeville** is another favorite. It's located several miles to the north, about midway up the island on scenic **Penn Cove.** Saratoga Passage lies to the east and Admiralty Inlet to the west. Look for a gaggle of mussel rafts floating out on Penn Cove where the famous Penn Cove mussels are grown and harvested. The annual **Penn Cove Mussel Festival** takes place the first weekend in March (thepenncovemusselfestival.com). Walk to the boat shed at the end of the town wharf to see the skeleton of a gray whale. The body of the nearly 3-year-old male was found on the island's southwestern shore in 1998. To learn about Coupeville's Native American, pioneer, and maritime history and to pick up a walking-tour guide, visit the **Island County Historical Museum** (908 NW Alexander St.; 360-678-3310; whidbeycamanoislands.com/island-county-historical-museum) at the end of Front Street near the wharf. The museum is open every day but check with the contacts for updated hours. After browsing the museum go across the street to the wharf, which overlooks Penn Cove and the mussel-growing rafts. Poke around the **Gallery at the Wharf.** Walk along Front Street and up Main Street to see more historic buildings. Stop at **Mariti Chocolate Co.** (17 Front St.; 360-678-5811) for locally made treats. Shopping and browsing could not be more fun than in **Far from Normal** (360-678-3799), **Penn Cove Gallery** (360-678-1176; penncovegallery.com), or **One More Thing** (360-678-1894), all on historic Front Street. If you are in the area on Saturday, take in the **Coupeville Farmers' Market** (Apr through Oct; 360-678-4288) on the corner of Alexander and 8th Streets, behind the town library, to mingle with friendly locals and load up on fresh berries, flowers, and vegetables. For fabulous freshly baked cinnamon rolls, soups, and salads, stop at **Knead & Feed** on Front and Main Streets (360-678-5431), a former storehouse and laundry built in 1871 and nestled one level down the bluff facing Penn Cove. Its original post-and-beam structure adds to the ambience of this pleasant waterside spot. Local folks swear by the steamed Penn Cove mussels and garlic bread at **Toby's Tavern** on Front Street (360-678-4222; tobysuds.com).

Not far from downtown Coupeville, **Ebey's Landing National Historical Reserve** (360-678-6084; nps.gov/ebla) protects a swath of historic farmland and waterfront that makes for spectacular hikes. Hike along wildflower-strewn bluffs overlooking beaches and crashing waves, go birdwatching around Crockett Lake, or explore the military history and Admiralty Head Lighthouse at Fort Casey State Park.

To stay overnight in the Coupeville area, contact **Anchorage Inn Bed & Breakfast** (807 N. Main St.; 360-678-5581; anchorage-inn.com), where children over 10 are welcome; the **Blue Goose Inn B&B,** which offers 3 historic Victorian homes at 702 N. Main (360-678-4284; bluegooseinn.com); and **Garden Isle Guest Cottages** (207 NW Coveland St.; 360-678-5641; gardenislecottages

.com) near the downtown area. The same managers also offer a 1-bedroom vacation rental in the town's old 1937 firehouse.

For evening dining in Coupeville, check out local restaurants that do great things with mussels, seafood, and steaks: **Oystercatcher** (901 NW Grace St.; 360-678-0683; oystercatcherwhidbey.com) and **Christopher's** (103 NW Coveland St.; 360-678-5480; christophersonwhidbey.com). A dining-and-lodging alternative is the 1907 **Captain Whidbey Inn** (2072 W. Whidbey Island Inn Rd.; 360-678-4097; captainwhidbey.com) on the west shore of Penn Cove. The lodge, built of madrona logs, has comfortable rooms, a cozy beachstone fireplace, and a restaurant. Newer cabins are also available.

The impressive **Admiralty Head Lighthouse** interpretive center is located near the Keystone landing at **Fort Casey State Park.** Call (360) 678-4519 for information on seasonal tours. The park is open year-round for camping available by reservation (888-226-7688; parks.wa.gov). There are old fort structures to explore and long stretches of undeveloped public beaches to walk.

Before continuing north to scenic Deception Pass at Whidbey Island's north end, a spectacular sight in practically any kind of weather, you can find pleasant eateries in the Navy town of **Oak Harbor.** The best place to discover local naval aviation history is in the 2,500 square feet of galleries at the **PBY Memorial Foundation,** covering wars in Vietnam, Korea, and Iraq (270 SE Pioneer Way; 360-240-9500; pbymf.org).

Or replenish your cooler, put together an impromptu picnic, and continue north to **Deception Pass State Park.** Pull into any large grocery outlet for supplies or **Seabolt's Smokehouse** (31640 Hwy. 20; 360-675-6485; seabolts .com) for fresh seafood deli fare. **Zorba's** (32955 Hwy. 20; 360-279-8322;

Deception Pass

Captain George Vancouver sailed through the narrow pass in 1792. He thought the crew would sail into a small bay, but was "deceived," finding instead another large channel between islands; thus, the name Deception. Joseph Whidbey was aboard Vancouver's ship. Before the bridge, a ferry took passengers for the 5-minute trip between islands. To bring the ferry to your side, you had to strike the mallet against a very large metal lumberjack saw and the sound would tell the ferry pilot that it was time to cross the challenging channel. For years, Berte Olson, the first female ferry captain in the state, and her husband ran the ferry at Deception Pass and Hood Canal. She later owned her own company and was in charge of four ferry routes in the 1920s into the 1950s. She had enough swing that she convinced the governor to veto a legislative bill to build a bridge across Deception Pass. But the bridge was still constructed, and put the ferry company out of business when it opened in 1935.

zorbasrestaurantblog.wordpress.com) offers Italian and Greek fare. For a special occasion, book a reservation at **Frasers Gourmet Hideaway** (1191 SE Dock St. #101; 360-279-1231; frasersgh.com). Promoting the bounty of the Northwest, Frasers specializes in local seafood, meats, game, and wines. Look for the large Dutch windmill to help find lodging at the **Auld Holland Inn** (33575 Hwy. 20; 360-675-2288; auld-holland.com).

Drop in at **A Knot in Thyme** (4233 De Graff Rd.; 360-240-1216; aknotin thyme.com), about 3 miles before Deception Pass. The acreage includes a holly farm for seasonal use, a lavender garden, and a quilted garden that's planted in designs. The nature-inspired gift shop has a few surprises, including bean pod candles. Stop between 9 a.m. and 5 p.m. Mon to Sat; or 1 p.m. to 4 p.m. on Sun.

One of the best ways to see spectacular Deception Pass, the deep, turbulent waters rushing between Whidbey's cliff-bound north end and Fidalgo Island, is aboard the *Island Whaler* with **Deception Pass Tours** (888-909-8687; deceptionpasstours.com). Take the 1-hour tour with an interpreter and keep an eye out for bald eagles and seals, and go under the **Deception Pass Bridge,** built with more than 1,500 tons of steel in 1935 over Deception and Canoe passes and named a National Historic Landmark in 1982. It now costs more to paint the bridge than it did to build it. There are parking areas and viewpoints as well as trails on either side of the bridge, and 3-foot-wide sidewalks on both sides allow for safe viewing.

Northern Sound

Just across the Deception Pass Bridge from Whidbey Island is **Fidalgo Island.** For a bird's-eye view of this island, turn west from Highway 20 just south of Pass Lake and follow Rosario Road as it forks right, away from Burrows Bay. After 4 miles take an acute left onto Heart Lake Road at the Lake Erie Grocery, then turn right to enter **Mount Erie Park.** The steep road (not recommended for trailers or RVs) has several trails and observation points along the way, and the wide-angle views of northern Puget Sound and its islands from the nearly 1,300-foot summit are spectacular. Continue north on Heart Lake Road toward **Anacortes,** which makes a great base camp for exploration. Leave your bags, drive to the ferry landing, leave your car, and walk on the ferry for a day trip to **Friday Harbor** on San Juan Island. But before you head for the ferry terminal, take time to explore.

Named one of the top small art towns in the US, Anacortes has a rich history and a wonderful ambience in part reflected in more than 100 murals. Bill Mitchell initiated the idea for the life-size cutouts accenting a century of the community's history. Pick up a map from the Anacortes Visitors Information Center at 819 Commercial Ave. (360-293-3832; anacortes.org) and go wandering. Mural subjects include Ann Bessner and the Guemes Island Girls, a self-portrait of Bill Mitchell with a 1954 Autoette electric cart and wheelchair, the Black Ball Line and Washington State ferries from 1928 to 1972, Edna Whitney with a tandem bicycle, and Wild Bill Bessner and his Indian motorcycle (1920).

Meander past the *Burlington Northern Railway Station* at 611 R Ave. The revitalized station housed the now-closed *Depot Arts Center.*

Located nearby and a local favorite, *Gere-a-Deli* (502 Commercial Ave.; 360-293-7383; gere-a-deli.com) offers clam chowder, salads, and sandwiches. *Calico Cupboard Cafe and Bakery* (901 Commercial Ave.; 360-293-7315; calicocupboardcafe.com) offers tasty luncheon fare and also has locations in La Conner and Mount Vernon. Washington Governor Jay Inslee once called the buttermilk pancakes at throwback *Dad's Diner* (906 Commercial Ave.; 360-899-5269) the best in the state. *Rockfish Grill & Anacortes Brewery* (320 Commercial Ave.; 360-588-1720; anacortesrockfish.com) is a longtime local favorite for microbrews and ales as well as seafood and pizza from a wood-fired oven. One of the best-kept secrets in Anacortes is *SeaBear Specialty Seafoods* off the main drag at 605 30th St. (360-293-4661; seabear.com). Here you'll discover alderwood-smoked salmon, soups, chowders, and barbecued salmon.

The older neighborhoods are just west of Commercial Avenue on 6th through 12th Streets. *Causland World War I Memorial Park,* on 8th Street between M and N Avenues, is a pleasant green hideaway surrounded by mosaic walls made of white quartz and red argillite swirling in brown and gray sandstone. Across the street you can review the history of Fidalgo Island at the *Anacortes Museum* (1305 8th St.; 360-293-1915; museum.cityofanacortes.org), once the town's Carnegie Library.

For an overnight stay, try the historic *Majestic Inn & Spa* (419 Commercial Ave.; 360-299-1400; majesticinnandspa.com), a 21-room inn restored in 2005. Other choices include *Ship Harbor Inn* (5316 Ferry Terminal Rd.; 360-293-5177; shipharborinn.com).

Way too early for the ferry to the San Juans? Take 12th Avenue westward as it becomes Oakes. Turn before the ferry exit to follow Sunset Avenue onto Loop Road around *Washington Park* and check out the beaches. At Fidalgo Head, stop at the viewpoint on a high promontory overlooking Burrows Island and Bay. When you can tear yourself away from the great views, circle back to Sunset Avenue.

All four major San Juan County islands with regular *Washington State Ferries* service from Anacortes—Lopez, Shaw, Orcas, and San Juan—offer

Orcas 101

It's no wonder that *Free Willy* was filmed in the San Juans, as three pods of the so-called Southern Resident Killer Whales make their home in these waters. You can watch for them by sea or land, and you might see one without even trying—though, sadly, their numbers are critically low, and just 75 individuals remain. You might still catch a glimpse of these incredible animals, if you keep a close eye out. Here are some facts you can use to embellish your own whale tales:

- Males can grow to 31 feet in length; females 26 feet. Females outnumber males four to one and usually live to age 50, but some can live into their 90s. The average male lives to about 30.

- Males weigh up to 12,350 pounds, females up to 8,375 pounds.

- Whales give birth to one calf at 3- to 10-year intervals.

- Typical diet for the Southern Resident Community (the local orcas) is fish, and most of that is salmon. Transient orcas sometimes eat other marine mammals. Orcas eat from 100 to 300 pounds of food a day.

- The whales "talk" to each other with a dialect unique to each pod.

- Orcas navigate the waters at speeds up to about 30 mph.

- Orcas are members of the dolphin and porpoise family.

exploration and relaxation. Lopez and Shaw Islands are the farthest off the beaten path, especially during the off-season. **Shaw,** the smallest San Juan Island accessible by state ferry and the most residential, offers a step back in time. Franciscan Sisters once ran the ferry dock and the **Shaw General Store** (360-468-2288), but it's now run by a local family, which maintains the tradition of running a tab for the locals. Old baskets, fruit boxes, and nautical paraphernalia decorate the walls, and a wide assortment of foods and beverages are part of the mix.

This is strictly a quick day trip because there are no motels or B&Bs on Shaw. The main roads run down the center of the island, past the **Shaw Island Library** (shawislandlibrary.org) at the intersection with Blind Bay Road. It's run by islanders and is open from 2 to 4 p.m. Tues; 11 a.m. to 1 p.m. Thurs; 10 a.m. to noon and 2 to 4 p.m. Sat. Ask the volunteer librarian for a key to the adjacent log-cabin museum. Opposite the library is the still-in-operation red schoolhouse, part of it more than 100 years old.

Head south by the school on Hoffman Cove Road, then left on Squaw Bay Road. Drive past scenic and secluded Squaw Bay to the turnoff to the 60-acre **Shaw Island County Park,** with 11 campsites overlooking the bay. The park has drinking water available for campers only in summer. Then follow Squaw Bay Road back to Blind Bay and right to the ferry dock.

Lopez Island is larger and more developed than Shaw but still offers many opportunities for quiet. Its rolling hills and agricultural views are attractive to bicyclists. Located 4 miles from the ferry landing, Lopez Village, with a museum, a store, and restaurants, is the island's commercial center. The *Lopez Island Historical Museum* (28 Washburn Place; 360-468-2049; lopezmuseum .org) is full of island history and lore and worth a stop. The museum is open from noon to 4 p.m. Wed through Sun May through Sept. For good food in the village, try *Holly B's Bakery* (360-622-8133; hollybsbakery.com), and *Isabel's Espresso* (360-468-4114; isabelsespresso.com). For a truly memorable meal, make a reservation at the lovely *Ursa Minor* (210 Lopez Rd.; 360-622-2730; ursaminorlopez.com), where every plate is a veritable love song to the island and its farmers, fishers, and foragers. At scenic *Fisherman Bay* try the *Galley* (360-468-2713; galleylopez.com) for the best water views along with tasty fish-and-chips, juicy hamburgers, and good Mexican dishes. Remember that island restaurants are rarely open seven days a week so call before counting on a meal. Visit the island's lone winery tasting room at *Lopez Island Vineyards* (724 Fisherman Bay Rd.; 360-468-3644; lopezislandvineyards.com) to sample organic estate wines. Call ahead to confirm hours.

For a comfortable overnight stay in *Lopez Village,* call *Edenwild Inn Bed & Breakfast* (132 Lopez Rd.; 360-468-3238; theedenwild.com). It has 8 guest rooms, cozy fireplaces, and delicious European-style breakfasts. At *MacKaye Harbor Inn Bed & Breakfast* (ca. 1904) at 949 MacKaye Harbor Rd. (360-468-2253; mackayeharborinn.com), travelers find 5 guest rooms and great water views along with kayak rentals and the use of the inn's mountain bikes. For a peaceful farmstay surrounded by animals, complete with DIY meals with farm-fresh products, try *Midnight's Farm* (3042 Center Rd.; midnightsfarm .com). *Lopez Islander Resort* (360-468-2233; lopezfun.com) is the largest accommodation on Lopez and also operates the 60-slip marina and store at the dock in Fisherman Bay. Or choose to be tucked in the woods with eagles and ravens as neighbors at *Ravens Rook Cabin* (58 Wildrose Ln.; 877-321-2493; ravensrooklodging.com), a secluded family-friendly cabin, done in rustic post-and-beam style. From here, a short walk through adjacent Shark Reef Sanctuary takes you to the scenic shoreline and perhaps sunning harbor seals on a nearby rock. Public beaches on Lopez Island include the west side of Fisherman Bay off Bay Shore Road, *Shark Reef Sanctuary* (good tide pools here) at the end of Shark Reef Road on the island's southwestern tip, and *Agate Beach* off MacKaye Harbor Road at the island's south end. *Spencer Spit State Park and Campground* (360-468-2251; parks.wa.gov) on the island's east shore is a very popular destination, very scenic, and with ample hiking trails and beaches. The park also has campsites. **Odlin County Park** (360-468-2496) is closest to the ferry landing and offers camping and RV spaces (no hookups and no showers).

An extremely popular destination is horseshoe-shaped **Orcas Island.** It's easy to spend two or more days on Orcas, the largest island of the four ferry-served islands. Drive over to popular **Moran State Park and Campground** (360-376-2326; parks.wa.gov), hike its many trails, and then drive up to **Mount Constitution.** One of the grandest views of the islands is from the top of its tower, especially fine at sunset. Poke into the small communities of **Deer Harbor, Eastsound, Westsound, Olga,** and **Doe Bay.** Have a picnic by the water. Visit art galleries and artists' studios.

Especially during the summer and shoulder-season weekends, call well in advance to make overnight reservations at one of the bed-and-breakfast inns or campgrounds. Not far from the ferry landing, **Turtleback Farm Inn** (1981 Crow Valley Rd.; 360-376-4914; turtlebackinn.com) offers guests pastoral views and excellent cuisine along with resident sheep and chickens. For those who like getting farther away from it all, contact the innkeepers at **Otters Pond Bed & Breakfast** (100 Tomihi Dr.; 360-376-8844; otterspond.com), located beyond Eastsound on the way to Moran State Park. At **Doe Bay Resort & Retreat** (107 Doe Bay Rd.; 360-376-2291; doebay.com) you can treat yourself to hot plunge pools situated in the forest over a waterfall, sleep in a yurt or cabin, and dine on farm-to-table meals with a waterfront view. There's also **Once in a Blue Moon Farm** (412 Eastman Rd.; 360-376-7035; onceinabluemoonfarm .com), where you can sleep surrounded by 35 bucolic acres of farmland and orchards—and make friends with the resident alpacas. Even if you're not sleeping here, you can take tours with the delightful owners.

If you're interested in private cottages available by the day or week on Orcas, call **Buckhorn Farm Bungalow** (17 Jensen Rd.; 360-376-2298; buck hornfarm.com). The bungalow is close to the beach, sleeps 4, and comes with a woodstove as well as electric heat, cozy sitting areas, and a cheerful kitchen. At the **Old Trout Bed & Breakfast** (5272 Orcas Rd.; 360-376-7474; oldtroutinn .com), ask about the **Water's Edge Cottage,** where a couple can snuggle up with a view of the pond.

For food and drink in and near Eastsound, the largest community on Orcas, try **The Kitchen** (249 Prune Alley; 360-376-6958; thekitchenorcas.com) for Asian dishes made with local produce. For morning, midday, or takeout, locals suggest **Roses Bakery & Cafe** (382 Prune Alley; 360-376-4292; roses bakerycafe.com). For dinner, try one of two locavore favorites from island farmer and acclaimed chef Jay Blackinton: **Aelder** and its more casual sibling **Hogstone's Wood Oven**, which both share space at 460 Main St. (hogstone

The Pig War

In 1859 on San Juan Island, a long-standing border dispute between British and American residents nearly resulted in an all-out war. The catalyst and only casualty, however, was an Englishman's pig. An American shot the pig when he found the errant animal rummaging in his potato patch. The resulting "Pig War" lasted until 1872, when the island's ownership was awarded to the US. Today you can visit American Camp at the south end of the island, where the US troops were stationed, and English Camp, on Garrison Bay near the north end, where the Royal Marines of Britain were posted. Both offer interpretive displays, hiking trails, and scenic beaches.

.com). In the mood for beer? Visit *Island Hoppin' Brewery* (33 Hope Ln.; 360-376-6079; islandhoppinbrewery.com), which pours island-inspired beer and snacks like cheese dip and smoked salmon.

For a comfortable overnight stay right in the village of Eastsound, contact the friendly innkeepers at *Kangaroo House Bed & Breakfast* (360-376-2175; kangaroohouse.com).

Bustling *Friday Harbor* is the only town on *San Juan Island,* the second largest of the ferry-served islands. Folks find a busy marina, the ferry landing, and a plethora of shops and eateries. From mornings to early evening try *San Juan Coffee Roasting Co.* at the Cannery Landing (360-378-4443; coffeesanjuan.com). Check out *Haley's Sports Bar & Grill* (175 Spring St.; 360-378-4434) near the local movie theater, *Vinny's Ristorante* (165 West St.; 360-378-1934; vinnysfridayharbor.com), and *Friday Harbor House* (130 West St.; 360-378-8455; fridayharborhouse.com) overlooking the harbor and marina. For fine dining away from town, try the much-loved *Duck Soup Inn* (50 Duck Soup Ln.; 360-378-4878; ducksoupsanjuans.com), a fixture for nearly 40 years, and, at *Roche Harbor Village* (rocheharbor.com) at the northwest tip of the island, *Madrona Bar & Grill* (360-378-7954). Also at Roche Harbor, enjoy *Lime Kiln Cafe* (360-378-9892) at the end of the wharf and a good spot for breakfast or lunch. *Note:* Some island eateries close during the winter months and reopen in the spring or are open a few days each week; call ahead.

For bedding down in Friday Harbor, call well ahead for information and reservations. Check with *Kirk House Bed & Breakfast* (595 Park St.; 360-378-3757; kirkhouse.net), which was a rich Seattleite's summer retreat in 1907; *Harrison House Suites* (235 C St.; 360-378-3587; harrisonhousesuites.com); or the neighboring *Tucker House Bed & Breakfast* (275 C St.; 360-378-2783; tuckerhouse1840.com), an 1898 B&B with cottages. The venerable *Friday Harbor House* is also a cozy place to spend a few nights—especially if you score a room overlooking the harbor. The dining room here is top-notch, too, and you can feast on excellently-prepared local specialties like fresh halibut and foraged mushrooms.

Outside of Friday Harbor try **Highland Inn Bed & Breakfast** (360-378-9450; highlandinn.com) near Lime Kiln Point State Park, also known as Whale Watch Park; **Trumpeter Inn** (318 Trumpeter Way; 360-378-3884; trumpeterinn.com); and **Lakedale Resort** (4313 Roche Harbor Rd.; 360-378-2350; lakedale.com), with log cabins and "glamping" tents accessible by float plane. Several miles from Friday Harbor is **Olympic Lights Bed & Breakfast** (146 Starlight Way; 360-378-3186; olympiclights.com), a renovated 1895 farmhouse that sits in a wide meadow near the bluff that overlooks the Strait of Juan de Fuca.

From here you can walk to the site of **American Camp** and enjoy scenic walks at 4th of July Beach.

Be sure to check out both American Camp in the southeast section of **San Juan Island National Historical Park** and **English Camp** near the northwest tip of the island. There are historic displays about the infamous **Pig War,** the 1859 boundary dispute when British and US forces clashed over the shooting of a pig—the animal being the lone casualty. The park also offers bird watching for more than 200 species of migratory birds, hiking in the park forests, and watching for whales from the American Camp bluffs.

Don't miss a visit to the **Whale Museum** in Friday Harbor (62 1st St.; 360-378-4710; whalemuseum.org). The public is encouraged to report any signs of stranded marine mammals to the San Juan County Marine Mammal Stranding Network, operated by the Whale Museum (800-562-8832).

Find scenic camping and RV sites on the island as well as other lodging options by checking with the San Juan Island Chamber of Commerce Visitor Information Center at 165 1st St. S in Friday Harbor (360-378-5240; sanjuan island.org) and with the San Juan Islands Visitors Bureau (360-378-3277; visit sanjuans.com).

Leaving the islands for Anacortes takes a bit of planning. Double-check the ferry departure times and plan to arrive at the ferry landing at least a couple of hours early (seriously) on summer weekends. Passengers can make advanced reservations, which are recommended during summer peak travel times. Others are accepted on a first-come, first-served arrangement. Remember to bring a book and entertainment for the kids.

After returning to the Anacortes ferry terminal from the **San Juan Islands,** head southeast for a few miles to La Conner or **Mount Vernon.** In March and April, about 1,100 acres are carpeted with blooming daffodils, tulips, and irises that thrive in the rich loamy soil of the lower Skagit Valley. On clear days,

A Moveable Winter Feast

During February on the tidal flats and fields of Fir Island, visitors can marvel at some 30,000 Arctic snow geese, 1,500 trumpeter swans, and hundreds of tundra swans in addition to more than 20 species of ducks that pause to munch and rest while winging it along the **Pacific Flyway.** For maps and directions to the best viewing spots, contact the La Conner Chamber of Commerce Visitor Center (511 Morris St.; 888-642-9284; laconnerchamber.com).

enjoy views of distant snowcapped *Mount Baker.* Check (360) 428-5959 and tulipfestival.org for information on the annual *Skagit Valley Tulip Festival* in April. If possible, visit midweek to avoid weekends when the narrow farm roads are often clogged with traffic. Umbrellas and rubber boots are standard attire for spring on the West Coast.

From Highway 20 heading east from Anacortes, turn right on LaConner-Whitney Road and drive to La Conner at the edge of the Swinomish Channel. The scenic waterway carries a parade of small boats between *Padilla Bay* to the north and Skagit Bay to the south. Once a quiet village serving local farmers and fishermen, *La Conner* is now a popular tourist destination with restaurants, antiques shops, and boutiques clustered along 1st and Morris Streets.

Be sure to stop and visit one of the town's three museums. The *Skagit County Historical Museum* (501 4th St.; 360-466-3365; skagitcounty.net/museum) houses exhibits on the area's history, industries, and lost towns. The museum is open from 11 a.m. to 5 p.m. Tues through Sun. Don't miss visiting the *Pacific Northwest Quilt & Fiber Arts Museum* in the 1891 Gaches Mansion (703 S. 2nd St.; 360-466-4288; qfamuseum.org). It's home to a wonderful collection of quilts from the Northwest and ongoing exhibits of quilts and fiber art throughout the year. It is open daily in Apr during the Skagit Valley Tulip Festival and Wed through Sun the rest of the year.

The *Museum of Northwest Art* (121 S. 1st St.; 360-466-4446; mona museum.org) features world-class art exhibits and educational programs. Its inspiration began with photographer Art Hupy in 1981, and in its first years it showed works from artists such as Mark Tobey, Clayton James, Philip McCracken, and Mary Randlett. The museum moved from the Gaches Mansion (now the quilt museum) into a stunning renovated building on Front Street. It is open daily, but does close for holidays and exhibition changes. Afterward, have a bite to eat at one of several fine cafes and restaurants along 1st and Morris Streets. Consider the wood-fired Greek pizza at *La Conner Brewery* (117 N. 1st St.; 360-466-1415; laconnerbrewery.com); the waterfront *Nell Thorn of La Conner* (116 1st St.; 360-466-4261; nellthorn.com), or *Calico Cupboard Cafe and Bakery* (720 S. 1st St.; 360-466-4451; calicocupboardcafe.com) for breakfast and lunch.

Head north from La Conner on La Conner-Whitney Road and cross Highway 20 onto Bayview-Edison Road, which offers views of the islands and Padilla Bay. Then pass Bay View State Park and Padilla Bay National Estuarine Research Reserve and stop at the remodeled *Breazeale–Padilla Bay Interpretive Center* (10441 Bayview-Edison Rd.; 360-428-1558; padillabay.gov). In addition to fish tanks and displays of local birds and mammals, children can enjoy environmental games and hands-on activities. Because of its fertile waters, Padilla Bay is a major stop for migrating birds. The center offers many programs for all ages and is open year-round from 10 a.m. to 5 p.m. Tues through Sat. Walk or bicycle along the 2.25-mile Padilla Bay Shore Trail, which starts 1 mile south of the interpretive center.

Small, comfortable inns entice travelers to rest in the Skagit Valley area. For a quiet stay where solitude is king, *Alice Bay Bed and Breakfast* offers an intimate vacation rental with waterside views (especially from the summer-only tent at the shoreline) at 11794 Scott Rd. on Samish Island, Bow (360-766-6396; alicebay.com), as does *La Conner Channel Lodge* (205 N. 1st St.; 360-466-1500; laconnerlodging.com), with all but 7 of its rooms at the edge of the Swinomish Channel.

It's impossible to not find the small artists' enclave of Edison endlessly charming. It takes only a few minutes to stroll the main street of Cains Court, where most businesses are clustered. Stop in for live music, coffee, and pastries at *Tweet's Café* (360-820-9912; tweetscafe.com), eat excellent tacos at *Mariposa* (360-820-9912), fill up on freshly baked treats and bread at *Breadfarm* (360-766-4065; breadfarm.com), shop for found-object art at *The Lucky Dumpster* (360-766-4049; luckydumpster.blogspot.com), and eat a leisurely meal on the back patio at *Slough Food* (360-766-4458; sloughfood.com).

Everyone should experience scenic *Chuckanut Drive* (Highway 11). Continuing north from Padilla and Samish Bays for about 20 miles, the winding road skirts high bluffs and offers breathtaking glimpses of the *San Juan Islands* before entering the *Fairhaven Historic District* of *Bellingham* soon after passing *Larrabee State Park* (parks.wa.gov). Many of Bellingham's old commercial and residential buildings have been renovated to their 19th-century grandeur, especially in Fairhaven and downtown Bellingham.

The college campus here is home to one of the best free attractions in the state: the *Western Washington University Outdoor Sculpture Collection* (360-650-3900; westerngallery.wwu.edu/sculpture.shtml) incorporates dozens of small and large works around the grounds. To reach Fairhaven more directly from I-5, take exit 250 and follow Highway 11 west to 12th Street. From 10th Street walk the South Bay Trail, which has a section called Taylor Dock that takes you over the water. Or take a San Juan Cruises' foot-passenger scenic cruise (800-443-4552; whales.com) from the Bellingham Cruise Terminal for a bird-watching, whale-watching, dinner, wine, and bicycle cruise. Or, 30 minutes west of downtown, follow signs to the Lummi Island ferry landing for a 5-minute ferry ride to enjoy a leisurely drive on this scenic little island.

While exploring the eclectic Fairhaven District near the waterfront, check out *Colophon Cafe* (1208 11th St.; 360-647-0092; colophoncafe.com), with its funky cow memorabilia and bovine decor, or *Skylark's Hidden Cafe* (1308 11th St.; 360-715-3642; skylarkshiddencafe.com), a casual restaurant along a cobblestone path. Skylark's also offers a saloon, late-night dining, live jazz, and a fantastic budget menu.

The *Whatcom Museum* (360-778-8930; whatcommuseum.org), in the Old City Hall at 121 Prospect St., is a good place to pick up a walking map of downtown Bellingham. But you'll want to spend most of your time exploring the nature, art, and history exhibits in the 2009 addition: the Lightcatcher Building with its 180-foot-long translucent wall. It's located at 250 Flora St. in the city's small but growing arts district. The museum is open noon to 5 p.m. Wed through Sun; admission includes entrance to both buildings. *Allied Arts of Whatcom County* operates a bright, friendly gallery at 1418 Cornwall St. Try to take the Whatcom Artist Studio Tour, over two weekends in Oct (360-676-8548; alliedarts.org).

Also check out the *SPARK Museum of Electrical Invention* (1312 Bay St.; 360-738-3886; sparkmuseum.org). From 11 a.m. to 5 p.m. Wed through Sun, history buffs can browse the museum's collection of more than 1,000 radios and broadcasting memorabilia dating through to the 1940s. This special museum also houses an FM station (KMRE-LP 102.3 FM) that locally broadcasts radio shows from the World War II era. Visit *Sehome Hill Arboretum*

Historic Fairhaven's Dirty Dan Harris

He sported the customary beard, mustache, and longish hair worn in the 1880s. It's said that he was a sailor, trader, and rumrunner. He wore a shabby frock coat over a red undershirt. A dusty black plug hat was jammed on his head. On his feet he wore a pair of unlaced dirty boots. He also didn't bathe very often. But Dirty Dan, or Daniel Harris, in 1883 filed the original plan to create the community of Fairhaven. Dirty Dan is memorialized at 1211 11th St. at the popular *Dirty Dan Harris Steakhouse* (360-676-1011; dirtydanharris.com), open daily at 5 p.m.

Lummi Island

Lummi Island, near Bellingham and a quick ferry ride from Gooseberry Point across Hale Passage, is one of the smaller populated San Juan isles. Only about 9 miles long and 2 miles wide, it offers a few surprises. For one, during the month of August, you can watch the ancient but extremely sustainable fishing technique of reef-netting from boats at Legoe Bay on the west side of the island. The *Nettles Organic Farm* and *Willows Inn,* a historic B&B retreat (2579 W. Shore Dr.; 888-294-2620; willows-inn.com), are a force in the island's farm-to-table movement, including sourcing reef-net-caught wild salmon. The dining room at Willows Inn has won national-tier awards for wild-foraged and locally farmed cuisine, served Thursday through Sunday evenings. There's also the more casual Taproot Cafe at the century-old inn. On Memorial Day weekend, Labor Day weekend, and a November weekend, attend the annual artist tours to see splendid watercolors, oils, sculpture, jewelry, glass, pottery, and fiber arts for sale at artists' studios around the island.

(360-778-7000; wwu.edu/share) on 180 acres with several miles of trails adjacent to Western Washington University. And don't miss the terrific *Bellingham Farmers Market* at 1100 Railroad Ave. (360-647-2060; bellinghamfarmers .org), 10 a.m. to 3 p.m. Sat, Apr through Christmas. Be sure to go early.

For dining in Bellingham, locals suggest finding fresh Southwestern fare at *Pepper Sisters* (1055 N. State St.; 360-671-3414; peppersisters.com) and drinks and food at *Boundary Bay Brewery* at 1107 Railroad Ave. (360-647-5593; bbaybrewery.com). *Chocolate Necessities* at 4600 Guide Meridian St. (360-676-0589; chocolatenecessities.com) offers decadent chocolate truffles. For a great view while dining, head to *Lighthouse Bar & Grill* (1 Bellwether Way; 360-392-3200; lighthousebarandgrill.com) in the Bellwether Hotel. Lodging options include the *Fairhaven Village Inn* (1200 10th St. S; 360-733-1311; fairhavenvillageinn.com), the upscale-with-Northwest-flair *Chrysalis Inn & Spa* on the waterfront (804 10th St.; 360-756-1005; thechrysalisinn.com), or the 65-room *Hotel Bellwether* (One Bellwether Way; 360-392-3100; hotelbell wether.com). If you're splurging, go all the way with the Bellwether's 3-story freestanding 900-square-foot Lighthouse Suite with a 360-degree observation deck. Hundred North at 100 N. Commercial St. (360-594-6000; hundrednorth .com) prepares seasonal, sustainable cuisine in an intimate dining room.

The small community of *Ferndale* just north of Bellingham is a great place to explore both history and nature. Two blocks south of Main Street on 1st Avenue, *Historic Pioneer Park* is home to the largest collection of 19th-century log structures in the state, maintained by the Ferndale Heritage Society (360-384-6461; ferndaleheritagesociety.com). Tour these sturdy buildings, hewn from giant cedars mid-May through mid-Sept from 11:30 a.m. to 4:30 p.m., daily except Mon. Two major green spaces lie along the Nooksack River: the 624-acre **Tennant Lake Park** and the 350-acre **Hovander Homestead Park.** Located 1 mile south of Ferndale along Hovander Road, Tennant Lake Park has the restored turn-of-the-20th-century farmhouse operating as a summer-only interpretive center. Next to the 1906 farmhouse, there are beds brimming with summer perennials, and visitors can stroll the paths of the Fragrance Garden, then follow the route past the viewing tower and toward the lake. Walk along the half-mile system of elevated boardwalks to see a variety of wetlands vegetation along with raptors and waterfowl, including large flocks of trumpeter swans in winter. Climb the 50-foot-tall observation tower and look for birds.

It's shorter to walk along the half-mile trail from Tennant Park to Hovander Homestead Park than to drive along Nielsen Avenue.

Hovander Homestead, at 5299 Nielsen Rd. (360-384-3444), is open year-round, 8:30 a.m. to 8 p.m. The restored family farmhouse was built in 1903 by Hakan Hovander, a Swedish architect who helped rebuild Chicago after the Great Fire of 1871. Volunteers show visitors through the elegant rooms (call for dates). There are farm animals on the grounds in summer and antique farm equipment at the big red barn, as well as a demonstration garden.

You could now detour from I-5 and head east into the Cascade Mountain foothills on Highway 542 (Mount Baker Highway) and follow the road for glorious views of 10,781-foot Mount Baker. At Glacier, near milepost 33, stop at the **Glacier Public Service Center** (360-599-2714) in late spring, summer, and early fall for information on scenic hiking trails and campgrounds in the North Cascades. From here it's an easy summer drive into the Mount Baker-Snoqualmie National Forest. The road winds up to the Shuksan Picnic Area with grills and restrooms near Hannegan Pass Road, Heather Meadows with trails and a visitor center at milepost 53, and on to **Artist Point Viewpoint** at road's end, 58 miles from Bellingham, at an elevation of 5,140 feet.

If you're not going east to Mount Baker, try sea level adventures by heading to **Birch Bay** just northwest of Ferndale (exit 270 from I-5) and close to the US–Canadian border. Plan your visit for Thurs through Mon from Mother's Day to Labor Day so that you can stop at the **C Shop** (4825 Alderson Rd.; 360-371-2070; thecshop.com), a Birch Bay institution and a combination bakery, candy shop, and hometown cafe. After munching the goodies, take a brisk walk along the beach at **Birch Bay State Park** (360-371-2800; parks.wa.gov) for spotting seabirds and shorebirds, beachcombing, and wonderful water views of Birch

Bay, Georgia Strait, and the San Juan Islands. Go to birchbaychamber.com (360-371-5004) for current tide tables and events.

Pause for good eats and wide-angle water views of Birch Bay at **Shores Restaurant** (7848 Birch Bay Dr.; 360-371-3464). For overnight stays inquire about a variety of modern condos and cozy cottages at **Birch Bay Getaway** (360-371-3730; birchbaygetaway.com) or **Cottages by the Beach** (360-927-1112; ilovecottages.com).

Lynden, a friendly community with a proud Dutch heritage, is located in the fertile Nooksack Valley farmlands east of Birch Bay. Stroll down Front Street, bedecked with flowers and quaint Dutch decor, and stop in for fresh pastries at a destination bakery—**Lynden Dutch Bakery** (421 Front St.; 360-354-3911; lyndenbakery.com), or authentic European cuisine at **Dutch Mothers Restaurant** (405 Front St.; 360-354-2174; dutchmothers.net).

Lynden Pioneer Museum (217 Front St.; 360-354-3675; lyndenpioneer museum.com) is open 10 a.m. to 4 p.m. Mon through Sat. Stroll through a re-created turn-of-the-20th-century main street with stores, a cafe, doctor and dentist offices, a school, a church, and a train station. Admire the collection of early automobiles, more than 40 restored horse buggies and wagons, and antique farm machinery. In midsummer, the steam tractors and threshing machines are fired up at the Puget Sound Antique Tractor and Machinery Association's **Threshing Bee.** The land around Lynden features well-kept working farms, many open seasonally for U-pick adventures.

One area really off the beaten path is a tiny peninsula situated just below the 49th parallel, south of British Columbia. Though part of Washington, this little geographical oddity is surrounded by Canadian territory. **Point Roberts** (population 1,314 in 2010) became US territory in the late 1840s. But before crossing the border, walk the gorgeous gardens of **Peace Arch International Park** (peacearchpark.org) by taking exit 276 in **Blaine.**

Pass through Canadian Customs at the border at Blaine, about 20 miles north of Bellingham on I-5. For border crossing requirements go to the US–Canadian Border Crossing website at cbp.gov or call (703) 526-4200.

Once in Canada, continue north into British Columbia and follow the signs to Tsawwassen, about 23 miles, then follow signs to Point Roberts and a small US Customs station used to reenter the US. For a spectacular water view, stop at Point Roberts' **Lighthouse Marine Park** (360-945-4911) at the peninsula's southwest corner. Check out the Orca Center on the boardwalk and 2-story whale-watching tower with its great views of Georgia Strait and the Canadian Gulf Islands.

At **Point Roberts Marina** (360-945-2255; pointrobertsmarina.com) at the south end of Tyee Drive, inspect a flotilla of sailboats and motor craft. A fine place to have dinner while taking in the splendid views is **South Beach House** (725 S. Beach Rd.; 360-945-0717; southbeachhousepointroberts.com), east of the marina. For more information visit pointrobertstourism.com and pointrobertschamberofcommerce.com.

Places to Stay on Puget Sound

ANACORTES

Fidalgo Bay Resort RV Park
4701 Fidalgo Bay Rd.
(360) 293-5353
fidalgobay.com

Majestic Inn & Spa
419 Commercial Ave.
(360) 299-1400
majesticinnandspa.com

Ship Harbor Inn
5316 Ferry Terminal Rd.
(360) 293-5177
shipharborinn.com

ANDERSON ISLAND & STEILACOOM

Above the Sound Bed & Breakfast
806 Birch St.
Steilacoom
(253) 589-1441
abovethesound.com

Inn at Burg's Landing Bed & Breakfast
8808 Villa Beach Rd.
(253) 884-9185
burgslandingbb.com

Inn at Saltar's Point
68 Jackson St.
(253) 588-4522
Steilacoom
innatsaltarspoint.com

ASHFORD & MOUNT RAINIER AREA

Alexander's Lodge at Mount Rainier
37515 Hwy. 706 E
(360) 569-2300
alexanderslodge.com

Alta Crystal Resort
68317 SR 410 E
(360) 663-2500
altacrystalresort.com

Mountain Meadows Inn
28912 Hwy. 706 E
(360) 569-0507
mountainmeadowsinn.com

Mounthaven Resort
38210 Hwy. 706 E
(360) 569-2594
mounthaven.com

Nisqually Lodge
31609 Hwy. 706 E
(360) 569-8804
whitepasstravel.com

Stormking Spa and Cabins
37311 Hwy. 706 E
(360) 569-2964
stormkingspa.com

Wellspring Spa and Retreat
54922 Kernahan Rd.
(360) 569-2514
wellspringspa.com

Whittaker's Historic Bunkhouse Motel
30205 Hwy. 706 E
(360) 569-2439
whittakersbunkhouse.com

BAINBRIDGE ISLAND

Eagle Harbor Inn
291 Madison Ave. S
(206) 842-1446
theeagleharborinn.com

BELLINGHAM

Chrysalis Inn & Spa
804 10th St.
(360) 756-1005
thechrysalisinn.com

Days Inn
215 Samish Way
(360) 734-8830
daysinn.com

Fairhaven Village Inn
1200 10th St. S
(360) 733-1311
fairhavenvillageinn.com

Hotel Bellwether on Bellingham Bay
One Bellwether Way
(360) 392-3100
hotelbellwether.com

BIRCH BAY

Beachside RV Park
7630 Birch Bay Dr.
(800) 596-9586
beachsidervpark.com

Birch Bay Getaway
(360) 371-3730
birchbaygetaway.com

Cottages by the Beach
(360) 927-1112
ilovecottages.com

Driftwood Inn Motel
7398 Birch Bay Dr.
(360) 371-2620
driftwoodinnmotel.com

GIG HARBOR

Best Western Wesley Inn
6575 Kimball Dr.
(253) 858-9690
wesleyinn.com

ISSAQUAH & NORTH BEND

Roaring River Bed & Breakfast
46715 SE 129th St.
(425) 888-4834
theroaringriver.com

LA CONNER/MOUNT VERNON/BOW

Alice Bay Bed and Breakfast
11794 Scott Rd.
Samish Island
(360) 766-6396
alicebay.com

Katy's Inn
503 S. 3rd St.
(360) 466-9909
bedandbreakfastlaconner
.com

La Conner Channel Lodge
205 N. 1st St.
(360) 466-1500
laconnerlodging.com

LOPEZ ISLAND

Edenwild Inn Bed & Breakfast
132 Lopez Rd.
(360) 468-3238
theedenwild.com

Lopez Islander Resort
2864 Fisherman Bay Rd.
(360) 468-2233
lopezfun.com

MacKaye Harbor Inn Bed & Breakfast
949 MacKaye Harbor Rd.
(360) 468-2253
mackayeharborinn.com

Midnight's Farm
3042 Center Rd.
midnightsfarm.com

Ravens Rook Cabin
58 Wildrose Ln.
(877) 321-2493
ravensrooklodging.com

LUMMI ISLAND

Willows Inn
2579 W. Shore Dr.
(888) 294-2620
willows-inn.com

OLYMPIA

Blueberry Hill Farm Guest House Bed & Breakfast
12125 Blueberry Hill Ln.
(360) 458-4726
blueberryhillfarmguest
house.com

Puget View Cottage
7924 61st Ave. NE
(360) 413-9474

Swantown Inn Bed & Breakfast
1431 11th Ave. SE
(360) 753-9123
swantowninn.com

ORCAS ISLAND

Bayside Cottages
65 Willis Ln.
(360) 376-4330
orcas1.com

Buckhorn Farm Bungalow
17 Jensen Rd.
(360) 376-2298
buckhornfarm.com

Doe Bay Resort and Retreat
107 Doe Bay Rd.
(360) 376-2291
doebay.com

Kangaroo House Bed & Breakfast
1459 N. Beach Rd.
(360) 376-2175
kangaroohouse.com

Old Trout Bed & Breakfast
5272 Orcas Rd.
(360) 376-7474
oldtroutinn.com

Once in a Blue Moon Farm
412 Eastman Rd.
(360) 376-7035
onceinabluemoonfarm.com

Otters Pond Bed & Breakfast
100 Tomihi Dr.
(360) 376-8844
otterspond.com

Turtleback Farm Inn
1981 Crow Valley Rd.
(360) 376-4914
turtlebackinn.com

POINT ROBERTS

Maple Meadows Inn
101 Goodman Rd.
(360) 945-5536
maplemeadowsinn.com

PORT LUDLOW

Resort at Port Ludlow
1 Heron Rd.
(360) 437-7000
portludlowresort.com

PORT ORCHARD

Reflections Bed and Breakfast
3878 Reflection Ln. E
(360) 871-5582

PORT TOWNSEND

Palace Hotel
1004 Water St.
(800) 962-0741
palacehotelpt.com

POULSBO

Manor Farm Inn
26069 Big Valley Rd. NE
(360) 779-4628
manorfarminn.com

Poulsbo Inn & Suites
18680 WA-305
(360) 779-3921
poulsboinn.com

SAN JUAN ISLAND

Friday Harbor House
130 West St.
(360) 378-8455
fridayharborhouse.com

Harrison House Suites
235 C St.
(360) 378-3587
harrisonhousesuites.com

Highland Inn Bed & Breakfast
439 Hannah Rd.
(360) 378-9450
highlandinn.com

Kirk House Bed & Breakfast
595 Park St.
(360) 378-3757
kirkhouse.net

Lakedale Resort
4313 Roche Harbor Rd.
(360) 378-2350
lakedale.com

Olympic Lights Bed & Breakfast
146 Starlight Way
(360) 378-3186
olympiclights.com

Trumpeter Inn
318 Trumpeter Way
(360) 378-3884
trumpeterinn.com

Tucker House Bed & Breakfast
275 C St.
(360) 378-2783
tuckerhouse1840.com

SNOQUALMIE

Salish Lodge & Spa
6501 Railroad Ave.
(425) 888-2556
salishlodge.com

TACOMA

Branch Colonial House Bed & Breakfast Inn
2420 N. 21st St.
(253) 752-3565
branchcolonialhouse.com

Chinaberry Hill Grand Victorian Inn and Cottage
302 Tacoma Ave. N
(253) 272-1282
chinaberryhill.com

VASHON ISLAND

Betty MacDonald Farm Bed & Breakfast
11835 99th Ave. SW
(206) 567-4227
bettymacdonaldfarm.com

WHIDBEY ISLAND

Anchorage Inn Bed & Breakfast
807 N. Main St.
(360) 678-5581
anchorage-inn.com

Auld Holland Inn
33575 Hwy. 20
(360) 675-2288
auld-holland.com

Blue Goose Inn B&B
702 N. Main
(360) 678-4284
bluegooseinn.com

Captain Whidbey Inn
2072 W. Whidbey Island Inn Rd.
(360) 678-4097
captainwhidbey.com

Comforts of Whidbey
5219 View Rd.
(360) 969-2961
comfortsofwhidbey.com

HELPFUL WEBSITES
IN THE PUGET SOUND REGION

Anacortes
anacortes.org

Bellingham, Whatcom County
bellingham.org

Blaine
blainechamber.com

Ferry Information
wsdot.wa.gov/ferries

Gig Harbor
gigharborguide.com

Kitsap Peninsula
visitkitsap.com

La Conner
laconnerchamber.com

Langley
visitlangley.com

Mount Rainier National Park
visitrainier.com
nps.gov/mora

Oak Harbor
oakharborcomeashore.com

Olympia-Lacey-Tumwater
visitolympia.com

Port Townsend Area
enjoypt.com

San Juan Islands
visitsanjuans.com

Seattle
visitseattle.org

Tacoma, Pierce County
traveltacoma.com

Washington State Parks
parks.wa.gov

Whidbey Island
whidbeycamanoislands.com

**Country Cottage of
Langley Bed & Breakfast**
215 6th St.
(800) 713-3860
acountrycottage.com

**Eagles Nest Inn Bed &
Breakfast**
4680 Saratoga Rd.
(360) 221-5331
eaglesnestinn.com

**Garden Isle Guest
Cottages**
207 NW Coveland St.
(360) 678-5641
gardenislecottages.com

Places to Eat on
Puget Sound

ANACORTES

**Calico Cupboard Cafe
and Bakery**
901 Commercial Ave.
(360) 293-7315
calicocupboardcafe.com

Dad's Diner
906 Commercial Ave
(360) 899-5269

Gere-a-Deli
502 Commercial Ave.
(360) 293-7383
gere-a-deli.com

Penguin Coffee House
2119 Commercial Ave.
(360) 588-8321

**Rockfish Grill &
Anacortes Brewery**
320 Commercial Ave.
(360) 588-1720
anacortesrockfish.com

ANDERSON ISLAND & STEILACOOM

De la Terre
1606 Lafayette St.
(253) 584-0258
restaurantdelaterre.com

ASHFORD & MOUNT RAINIER AREA

Base Camp Grill
300027 Hwy. 706 E
Ashford
(360) 569-2727
basecampgrill.com

Copper Creek Inn Restaurant
35707 SR 706 E
(360) 569-2799
coppercreekinn.com

Mount Rainier Railroad Dining Company
54106 Mountain Hwy. E
(360) 569-2505
rrdiner.com

National Park Inn Restaurant
47009 Paradise Rd. E
(360) 569-2275
mtrainierguestservices.com

Scaleburgers
54109 Mountain Hwy.
(360) 569-2247

BAINBRIDGE ISLAND

Blackbird Bakery
210 Winslow Way E
(206) 780-1322
blackbirdbakery.com

Bruciato
236 Winslow Way E
(206) 201-3462
pizzeriabruciato.com

Hitchcock
133 Winslow Way E,
Ste. 100
(206) 201-3789
hitchcockrestaurant.com

Hitchcock Deli
129 Winslow Way E
(206) 451-4609
hitchcockdeli.com

Mora Iced Creamery
139 Madrone Ln.
(206) 855-1112
moraicecream.com

Pegasus Coffee House
131 Parfitt Way
(206) 201-3606
pegasuscoffeehouse.com

Streamliner Diner
397 Winslow Way E
(206) 842-8595
streamlinerdiner.com

BELLEVUE/REDMOND

District One Saigon
2720 152nd Ave. NE #150
(425) 202-7150
districtonesaigon.com

Facing East
1075 Bellevue Way NE B2
(425) 688-2986
facingeastbellevue.com

Monsoon
10245 Main St.
(425) 635-1112
monsoonrestaurants.com

Tipsy Cow
16325 Cleveland St.
(425) 896-8716
tipsycowburgerbar.com

BELLINGHAM

Boundary Bay Brewery
1107 Railroad Ave.
(360) 647-5593
bbaybrewery.com

Colophon Cafe
1208 11th St.
(360) 647-0092
colophoncafe.com

Hundred North
100 N. Commercial St.
(360) 594-6000
hundrednorth.com

Lighthouse Bar & Grill
1 Bellwether Way
(360) 392-3200
lighthousebarandgrill.com

Pepper Sisters
1055 N. State St.
(360) 671-3414
peppersisters.com

Skylarks Fairhaven Cafe
1308 11th St.
(360) 715-3642
skylarkshiddencafe.com

BIRCH BAY

The C Shop
4825 Alderson Rd.
(360) 371-2070
thecshop.com

Shores Restaurant
7848 Birch Bay Dr.
(360) 371-3464

CHIMACUM

Farm's Reach Café
8972 Beaver Valley Rd.
(360) 732-4200

EDISON

Mariposa
14003 Gilmore Ave.
(360) 820-9912

Slough Food
5766 Cains Ct.
(360) 766-4458
sloughfood.com

Tweets
5800 Cains Ct.
(360) 820-9912
tweetscafe.com

GIG HARBOR

Java & Clay Cafe
3210 Harborview Dr.
(253) 851-3277
javaclaycafe.com

Table 47
5268 Point Fosdick Dr. NW
(253) 857-4777
t47.com

Tides Tavern
2925 Harborview Dr.
(253) 858-3982
tidestavern.com

ISSAQUAH & NORTH BEND

Boehm's Candies at Gilman Village
255 NE Gilman Blvd.
(425) 392-6652
boehmscandies.com

Dough Zone Dumpling House
1580 NW Gilman Blvd.
(425) 427-5555

Noodle Boat Thai Restaurant
700 NW Gilman Blvd.
#E104b
(425) 391-8096
noodleboat.com

LA CONNER

Calico Cupboard Cafe and Bakery
720 S. 1st St.
(360) 466-4451
calicocupboardcafe.com

La Conner Brewery
117 N. 1st St.
(360) 466-1415
laconnerbrewery.com

Nell Thorn of La Conner
116 1st St.
(360) 466-4261
nellthorn.com

LOPEZ ISLAND

The Galley
Fisherman Bay
(360) 468-2713
galleylopez.com

Holly B's Bakery
Lopez Plaza
(360) 622-8133
hollybsbakery.com

Isabel's Espresso
(360) 468-4114
isabelsespresso.com

Ursa Minor
210 Lopez Rd.
(360) 622-2730
ursaminorlopez.com

LYNDEN

Dutch Mothers Restaurant
405 Front St.
(360) 354-2174
dutchmothers.net

Lynden Dutch Bakery
421 Front St.
(360) 354-3911
lyndenbakery.com

OLYMPIA

Budd Bay Cafe
525 Columbia St. NW
(360) 357-6963
buddbaycafe.com

Chelsea Farms Oyster Bar
222 Capitol Way N
(360) 915-7784
222market.com

Three Magnets Brewing Company
600 Franklin St. SE #105
(360) 972-2481
threemagnetsbrewing.com

Wagner's European Bakery & Cafe
1013 Capitol Way
(360) 357-7268
wagnersoly.com

ORCAS ISLAND

Aelder and Hogstone's Wood Oven
460 Main St.
hogstone.com

Doe Bay Café
107 Doe Bay Rd.
(360) 376-8059
doebay.com

Island Hoppin' Brewery
33 Hope Ln.
(360) 376-6079
islandhoppinbrewery.com

The Kitchen
249 Prune Alley
(360) 376-6958
thekitchenorcas.com

Roses Bakery & Cafe
382 Prune Alley
(360) 376-4292
rosesbakerycafe.com

POINT ROBERTS

South Beach House
725 S. Beach Rd.
(360) 945-0717
southbeachhousepoint
roberts.com

PORT HADLOCK

Ajax Cafe
21 Water St.
(360) 385-1965
ajaxcafe.com

PORT LUDLOW

Resort at Port Ludlow
1 Heron Rd.
(360) 437-7000
portludlowresort.com

PORT TOWNSEND

**Elevated Ice Cream &
Candy Shop**
631 Water St.
(360) 385-1156
elevatedicecream.com

Finistère
1025 Lawrence St.
(360) 344-8127
restaurantfinistere.com

Fountain Cafe
920 Washington St.
(360) 385-1364

Nifty Fifties
817 Water St.
(360) 385-1931
niftyfiftyspt.com

POULSBO

Cups Espresso
18881 Front St.
(360) 697-2559

JJ's Fish House
18881 Front St.
(360) 779-6609
jjsfishhouse.com

**Poulsbohemian
Coffeehouse**
19003 Front St.
(360) 779-9199

Sluy's Poulsbo Bakery
18924 Front St.
(360) 779-2798

SAN JUAN ISLAND

Duck Soup Inn
50 Duck Soup Ln.
(360) 378-4878
ducksoupsanjuans.com

Friday Harbor House
130 West St.
(360) 378-8455
fridayharborhouse.com

Haley's Sports Bar & Grill
175 Spring St.
(360) 378-4434

Lime Kiln Cafe
248 Reuben Memorial Dr.
(360) 378-9892

The Madrona Bar & Grill
310 Main St. #105
(360) 378-7954

**San Juan Coffee
Roasting Co.**
18 Cannery Lndg.
(360) 378-4443
coffeesanjuan.com

Vinny's Ristorante
165 West St.
(360) 378-1934
vinnysfridayharbor.com

SEATTLE

Pike Place Market
1501 Pike Pl.
(206) 682-7453
pikeplacemarket.org

SNOQUALMIE

**Snoqualmie Brewery and
Taproom**
8032 Falls Ave. SE
(425) 831-2357
fallsbrew.com

**Snoqualmie Falls Candy
Shoppe**
8102 Railroad Ave. SE
(425) 888-0439
snofallcandyshoppe.com

TACOMA

**Antique Sandwich
Company**
5102 Pearl St.
(253) 752-4069
antiquesandwichcompany
.com

The Chili Parlor
5640 S. Tacoma Way
(253) 472-6829

Dirty Oscar's Annex
2309 6th Ave.
(253) 572-0588
dirtyoscarsannex.com

Engine House #9
611 N. Pine St.
(253) 272-3435
ehouse9.com

Indo Street Eatery
110 N. Tacoma Ave.
(253) 503-3527
indostreeteatery.com

Marzano
516 Garfield St.
(253) 537-4191
dinemarzano.com

Over the Moon Cafe
709 Opera Alley
(253) 284-3722
overthemooncafe.net

Red Wagon
2315 N. Pearl St.
(253) 212-3705
redwagonburgers.com

Social Bar and Grill
1715 Dock St. E
(253) 301-3835
thesocialbarandgrill.com

Spar Tavern
2121 N. 30th St.
(253) 627-8215
the-spar.com

The Swiss
1904 Jefferson Ave.
(253) 572-2821
theswisspub.com

VASHON ISLAND

Gravy
17629 Vashon Hwy. SW
(206) 463-0489
gravyvashon.com

May Kitchen + Bar
17614 Vashon Hwy. SW
(206) 408-7196
maykitchen.com

Snapdragon
17817 Vashon Hwy. SW
(206) 463-1310
vashonsnapdragon.com

The Ruby Brink
17526 Vashon Hwy. SW
therubybrink.com

Zombiez
17705 Vashon Hwy. SW
(206) 463-7777

WHIDBEY ISLAND

Braeburn Restaurant
197 2nd St.
(360) 221-3211
braeburnlangley.com

Christopher's
103 NW Coveland St.
(360) 678-5480
christophersonwhidbey
.com

**Fraser's Gourmet
Hideaway**
1191 SE Dock St. #101
(360) 279-1231
frasersgh.com

**Gordon's on Blueberry
Hill**
5438 Woodard Ave.
(360) 331-7515

SELECTED INFORMATION CENTERS

Anacortes
(360) 293-3832

Bellingham, Whatcom County
(360) 671-3990

Blaine
(800) 624-3555

Gig Harbor
(253) 857-4842

Kitsap County
(800) 337-0580

La Conner
(888) 642-9284

Langley
(360) 221-6765

Oak Harbor
(360) 675-3535

Olympia-Lacey-Tumwater
(877) 704-7500

Port Townsend
(888) 365-6978

San Juan Islands
(888) 468-3701

Seattle
(206) 461-5840

Tacoma, Pierce County
(800) 272-2662

Island Nosh
8898 WA-525
(360) 341-3828
islandnosh.com

Knead & Feed
4 Front St.
(360) 678-5431

Orchard Kitchen
5574 Bayview Rd.
(360) 321-1517
orchardkitchen.com

Oystercatcher
901 NW Grace St.
(360) 678-0683
oystercatcherwhidbey.com

Prima Bistro
201½ 1st St.
(360) 221-4060
primabistro.com

Roaming Radish
5417 S. Crawford Rd.
(360) 331-5939
roamingradish.com

Seabolt's Smokehouse
31640 Hwy. 20
(360) 675-6485
seabolts.com

Toby's Tavern
8 Front St.
(360) 678-4222
tobysuds.com

Useless Bay Coffee Company
121 2nd St.
(360) 221-4515
uselessbaycoffee.com

Village Pizzeria
106 1st St.
(360) 221-3363

Zorba's
32955 Hwy. 20
(360) 279-8322
zorbasrestaurantblog
.wordpress.com

North Cascades & North Central Washington

Tremendous geological forces shoved huge chunks of granite thousands of feet into the air to form the far north section of the Cascade mountain range. We're talking mountains that reach 8,000 or more feet topped off with craggy snow-covered peaks, a picket fence that divides the wet western third from the drier two-thirds of the state.

Abundant water, rich volcanic soil, and hot summers make the Okanogan, Chelan, and Wenatchee river valleys on the east side of the Cascades ideal for fruit growing. Depending on the season, you'll find juicy cherries, apples, pears, and peaches, as well as field-ripened vegetables.

Farther east, the landscape mellows into dry, tan hills covered with sagebrush or bitterbrush. Explore back roads, ghost towns, and a scattering of small lakeside fishing resorts. National forests and state parks offer thousands of miles of trails, making it easy to hike, cross-country ski, trail ride, or mountain bike your way off the beaten path.

North Cascades

The North Cascades puncture the skyline, covered with forests up to the higher elevations and cut by dozens of rivers,

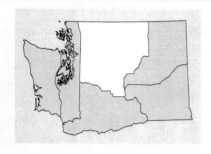

CANADA
UNITED STATES

Oroville

Mount Baker,
10,781 feet
+

NORTH CASCADES

Okanogan R.

97

Tonasket

20

Baker
Lake

Newhalem

20

20

OKANOGAN
VALLEY

Winthrop

Twisp

Okanogan

Stehekin

CASCADE RANGE

Glacier Peak
10,541 feet
+

Columbia R.

155

153

97

Lake
Chelan

17

174

MOUNTAIN PASSES,
VALLEYS
&
CANYONS

2

97A

Chelan

17

202

2

Leavenworth

97

Wenatchee

18

90

169

WENATCHEE MOUNTAINS

28

410

N

0   35 mi

Ellensburg

90

0   35 km

82

waterfalls, and lakes. At the timberline between 4,500 and 5,500 feet, alpine meadows carpeted with brightly colored wildflowers draw hikers. Crossing over the passes to the eastern side of the Cascades, you'll see how the mostly blocked clouds leave the hills and canyons to drought-tolerant species of lodgepole, Western white, and ponderosa pine.

Highway 20, Washington's only paved road across this northern wilderness, was completed in 1972. It connects north-western Washington and the north-central section of the state. The highway closes with the first heavy snowfall, usually around Thanksgiving. It normally opens again in late April or May. But the dates swing widely from year to year. For current highway conditions call the Washington State Department of Transportation at (800) 695-7623, or check for travel alerts on their website wsdot.com/traffic. Late

NORTH CENTRAL WASHINGTON'S FAVORITE ATTRACTIONS

Baker Lake
Concrete

Cascadian Farm Organic Market
cascadianfarm.com

Chimposiums
Ellensburg
friendsofwashoe.org

Ginkgo Petrified Forest
Vantage
parks.wa.gov

John Wayne Pioneer Trail
Central and eastern Washington
parks.wa.gov/trails

Lake Chelan and Stehekin
Chelan
nps.gov/noca
lakechelan.com

Molson School Museum
Molson
okanogancountry.com

North Cascades National Park
North Cascade Mountains
nps.gov/noca

Ohme Gardens and Rocky Reach Dam
Wenatchee
ohmegardens.com
chelanpud.org/visitor-center.html

Ross Lake Resort
Diablo Lake
rosslakeresort.com

Run of the River Inn and Refuge
Leavenworth
runoftheriver.com

Skagit River Bald Eagle Viewing
Rockport
skagiteagle.org

Winthrop and Methow Valley
Hwy. 20
winthropwashington.com

Yakima River Canyon
Yakima
visityakima.com

Nature Classes

An excellent adventure is to incorporate a nature or natural history class into your vacation plans. The premier organization to offer a wide range of weekend classes and field experiences, many designed with the family in mind, is the nonprofit **North Cascades Institute** (360-854-2599; ncascades.org). NCI has an $11.6 million learning center in partnership with North Cascades National Park and Seattle City Light, giving it a base high in the mountains.

Topics range far and wide: outdoor photography, high desert ecology, spring birding, nature journaling, poetics of the wild, landscape watercolor, Ross Lake by boat and boot, volcanic geology of Mount Baker, and treetop forest ecology are just skimming the surface of a long list of experiences. Check out NCI's website or call for a catalog.

spring (wildflowers) or early fall (fall color) are the best times to view nature's displays. The **North Cascades National Park** office complex at 810 Hwy. 20 in **Sedro-Woolley** (360-854-7200) is a good place to stop for information as you approach from the west. The office is open daily 8 a.m. to 4:30 p.m. from Memorial Day weekend through early Oct and Mon through Fri (same hours) the rest of the year. Visit nps.gov/noca for full park information. Rangers for the Mount Baker-Snoqualmie National Forest are based in the same building, and can be reached at (360) 856-5700 or fs.usda.gov/mbs.

Many visitors to north-central Washington enjoy river-rafting adventures. More than a dozen rivers are popular for rafting, ranging from a relaxing Class I to suicidal Class VI. Several professional rafting companies supply the equipment, information, and confidence beginners need to tackle a river. Most guided rafting trips concentrate on Class III and IV rivers—that is, rivers that have enough riffles, rapids, and whitewater to guarantee a great adventure. Some easy float trips are also scheduled to observe eagles. For current information about trips on the Skagit, Twisp and Methow Rivers, contact the North Cascades National Park office complex in Sedro-Woolley (360-854-7200). Another good contact is the **Washington Outfitters & Guides Association** (509-997-1080; woga.org), the only industry organization in the state that represents outfitters, sport-fishing guides, horse and llama packers, whitewater rafters, hunting guides, and other outdoors professionals.

Traveling east on Highway 20 from Sedro-Woolley, follow the winding Skagit, a National Wild and Scenic River that's colored blue-green with glacial meltwaters. Just before the small town of Concrete, take the turnoff north on Baker Lake Road to visit the 9-mile **Baker Lake,** a lovely mountain reservoir with campsites, trails, and boating access. Enjoy spectacular views of Mount Baker, known to the local Nooksack Tribe as Koma Kulshan, "Great White Watcher." *Shadow of the Sentinels,* on your right just past the Koma Kulshan Guard Station at Baker Lake's south end, is a pleasant half-mile, wheelchair-accessible trail and interpretive hike through old-growth forest. For information about forest and lakeside campgrounds in the North Cascades, stop in or contact the North Cascades Visitor Center on Highway 20 in Newhalem (206-386-4495 ext.11; nps.gov/noca).

Located about 28 miles east of I-5, the town of *Concrete* is worth a stop before continuing east on Highway 20. The Superior Portland Cement plant here was once the largest in the state, producing nearly half the cement used in the Grand Coulee Dam and supplying plenty more for construction of the local dams on Diablo and Ross Lakes. The plant closed in 1968. Concrete now serves as a jumping-off point for recreation in the Upper Skagit Valley and North Cascades. The 1916 concrete bridge that spans the Baker River at the town's east end is listed in the National Register of Historic Places. A jaunt across the bridge leads to E. Shannon Road and an overlook to Baker Dam.

didyouknow?

Water that feeds the North Cascades' rivers and lakes comes from melting glaciers. The milky blue or green or gray color of the lakes is caused by rock flour, what's left after rocks are ground down underneath the glaciers' movements. The fine powder is suspended and refracts sunlight, producing the colors.

Staying here is an option before exploring the scenic North Cascades Highway and mountainous regions to the east. At *Ovenell's Heritage Inn* (46276 Concrete-Sauk Valley Rd.; 360-853-8494; ovenells-inn.com), travelers are greeted by a noisy but cheerful welcoming committee of ducks, geese, and other farm animals. There are 4 comfortable guest rooms in the main house and 7 log cabins on the 580-acre cattle ranch that's been in the family for four generations. Enjoy views of Mount Baker—when it's "out."

Food options along Highway 20 in the Concrete area include *Annie's Pizza Station* (44568 Hwy. 20; 360-853-7227; anniespizzastation.net) for good pizza and other Italian fare and, a bit farther east, *Perks* (360-853-9006) for espresso drinks and sandwiches.

Rockport, 8 miles east of Concrete, has excellent off-the-beaten-path credentials. *Rockport State Park,* opened in 1961, is a 670-acre park in an ancient forest, although the camping area has been closed because of hazardous conditions. The trees are worth the stop in this rare never-logged forest with a dense canopy at the foot of Sauk Mountain. Folks can thank the old

Sound Timber Company owners who declined to log the old-growth trees, selling the almost 600 acres to the state for $1.

The **Skagit River Bald Eagle Interpretive Center** (open weekends from Dec to Jan) is located in Rockport, 2 blocks south of Highway 20 at 52809 Rockport Park Rd. (360-853-7626; skagiteagle.org). Contact the center for information about guided eagle-watching walks. The **Upper Skagit Bald Eagle Festival** (concrete-wa.com) happens every January. Guided float trips on the Skagit River allow folks to see the eagles. This is home to one of the largest wintering bald eagle populations in the continental US. Hundreds of eagles are counted here annually by expert birders, with mid-December to mid-January being the best times to see the majestic birds on the Upper Skagit. On any given day, visitors might see up to 100 eagles from pullouts off Highway 20.

Between Rockport and Marblemount is the **Skagit River Bald Eagle Natural Area** with its viewpoints and interpretive signs overlooking the river. Designated sites such as this are the best places to watch eagles without disturbing them. Volunteers from the Eagle Watchers program provide information and birding scopes at the best sites. The eagles start heading here in late autumn from as far away as Alaska to feast on chum salmon that are exhausted and dying after navigating many miles upstream from the Pacific Ocean.

At milepost 101 is the **Cascadian Farm Organic Market** (55749 Hwy. 20; 360-853-8173; cascadianfarm.com), a roadside stand that sells the company's outstanding organically grown products; the organic foods are shipped all over the country. At this busy little stand, taste delicious berry shortcakes, low-sodium pickles and sauerkraut, fresh salads, sweet corn, all-fruit sorbets, and espresso. There are shaded picnic tables and self-guided tours of the experimental gardens. The market is open May through mid-Sept from 10 a.m. to about 6 p.m. weekdays and to 9 p.m. on weekends.

Glacier Peak Resort (58468 Clark Cabin Rd.; 360-873-2250; glacier peakresort.com) near Rockport, offers cabins, cottages, lodge rooms, riverside camping, and RV sites, plus spa and hot tub access. The on-site restaurant, The Eatery, has hearty breakfast, burgers, and entrées.

Near the confluence of the Skagit and Cascade Rivers, **Marblemount** has been the last-chance stop for food, fuel, and news for travelers heading into the high country ever since miners trekked through these rugged mountains in the 1880s. **Buffalo Run Restaurant** (60084 Hwy. 20; 360-873-2461; buffalo runinn.com), open for breakfast, lunch, and dinner, features buffalo steaks and burgers as well as venison and elk. For a more traditional menu, stop at **Marblemount Diner** (360-873-4503) at the east end of town. If you're not fond of tents, check out the **Buffalo Run Inn** (60117 Hwy. 20; 360-873-2103), originally an 1889 roadhouse and a watering hole for gold miners and traders.

Birding on the North Cascades Loop

The *Great Washington State Birding Trail* includes the *Cascade Loop,* featuring 225 out of the state's 346 annually recorded bird species from inland coastal waters through conifer forests and over high passes of the Cascade Mountains to sagebrush and grassland plateaus, desert canyons, and the Columbia River. The state is known for its large populations of shorebirds and waterfowl, bald eagles, snow geese, neotropical migrants, and trumpeter and tundra swans. Grab your binoculars, scope, and bird book and hit the road, or incorporate some of these stops into one of your outings. The best birding times are generally early mornings and late afternoons and in spring and fall.

Barn Beach Reserve (leavenworth.org) in Leavenworth is home to an environmental learning center, arts facility, and museum. The reserve and an adjacent park create a 50-acre greenbelt along the river, including a mature streamside forest and Blackbird Island.

Bayview State Park (parks.wa.gov), part of the more than 11,000-acre Padilla Bay National Estuarine Sanctuary near Mount Vernon, offers an interpretive center, gravel beaches, a salt marsh, and mudflats.

Larrabee State Park (parks.wa.gov), north of Mount Vernon via scenic Chuckanut Drive, offers 2,683 acres of mountain lookouts, lakes, conifers, saltwater coves with fascinating rock formations, and tide pools. Watch for waterfowl and shorebirds. Explore 15 miles of trails that start at the day-use area.

Pearrygin Lake State Park (parks.wa.gov), north of Winthrop, is a more than 1,200-acre park with a large lake; bird viewing is best along its east side. Try spring and summer mornings.

Rockport State Park (parks.wa.gov), near Rockport, has 670 acres with 5 miles of trails through old-growth conifers. Spring visits are best except for December through February when it becomes bald eagle country with eagles converging to feed on salmon coming up the Skagit River to spawn.

Tennant Lake (wdfw.wa.gov) is near Ferndale, northwest of Bellingham. Use the 1.4-mile-long elevated boardwalk Loop Trail around lush wetlands and a marshy lake, and climb the observation tower.

Get a copy of the *Great Washington State Birding Trail* map or birding checklists through wa.audubon.org; wos.org; birdweb.org; or the Washington Department of Fish and Wildlife in Mount Vernon, (360) 445-4441.

This area is a backpacker's nirvana. If you don't mind steep trails of 3 to 5 miles in length that end in superb views of alpine lakes, jagged peaks, and long-range vistas, contact the visitor center in Marblemount at 59831 Hwy. 20 (360-873-4150; marblemount.com) or the **Wilderness Information Center** (7280 Ranger Station Rd.; 360-854-7245) for maps, advice, and backcountry permits for the Pasayten Wilderness and North Cascades National Park. Also ask about hiking trails to high vistas from nearby Cascade Pass and Thornton Lakes trailheads. *Note:* Do not attempt backcountry hikes without being completely prepared. See "Ten Essentials for Backcountry Hikers" on page 100.

The Skagit River Valley widens at milepost 120 at *Newhalem,* a company town on Highway 20. Stop at the 1922 *Skagit General Store* (206-386-4489) to gather picnic goodies and try samples of the Skagit fudge that's made on the premises. Find a shady picnic spot near Old Number Six, the restored Baldwin locomotive engine that ran between Newhalem and Rockport before the highway was built.

The North Cascades Visitor Center and Ranger Station (206-386-4495 ext. 11) is located off Highway 20, behind the Newhalem Creek Campground. It's open daily at 9 a.m. from mid May to late Oct with hiking and camping information, helpful maps, and wildlife information.

Just past Skagit General Store, cross the Skagit River on a small suspension bridge and walk the third of a mile self-guided and wheelchair-accessible nature trail that loops through old-growth forest. Cross the river on another pedestrian suspension bridge next to the gorge powerhouse and continue a short distance on a woodland trail with benches and native plantings for close-up views of *Ladder Creek Falls,* which plunges in tiers more than 70 feet through a narrow chasm of basalt.

The open-grate bridge at *Gorge Creek Falls,* between mileposts 123 and 124 on Highway 20, provides breathtaking views of the 242-foot waterfall. The big parking lot makes this spot easily accessible to highway travelers. On the other side of the highway, walk to a viewpoint over *Gorge Creek Dam,* the first in a series of three successively larger dams.

Call *Skagit Tours* (360-854-2589; skagittours.com) to inquire about scenic cruises on *Diablo Lake.* On the 75-minute tour, you'll see Diablo Dam, craggy mountain peaks, North Cascades wildlife, and learn the history of the Skagit hydroelectric project including the old Incline Railway, which took loaded freight cars about 600 feet up and back down Sourdough Mountain from the 1920s. The boat tours are offered Thurs through Mon from late June to early Sept. Contact the Skagit Information Center (206-233-2709) in Newhalem with questions about the area.

unpassable

Highway 20 can close from milepost 134 at Ross Dam east over 5,477-foot Washington Pass and down to milepost 178 near Mazama. It's a seasonal closure, with the first large snowstorms in mid November to mid December and deep snowfalls through to when the highway can be plowed again in April or May.

To get farther from the crowds and thoroughly enjoy yourself in the process, stay at the floating **Ross Lake Resort** (503 Diablo St., Rockport; 206-386-4437; rosslakeresort.com) as thousands have done since 1950. Eleven cabins and three bunkhouses built on cedar log floats are on the west side of Ross Lake just north of Ross Dam. It's the only resort on the lake and has no direct road access. To reach the resort, meet the passenger ferry (for a nominal fee) and truck that delivers guests to the resort in less than an hour or hike a 2-mile mountain trail from Highway 20. It's open mid-June to Oct.

Piles of food (there is no store or restaurant at the resort), ice chests, baggage, and people all jumble together in the Seattle City Light boat as it chugs past rocky islands and into a narrow passageway between steep canyon walls up to Ross Dam. Then, with gear and everyone safely loaded onto open trucks, it's a short but bumpy ride up switchbacks through the forest to Ross Lake. Speedboats from the resort ferry guests across the lake to the cluster of lodgings.

The cabins, built in the 1930s for logging crews, have been modernized with kitchens, plumbing, and electricity. Hardy hikers can arrange water-taxi service to trailheads for backcountry adventures. Pets are not allowed, and boat rental is available for guests and nonguests; rentals include boats with outboard motors, aluminum canoes, and single and double kayaks.

Back on Highway 20 heading east, you can stop for sweeping views of Diablo Lake, the hanging Colonial Glacier, and 7,182-foot Pyramid Peak from the overlook just before milepost 132. A couple of miles farther, the very short **Happy Creek Forest Walk,** south of the highway, provides a barrier-free boardwalk past huge fallen and standing old-growth trees. Interpretive signs tell the forest's story amid the sounds of the bubbling creek. Ross Lake stretches before you from the two **Ross Lake Overlooks,** north of the highway.

A few miles farther east, at the **East Bank trailhead,** a quarter-mile hike will take you to Ruby Creek, an important spawning area for native trout (no fishing allowed). After 3 miles on the trail, you reach the shore of **Ross Lake,** and in 31 miles hardy backpackers can get to **Hozomeen Lake** near the Canadian border. The roadside scenery gets even more spectacular as you approach the high mountain passes. Creeks cascade down steep gullies; alpine meadows are dotted with purple fireweed and red Indian paintbrush in the summer; and avalanches have left their mark on hillsides by sweeping away trees and bushes. There are several places to pull off the road to ogle at the awesome mountain views, such as the **Whistler Basin Overlook** at milepost 160, the barrier-free **Rainy Lake Trail,** or the point at which the 2,600-mile **Pacific Crest National Scenic Trail** from Mexico to Canada crosses the highway at 4,855-foot-high Rainy Pass.

Creative Vacations

One way to wander the state is to attend a creative workshop, conference, or personal retreat that would take you to a part of the state that is not familiar. Set aside a few days after that experience and explore the area before heading home.

Centrum. Port Townsend, (360) 385-3102, centrum.org

Earth Sanctuary. Freeland, (360) 637-8777, earthsanctuary.org

Field's End. Bainbridge Island, (206) 842-4162 (leave a message with the public library), fieldsend.org

Get Lit! Programs, Eastern Washington University. Spokane, (509) 359-6447, outreach.ewu.edu/getlit

Hedgebrook. Whidbey Island, (360) 321-4786, hedgebrook.org

North Cascades Institute. North Cascades National Park, (360) 854-2599, ncascades.org

Northwind Arts Center. Port Townsend, (360) 379-1086, northwindarts.org

Pacific Northwest Art School. (866) 678-3396, pacificnorthwestart school.org

Pacific Northwest Writers Conference. Issaquah, (425) 673-2665, pnwa.org

Port Townsend Writers Conference. (360) 385-3102, centrum.org

Puget Sound Guitar Workshop. psgw.org

Whidbey Institute. Clinton, (360) 341-1884, whidbeyinstitute.org

Whidbey Island Writers Conference. (360) 331-6714

Write on the Sound. Edmonds, (425) 771-0228, writeonthesound.com

Cast your gaze on 7,740-foot Liberty Bell Mountain, a jagged-edged precipice that looms above the don't-miss **Washington Pass Overlook** (milepost 162), a spot with some of the most spectacular views in the state from 700 feet above the highway. The wheelchair-accessible loop path to the overlook offers close-up views of alpine plants and geology, from spiral-grained trees to smooth, glacier-carved rocks. At 5,477 feet above sea level, Washington Pass is the North Cascades Highway's highest point. From here it winds down a steep U-shaped valley into the terrain of central Washington, drier because the Cascade Mountains block most of the rain clouds coming from the west.

Driving into east-of-the-mountains landscape is a surprise to most newcomers. This land is dominated by tall cinnamon-barked ponderosa pine on the eastern slopes as you descend into the **Methow Valley.** There are pleasant, streamside campgrounds along the way at **Klipchuck** and **Early Winters** in the Okanogan-Wenatchee National Forest.

Tiny **Mazama** is located a half-mile north of Highway 20 at the upper end of the scenic Methow Valley. Its country store, gas station, and post office appear to be all that is left of this once-booming mining town. **Mazama Country Inn** (509-996-2681; mazamacountryinn.com), an all-season retreat nestled in the forest between mountains, has a restaurant that's open to travelers as well as overnight guests. Located at the edge of the **Pasayten Wilderness,** the inn's 18-room lodge and comfortable cabins open onto miles of hiking and mountain-bike trails. In the winter, you can cross-country ski out your door on one of the largest groomed trail systems in the US or book a helicopter to fly you in to ski trackless snow higher in the Cascades.

For advice, information, and maps on hiking and camping in the North Cascades, call the Mount Baker Ranger District, (360) 856-5700, at the complex that also houses the **North Cascades Institute** (360-854-2599; ncascades .org), or go to the **Mount Baker–Snoqualmie National Forest** website, fs .usda.gov/mbs. Another option is to contact the Golden West Visitor Center of North Cascades National Park at (360) 854-7365 ext. 14, nps.gov/noca, which also provides information on Stehekin and the Ross Dam.

In Mazama, eateries—besides the restaurant at Mazama Country Inn— include the **Sandy Butte Bistro & Bar** (31 Early Winters Dr.; 509-996-3906; freestoneinn.com) for Northwest gourmet specialties and the **Mazama Store** (50 Lost River Rd.; 509-996-2855; themazamastore.com), which offers home-made soups and baked goods along with deli sandwiches, pizza, and information about seasonal recreation. During the winter when Highway 20 is closed, Mazama is accessible only from Highways 97 and 153 from Wenatchee.

Activities abound in this area during all four seasons. **Rendezvous Huts** (509-996-8100; rendezvoushuts.com) offers backcountry hut-to-hut cross-country ski touring on the **Methow Valley Trail System** (mvsta.com) in the Okanogan National Forest for a combination of daytime adventure and overnight comfort. If scenic horseback-riding adventures are more your style, consider a wilderness pack trip with **Early Winters Outfitting** in Mazama

Peak Driving

From Mazama, take Hart's Pass and Slate Peak Roads to the highest point one can drive to in Washington State. RVs—don't. This drive is an altitude-gaining, switch-backing, sometimes edge-of-the-cliff, asphalt or gravel road with occasional blind curves. The reward is **Slate Peak** (7,440 feet), a fire lookout and 360 degrees of spectacular views of peaks and valleys. The best time is late July to September (call the Twisp Ranger Station at 509-997-2131 to check the snow level).

(509-996-2659; earlywintersoutfitting.com). Scenic horseback rides are also an option for guests staying at **Freestone Inn** (31 Early Winters Dr., near Mazama; 509-996-3906; freestoneinn.com) and at the excellent mountaintop **Sun Mountain Lodge** (509-996-2211; sunmountainlodge.com), about 10 miles from Winthrop via Twin Lakes and Patterson Lake Roads.

Hikers and mountain bikers can obtain current information for all types of trails from the Methow Valley Visitor Information Center and US Forest Service Ranger District in Winthrop (509-996-4000) and from **Methow Valley Sports Trails Association** (509-996-3287; mvsta.com).

Even if you're not camping, the **Winthrop KOA Campground** (509-996-2258; koa.com) is worth a detour from Highway 20 about a mile east of Winthrop for a look at its display of license plates from around the world, all collected by local resident Mike Meyers.

Highway 20 traffic slows as it winds through the small town of **Winthrop,** a late 1800s trading post now spruced up with a touristy Western theme (winthrop washington.com). The **Shafer Museum,** in a historic log home on the hill 1 block above town, is worth a visit to glimpse some of the early history. It's open from 10 a.m. to 5 p.m. daily from Memorial Day to Labor Day (509-996-2712; shafermuseum.com).

Ten Essentials for Backcountry Hikers

1. Flashlight or headlamp, spare batteries

2. Map of your hiking area

3. Compass or GPS (global positioning system) device

4. Extra food

5. Extra clothing

6. Sunglasses and sunscreen

7. First aid supplies and medications

8. Pocketknife

9. Matches in waterproof container

10. Fire starter

We suggest adding a few more items to the traditional 10: extra water or a water filter, a whistle, insect repellent, emergency shelter, and a tool kit for basic repairs. But the most important "essential" is common sense, which includes making thoughtful decisions and erring on the side of safety, especially with children in tow.

Eateries along Winthrop's main street, Riverside Avenue (Highway 20), include **Rocking Horse Bakery** (509-996-4241; rockinghorsebakery.com) for awesome baked goods and java; **Boulder Creek Deli** (509-996-3990) for great specialty sandwiches; **Sheri's Sweet Shoppe** (509-996-3834; sherissweetshoppe .com) for freshly made fudge, chocolates, cinnamon rolls, and handmade ice cream; and **Old Schoolhouse Brewery** (509-996-3183; oldschoolhousebrewery .com), located in a wedge-shaped building that was once a schoolhouse, for fine handcrafted ales and tasty pub fare. For a gourmet feast at a crisp altitude of 2,850 feet with a great view of the **Methow Valley,** 1,000 feet below, try the elegant **Wolf Creek Bar & Grill at Sun Mountain Lodge,** or the dining room in the 5,000-bottle wine cellar (509-996-2211; sunmountainlodge.com/dining).

Comfortable places to bed down in the scenic Winthrop area include the inviting, family-oriented **Wolf Ridge Resort** (509-996-2828; wolfridge-resort .com), the casually elegant **Chewuch Inn Bed & Breakfast** (509-996-3107; chewuchinn.com), and **River Run Inn & Cabins** (800-757-2709; riverrun-inn .com), close to the Methow River.

The Winthrop–Twisp Eastside Road, which runs parallel to Highway 20, is a pleasant, less-traveled route to the small community of Twisp. On the way, about 5 miles southeast of Winthrop, explore the world of firefighting at the **North Cascades Smokejumpers Base** operated by the US Forest Service.

bookworms

Winthrop was named after Theodore Winthrop, a 19th-century Yale graduate and author. And the town has a connection to another prominent author of the era: Owen Wister, town founder Guy Waring's Harvard roommate, spent his honeymoon here and came up with ideas for his first Western novel, *The Virginian.*

Contact the base (509-997-2031; north cascadessmokejumperbase.com) to take a daily tour from June to Oct 1. The USDA Forest Service Methow Valley Ranger Station (509-996-4003) offers maps and information for backcountry hikes in the region.

In the small community of **Twisp,** pause for espresso drinks and superb pastries at **Cinnamon Twisp Bakery** (116 N. Glover St.; 509-997-5030), and for waist-bulging entrees at **BJ's Branding Iron Restaurant & Saloon** (123 N. Glover St.; 509-997-0040). For an overnight stay here in the scenic Twisp Valley, call **Methow Valley Inn Bed & Breakfast** (234 2nd Ave.; 509-997-2253; methowvalleyinn.com). Stop in for excellent espresso and pastries at **Blue Star Coffee** (3 Twisp Airport Rd.; 509-997-2583; bluestarcoffeeroasters.com), a charming café with a patio.

The highway forks a couple of miles past Twisp, and Highway 20 continues east to Okanogan. Highway 153 proceeds southeast along the Methow

River as it winds and bubbles over its pebbly bed to Pateros. On this route you'll pass the pleasant community of Methow, then plunge into orchard country as the river gorge deepens before its confluence with the Columbia River.

Okanogan Valley

The Okanogan Valley stretches from the British Columbia border at **Oroville** south to the Columbia River. Much of the land along the river is planted with fruit orchards. The area above the river valley is drier, covered with rolling grass and sagebrush meadows dotted with occasional stands of ponderosa pine, glacially deposited boulders, and pristine lakes. **Okanogan** is the Kalispel Tribe's word for "rendezvous," or "gathering place."

Highway 20 merges with US 97 just south of the city of Okanogan, where you can find out more about this isolated region at the **Okanogan County Historical Museum** (1410 2nd Ave. N; 509-422-4272; okanoganhistory.org) adjacent to Legion Park. Fine displays cover local geography and history of Indian and pioneer life. Outside, inspect a collection of log buildings, including a settler's cabin, a blacksmith's shop, and a saloon. Contact the Okanogan County Tourism Council (509-826-5107; okanogancountry.com) or the Okanogan Chamber of Commerce (visitokanogan.com) for more information about town attractions and events.

Dining choices are slim in number but high in quality. A few miles north is **Omak** with its highly thought of **Breadline Cafe** (102 S. Ash St.; 509-826-5836; breadlinecafe.com). The Breadline offers locally grown beef and occasional live blues and folk music. It's in the former Omak Beverages building that bottled soda pop from the 1920s through the 1950s. Locals suggest **Rancho Chico** (22 N. Main St.; 509-826-4757) for an excellent Mexican feast. Find home knick-knacks and a mini-soda fountain at **Grandma's Attic** (12 N. Main St.; 509-826-4765). You can also browse the large selection of used books. **Magoo's Restaurant** (24 N. Main St.; 509-826-2325) is a good choice for breakfast and lunch.

No words can be written about this town without mentioning the Big Show, the **Omak Stampede** (800-933-6625; omakstampede.org), which includes a rodeo and the **World-Famous Omak Suicide Race,** in which horses and their Native American riders plunge down impossibly steep 200-foot-long Suicide Hill into the Okanogan River. It's become infamous, too, because more than 20 horses have died since 1983, including three in 2004 and one in 2012.

Heading north again on US 97, stop at **Riverside** on any day except Saturday to browse **Historic Detro's Western Store** (107 Main St.; 509-826-2200). The all-purpose outfitter offers clothes and gear for tourists, residents, and professional cowboys and cowgirls. Although the structure was rebuilt as a store after a fire in 1916, it became Detro's Western Wear in 1946, making it one of Washington's oldest and largest historic stores. Pick up some food at **Riverside Grocery** (102 N. Main St.; 509-826-2049) and check out its collection of antiques.

For a pleasant overnight campout, head about 18 miles northwest of Omak to **Shady Pines Resort** (125 W. Fork Rd.; 509-826-2287; shadypinesresort .com) on the shores of 350-acre Conconully Reservoir. Four small cabins each sleep 4, and a log cabin duplex sleeps 6, all shaded from summer's heat by tall pines. Appreciate full kitchens, queen-size beds, and cozy sitting areas. Beachfront RV sites offer full hookups, and a few tent sites are also available. Rent a boat to go fishing for rainbow trout or just a relaxing row around the scenic lake. And yes, wireless Internet service has come to **Conconully.**

cowboycaviar

Conconully has gone upscale with its **Cowboy Caviar Fete** in June. Local restaurants compete for the best dish made with bull testicles, otherwise known as cowboy caviar. Try the spicy Great Balls of Fire.

Head into the town of Conconully and catch one of the small town's many festivals: **Miners Day, Grubstake Open Golf Tournament, Outhouse Races** (since 1983), **Snow Dog Super Mush,** and the ever-popular **Cowboy Caviar Fete** (see sidebar). For a quieter way to spend your time, check out the **Conconully Museum** (509-826-4308; conconully.com/museum.php); hours are 10 a.m. to 4 p.m. weekends and holidays. The town was nearly destroyed three times in its youth: an 1892 fire, an 1893 mining depression, and an 1894 flood.

Conconully's culinary options include the **Red Rock Saloon** (316 N. Main St.; 509-557-4993), which specializes in pizza, mozzarella sticks, and steaks.

About 25 miles east of Tonasket on Highway 20, the tiny community of **Wauconda** offers a great introduction to the open beauty of the Okanogan high desert. You'll pass a scattered collection of homes, old homestead cabins, and barns on the 3,000-foot-high plateau. **Bonaparte Lake Resort,** located near Tonasket at 615 Bonaparte Lake Rd. (509-486-2828; bonapartelakeresort .com), has cabins with kitchens, camping, gas, and a lodge with a small store and cafe famous for its great hamburgers. To get there, take Highway 20 3 miles west of Wauconda, then turn north onto Bonaparte Lake Road, a 6-mile-long country road that winds along Bonaparte Creek through meadows and forests to the lakeshore. The Okanogan National Forest also has several campgrounds in the area, including one at Bonaparte Lake. **Lost Lake Campground,** about 8 miles beyond the resort, offers several fine hiking trails, including the easy

Conconully Jail, Sam's Story

Although it was built for impenetrability, the Conconully jail became the butt of many a local joke for the frequent prisoner escapes between 1891 and 1915. Perhaps the most amusing is the story of **Sam Albright,** who found out that two of his friends were guests of the hoosegow and went with another man to pay them a visit. Finding the jailer absent, he and his partner unlatched the window and climbed through. The four friends then engaged in a lively poker game, after which Sam and his friend left candy and books for the inmates, then exited back through the window, latching it behind them.

Big Tree Trail with 600-year-old Western larches, and the Strawberry Mountain Trail, offering panoramic views of Bonaparte Mountain and Lost Lake from hillsides covered with wild strawberries. For information, contact the Tonasket Ranger Station at 1 W. Winesap (509-486-2186; fs.usda.gov/okawen).

Located about 16 miles east of Oroville, and right on the US–Canada border, **Molson**'s two historical museums (molsonmuseums.org) are worth seeing. The **Molson School Museum,** open daily from 10 a.m. to 5 p.m. Memorial Day weekend through Labor Day, offers three floors of well-organized displays. After browsing through the classrooms and library upstairs, the vintage clothing and furniture on the main floor, and the huge tool collection downstairs, enjoy homemade treats provided by museum volunteers. The **Old Molson Ghost Town** (539 Molson Rd.; 509-485-3292), open during daylight hours for self-guided tours Apr through Dec, exudes an Old West feeling with its 19th-century cabins, original bank building, mining and farm tools, and storefronts. Both museums are free, but donations are appreciated. **Sidley Lake** and **Molson Lake,** just north of town, are popular with travelers who like to fish. Bird-watchers also delight in the array of waterfowl, from blue-billed ruddy ducks to canvasbacks, feeding amid reeds and islands in the tiny lakes.

From Molson retrace your route back to Oroville and US 97. *Oro,* Spanish for gold, links us to the town's early history as a miners' mecca. But in 1925 it was nicknamed Queen Tomato for its large tomato-canning factory, and it was an honor for a young woman to be elected Tomato Queen.

Oroville's original Great Northern Depot has been restored as a museum and community hall on the corner of 12th and Ironwood Streets. The **Old Oroville Depot Museum** (509-476-2739), open 9 a.m. to 4 p.m. Mon through Sat from the first weekend in May to the second weekend in Sept, provides insight into the town's history as a railroad, mining, and agricultural center buffeted by changing times.

TOP ANNUAL EVENTS IN NORTH CENTRAL WASHINGTON

JANUARY

Upper Skagit Bald Eagle Festival
Rockport
skagiteagle.org

FEBRUARY

Spirit of the West Cowboy Gathering
Ellensburg
ellensburgcowboygathering.com

MAY

'49er Days
Winthrop
winthropwashington.com

Leavenworth Spring Bird Fest
leavenworthspringbirdfest.com

SEPTEMBER

Ellensburg Rodeo
Ellensburg, Labor Day weekend
ellensburgrodeo.com

For meals, try *America's Family Grill* (1518 Main St.; 509-476-4500) for hamburgers, malts, and shakes amid a nostalgic 1950s decor; *Expressions Espresso* (718 Apple Way St.; 509-476-2970) for light sandwiches, baked goods, and soft ice cream; or *Hometown Pizza, Pasta & Bakery* (1315 Main St.; 509-476-2410) for made-from-scratch pizza, Italian pastas, and gourmet desserts to die for.

Continue southwest to *Loomis,* traversing dry hillsides above the green Sinlahekin Valley. Loomis is another quiet village that boomed during the gold rush of the 1890s and busted soon after. You'd never know from the orchards, old houses, and 1-block-long main street that this was once the largest city in the county. South from Loomis take the primitive but scenic Sinlahekin Road through the *Sinlahekin Wildlife Area* (509-223-3358), the oldest (1939) wildlife area in the state, back to Conconully.

East of Loomis on the Loomis–Oroville Road is narrow *Spectacle Lake,* rimmed with cattails, dry hills, and remnants of an old wooden irrigation flume. There are several rustic resorts along this roadside lake, but the best one is hidden away to the north on secluded Wannacut Lake. Watch for the sign past spring-fed Spectacle Lake for *Sun Cove Resort and Guest Ranch* (93 E. Wannacut Ln.; 509-476-2223; thesuncoveresort.com). Or arrive directly from Oroville on an 8-mile, partially graveled road by following signs on 12th Avenue west of the Oroville Depot Museum. There are RV sites, campsites, log cabins, and larger cottages with splendid lake views, excellent fishing opportunities, wooded grounds that provide plenty of fun activities for both children and adults, including hiking trails, a heated swimming pool, a playground, and sports equipment. The resort is open from Apr through Oct.

If you don't take the turnoff to Sun Cove, you can continue straight along the shore of Wannacut Lake south to the Loomis–Oroville Road. Follow the road east past Whitestone Lake and merge right onto Highway 7, or the Tonasket–Oroville Road. This less-traveled route traverses the hills west of the Okanogan River, parallel to US 97. During summer, keep an eye out for fresh-fruit stands along the way to refill your picnic hamper with locally grown apples, pears, peaches, cherries, and apricots.

fruits&veggies

Washington grows 51 percent of all sweet cherries, almost 60 percent of the country's apples (including two-thirds of the US organic crop), almost 50 percent of our pears, 91 percent of red raspberries in the US, and more Concord and Niagara grapes than any other state in the country. It's also a top producer of lentils, dry peas, and hops.

Cross the river to US 97 at *Tonasket;* before heading south toward *Lake Chelan,* pause for refreshments at *Shannon's Cafe & Deli* (626 S. Whitcomb Ave.; 509-486-2259). You'll find many flavors plus tasty sandwiches, soups, salads, and desserts in this welcoming oasis. Or try the Mexican dishes at *Rancho Chico* (312 Hwy. 97; 509-486-4030). An option for hearty meals is *Whistler's Family Restaurant* (616 N. Whitcomb Ave.; 509-486-2568) and there's also *The Kubler* (302 S. Whitcomb Ave.; 509-486-2996), formerly the historic Tonasket Saloon.

Two lodgings in the lightly populated area to the east and south of Tonasket deserve mentioning: to the east, Canaan Guest Ranch Bed & Barn, between Tonasket and *Republic;* to the south, Eden Valley Ranch. Both are year-round operations with activities that fit snow and sun. The 500-acre *Canaan Guest Ranch* (474 Cape LaBelle Rd., Tonasket; 509-486-1191; canaanguestranch .com), sits at a 3,500-foot elevation. Bring your horses or ride the ranch's stock; enjoy the beautiful gardens and use the ranch as a base to explore the area. The 900-acre *Eden Valley Ranch* (31 Eden Ln., Oroville; 509-485-4002; edenvalleyranch.net), offers 10 deluxe cabins. It's adjacent to the Okanogan National Forest.

If you are in the area during the winter ski season, the Tonasket District ranger station at 1 W. Winesap (509-486-2186; fs.usda.gov/okawen) can provide information about the *Sitzmark Ski Area* (skisitzmark.org), and the *Highlands Sno-Park* for cross-country skiing, and nearby snowmobile trails.

Mountain Passes, Valleys & Canyons

If you like being surrounded on three sides by rugged, 8,000-foot-high mountain peaks, dense alpine forests, and miles of hiking trails; don't mind a long boat ride to the end of a 55-mile-long lake that reaches deep into the Lake Chelan National Recreation Area and the Sawtooth Wilderness; love the allure of winter moonlight snowshoe treks and staying overnight in rustic tent-cabins or cozy lodge rooms without TVs, telephones, daily newspapers, or Internet access, do we have a destination for you.

It's an extraordinary adventure to *Stehekin* and the scenic Stehekin Valley, one of the most isolated outposts in the state. The good news is that Stehekin also offers a small restaurant (in the North Cascades Lodge at Stehekin run by the national park), a bakery, mountain-bike rentals, and shuttle van rides up-valley to trailheads. We're talking small, low key and down-home friendly. And it's possible to see the immediate area in a few hours, or stay for a vacation.

Two passenger ferries leave daily from the town of Chelan to the village of Stehekin. The *Lady of the Lake* takes 4 hours to travel each way with a 1.5-hour stopover in Stehekin. The *Lady Express* does the same trip in 2.5 hours with an hour stopover. Or go on the *Lady Express* and back on the *Lady of the Lake* and earn a 3-hour layover, although this is only available in peak season when both boats are running. During the trip, a guide comments on natural history and the wilderness environment. For schedules, contact *Lake Chelan Boat Company* (509-682-4584; ladyofthelake.com).

If you're interested in camping, hiking, and other recreational activities in the Stehekin Valley area, start with nps.gov/noca and stehekinvalley .com. Then call the National Park Service's *Golden West Visitor Center* in Stehekin (360-854-7365 ext. 14). Rangers can help with trail maps, weather

thehousethat jackbuilt

The House That Jack Built, a small log cabin and craft cooperative located near the Golden West Visitor Center in Stehekin, is popular with long-distance hikers because of its gear-mending kits and other hiking items. It's also a draw for locally made gifts.

conditions, campgrounds and camping sites, other lodging in Stehekin, equipment lists, guide services, and permits for backcountry excursions. The center is open daily from 8:30 a.m. to 5 p.m. from late-May through Sept and at reduced hours year-round on any days there is ferry service. There is also an Okanogan-Wenatchee National Forest and *Lake Chelan Recreation Area* information center in Chelan (428 W. Woodin Ave.; 509-682-4900).

Skiing Washington

Individual websites offer specific information about downhill runs; the extent of cross-country trail systems; snowboarding areas; snowshoeing; day lodge amenities; directions, weather, snow conditions, Sno-Park fees, and overnight accommodations in the area. For additional information, visit skiwashington.com.

49 Degrees North Mountain Resort
Flowery Trail Road, Chewelah
58 miles north of Spokane via US 395
(509) 935-6649
ski49n.com

Hurricane Ridge
17 miles south of Port Angeles in
Olympic National Park
(360) 565-3131
hurricaneridge.com

Loup Loup Ski Bowl
Between Okanogan and Twisp
off Hwy. 20
(509) 557-3405
skitheloup.com

Methow Valley Trail System
North of Wenatchee and near Mazama
and Winthrop via
Hwys. 97, 153, and 20
(509) 996-3287
mvsta.com

Mission Ridge Ski and Board Resort
12 miles from Wenatchee
(509) 663-6543
missionridge.com

Mount Baker
56 miles east of Bellingham
via Hwy. 542
(360) 734-6771
mtbakerskiarea.com

Mount Spokane Ski & Snowboard Park
23 miles north of Spokane
(509) 238-2220
mtspokane.com

Sitzmark Ski Area
20 miles northeast of Tonasket off
US 97
(509) 485-3323
skisitzmark.org

Stevens Pass
between Seattle and Leavenworth via
Hwy. 2
(206) 812-4510
stevenspass.com

Summit at Snoqualmie
52 miles east of Seattle via I-90
(425) 434-7669
summitatsnoqualmie.com

White Pass
120 miles southeast of Olympia near
Mount Rainier National Park via I-5 and
Hwy. 12
(509) 672-3101
skiwhitepass.com

Note: Do not hike into wilderness areas without being fully equipped and fully informed about the areas you plan to explore. See "Ten Essentials for Backcountry Hikers" on page 100.

For a gentler outdoor adventure, try the ***Stehekin Valley Ranch*** (509-682-4677; stehekinvalleyranch.com or stehekin.biz), open from mid June to early Oct. At the ranch 9 miles up-valley from the boat landing, the Courtney family offers rustic one-room tent-cabins, which have canvas roofs. There are also ranch cabins with private bathrooms and new-in-2007 kitchen cabins. In the open-air dining lodge, guests hunker down at huge log slab tables to enjoy steaming cups of coffee and hearty meals cooked by ranch staff. There are no water views here, but you can arrange for scenic horseback rides and rafting trips. Guests have meal plan dining, but day-guests can also make reservations to dine at the ranch.

Another option is the ***North Cascades Lodge at Stehekin*** (509-682-4494; lodgeatstehekin.com) near the boat landing. The lodge offers a restaurant and a small convenience store. ***Silver Bay Inn*** (10 Silver Bay Rd.; 509-670-0693; silverbayinn.com) has cozy and self-contained accommodations in the Lake Cabin (sleeps 4), the Bay Cabin (sleeps 6 to 8), the River View Room (sleeps 2), and the Lake-view House (comes with 2 bedrooms, 2 baths, and a full kitchen). The property offers panoramic views of Lake Chelan and those 8,000-foot-high steep mountains. The inn is close to restaurants, a bakery, and the Stehekin Valley shuttle bus.

Bring sturdy walking shoes and water on the easy 3.5-mile hike to ***Rainbow Falls*** (or take the shuttle bus). Just a short walk from the main road brings you to a good view of 312 feet of cascading water. For a taste of history, explore the old one-room Stehekin School, down the road from the falls, then

Recreation & Picnicking in the Lake Chelan Area

Chelan Falls Park
Picnic area, swimming beach, boat ramp, and docks 5 miles southeast of Chelan.

Chelan Riverwalk Park
Scenic 1-mile shoreline trail along the Chelan River near downtown.

Lake Chelan Mural Walk
Over a dozen murals in and around the downtown area, each containing an apple in some form. Pick up a mural map from the visitor information center.

Old Mill Park
Picnic sites, boat launch, short-term moorage, and marine wastewater station located in the Manson area, 6.5 miles up the north lakeshore.

Willow Point
Scenic and quiet lakeside spot near Manson.

Dammed River

The Columbia River is tamed in the center of the state by the Rocky Reach, Rock Island, Wanapum, and Priest Rapids dams, which create long, narrow reservoirs, generate electricity, and provide irrigation for the Wenatchee Valley region. Like the Okanogan Valley to the north, nearly all available plots of land along the east side of the Columbia River and several smaller valleys to the west toward Cashmere are planted in orchards, making this one of the nation's prime sources of apples, pears, peaches, and apricots. Boating, swimming, fishing, and bicycling are popular during the long, sunny summers; skiing and snowshoeing are popular in winter.

walk a short distance to the Buckner Orchard and their early 1900s Buckner Homestead (bucknerhomestead.org). On your return walk, stop at the **Stehekin Bakery** (509-682-7742; stehekinpastry.com) for delicious, fresh-baked treats (open June 15 through Oct 15). If you can hold off munching everything, carry your snack the 2 miles back to Stehekin and enjoy your pastries with grand views of the lake at one of the picnic tables on the large deck near the boat landing.

On the populated end of the lake is **Chelan.** The downtown area is a pleasant place for strolling, shopping, and leisurely eating. **Chelan Riverwalk Park** offers a shoreline walking trail and a pavilion where outdoor concerts are scheduled during the summer. There are many good eating options in the area, including the historic **Campbell's** (104 W. Woodin Ave.; 509-682-4250 or 509-682-2561; campbellsresort.com) in downtown Chelan, which has a full-service dining room on the main floor. But the best place to eat is in the pub on the second floor, which offers outdoor seating on its veranda along with superb views of the lake. For a casual family-style eatery, stop at **Apple Cup Cafe** (804 E. Woodin Ave.; 509-682-5997; applecupcafe.com), which serves breakfast all day; for good takeout pizza try **Local Myth Pizza** (122 S. Emerson St.; 509-682-2914; localmythpizza.com); and **Vin du Lac Winery** (105 WA-150; 509-682-2882; chelanwine.com) where top-notch plates are paired with wines made on site and views of the lake.

deliciousapples

The world's oldest strain of Delicious apples, a green-and-red-striped one called Common Delicious, grows in the abandoned Buckner Orchard, about 3 miles up the Stehekin Valley. Be prepared to share the orchard with black bears.

In the **Manson** area on Lake Chelan's north shore, a few miles from Chelan, sample Mexican specialties at **El Vaquero Restaurant** (75 Wapato Way;

509-687-3179). If you have a deli picnic planned, follow the signs to scenic *Willow Point Park* near Manson. While city parks can get lively and noisy with kids and families, this small shoreside park offers a quiet alternative and great views of the lake. While in Manson, don't miss *Blueberry Hills Farm,* a popular U-pick blueberry farm and restaurant featuring from-scratch cooking surrounded by more than 10 acres of berry fields (509-687-2379; wildabout berries.com).

For a leisurely few hours on the lake, try stand-up paddleboarding or kayaking. You can rent gear from the friendly staff at *Lake Rider Sports* (409 W. Manson Hwy.; 509-885-4767; lakeridersports.com). For a side trip, head south of Chelan on US 97 east and then along US 2, about 35 miles to *Waterville.* The Douglas County seat since 1887, its cattle-based economy changed in the course of the terrible winter of 1889–90, when temperatures were subzero and snowdrifts continued into April. The cattle industry was essentially wiped out, and farmers turned to wheat.

Waterville's *Douglas County Historical Museum* on US 2 has interesting displays, including an extensive rock collection. But its main claim to fame is

sky high

The sunny oasis of Waterville, where grain fields have replaced sagebrush and cattle, claims the distinction of being the town with the highest altitude in the state: 2,622 feet above sea level.

the state's first recovered meteorite, found by a farmer in 1917 and weighing 84 pounds. In front of the museum rests a large metal bucket, once part of an overhead conveyor system that in the early 1900s carried wheat 2,400 feet

Eating the Slow Food Way

Many Washington inns, B&Bs, and restaurants are embracing the Slow Food movement that originated in 1986 in Italy with Carlo Petrini, who recognized that the industrialization of food was standardizing and limiting options and tastes while eliminating varieties. The supporters appreciate the concept of leisurely dining with family and friends, sustainable agriculture, experimenting with new foods and flavor, eating locally produced food, protecting the environment from chemicals by eating organic, and recognizing the cost of importing food hundreds or thousands of miles. A combination of positive steps can help create good, clean, and fair (field workers should be adequately compensated) food. The *Slow Food movement* also includes wines and meat. Yakima-area hosts speak of visitors coming from Portland and Seattle to enjoy the ambience and community-supported agriculture; there are about a dozen Slow Food USA chapters in Washington state.

down to the river, where it was loaded onto grain barges. The museum also has a two-headed calf and a horse mannequin that was used to model saddles and bridles.

Waterville is a pleasant community with many old houses and a fine county courthouse. Directly across from the museum, the 1903 **Waterville Historic Hotel** (102 E. Park St.; 509-745-8695; watervillehotel.com) has been restored by owner Dave Lundgren. One large suite, a smaller suite, and 7 comfortable rooms (some with private baths and claw-foot tubs) are available. Some of the original oak and leather Mission-style furnishings are on the main floor in the cozy lobby and library area. The hotel is open seasonally. Ask about the old 1919 vaudeville house, the Nifty Theater, which occasionally hosts plays and musical acts.

From Chelan, head south to **Wenatchee** on US 97A on the west side of the Columbia River. Tan-colored hills looming on your right (west) are now clothed in sagebrush, bitterbrush, and aromatic juniper. But across the river to the east, you see compact orchards that are lush and green from irrigation. Detour at **Rocky Reach Dam** (509-663-7522; chelanpud.org) and enjoy a rest stop and perhaps an impromptu picnic amid a splendid perennial garden, hanging baskets of summer flowers, and a children's playground. With camera in hand, climb the steps to the top of the children's slide and snap a picture of the large floral US flag in the **Old Glory Garden,** planted in red, white, and blue annuals. More than 8,000 annuals bloom on Petunia Island surrounding the fish ladders. Take a tour of the dam, check out the visitor center, and watch migrating fish through a viewing glass.

Just prior to reaching Wenatchee, look for the sign to **Ohme Gardens** (3327 Ohme Rd.; 509-662-5785; ohmegardens.com) and detour to visit this lush and cool alpine wonderland. Herman and Ruth Ohme started to develop the family gardens on their barren hilltop 600 feet above the Columbia River in 1929. Ten years later, friends and community members urged the Ohmes to allow public visits to their splendid creation. Travelers still flock to this 9-acre alpine garden atop the bluff that allows wide views of the Columbia River, Cascade Mountains, and **Wenatchee Valley.** Irregular stepping-stones and narrow flagstone pathways meander up, down, and around shaded fern-lined pools, next to large ponds, and around immense boulders. You'll see many varieties of sedum along with creeping thyme, creeping phlox, alyssum, and dianthus. Tall western red cedar, mountain hemlock, grand fir, Douglas fir, and alpine fir grow around the garden's perimeter. The garden is open from Apr 15 to Oct 15, 9 a.m. to 6 p.m. (until 7 p.m. from Memorial Day to Labor Day). There's a nominal admission fee.

For other activities, stop by the **Wenatchee Valley Visitor Bureau** at 5 S. Wenatchee Ave. (509-662-2116; wenatcheevalley.org). A pleasant overnight option is ***Apple Country Bed & Breakfast*** (524 Okanogan Ave.; 509-972-3409; applecountryinn.com). The innkeepers welcome guests to their 1920 Craftsman-style home with its deep and inviting porch. Guest rooms in the main house are named for the apples that grow in the valley—Gala, Fuji, Red Delicious, Golden Delicious, and Cameo. A separate carriage house is a cozy and private haven. For basic motel accommodation, try ***Moonlight Motor Lodge*** (2921 School St.; 509-663-5157; moonlightmotorlodge.com), which has a slightly 1950s feel with a batting cage, outdoor pool, and cinder-block walls. Worth stopping into is the relatively new ***Pybus Market*** (3 N. Worthen St.; 509-888-3900; pybuspublicmarket.com), a charming collection of small shops and restaurants. The building sits on the Wenatchee River and also hosts a farmers market every Wednesday and Saturday in summer. Inside the market, an outpost of ***Arlberg Sports*** (509-888-7433; arlbergsports.com) offers bike rentals in spring and summer for rides along the Apple Capital Recreation Loop, one of the state's longest paved paths.

For good eats in the Wenatchee area, try ***McGlinn's Public House*** (111 Orondo St.; 509-663-9073; mcglinns.com) for pastas, gourmet pizza, and home-made desserts; and the ***Windmill*** (1501 N. Wenatchee Ave.; 509-665-9529; thewindmillrestaurant.com) for legendary steaks and freshly baked pies to die for. ***Wild Huckleberry*** (302 S. Mission St.; 509-663-1013; wildhuck.com) serves reliable breakfasts downtown.

Walk off the calories on a scenic section of the 10-mile ***Apple Capital Recreation Loop Trail*** that skirts both banks of the Columbia River. Find parking and trail access at Riverfront Park at the end of 5th Street in downtown Wenatchee or at Walla Walla Point Park off Walla Walla Avenue at the north end of town. The path is wheelchair accessible.

As you head northwest on US 2 from Wenatchee toward Leavenworth, detour first at the small town of ***Cashmere*** to tour the ***Liberty Orchards' Aplets & Cotlets Candy Factory*** (117 Mission Ave.; 509-782-2191; liberty orchards.com). The tour includes samples of the delicious fruit and nut confections. If time allows, plan an hour or so to tour Cashmere's ***Historic Museum and Pioneer Village,*** located at 600 Cotlets Ave. (509-782-3230; cashmeremuseum.org; there is a nominal admission fee). Volunteers in pioneer dress encourage you and the kids to snoop into some 20 pioneer structures dating from the 1800s that are outfitted with vintage furniture, linens, dishes, kitchenware, clothing, and accessories of those earlier times. For a bite to eat in Cashmere, try the pit-smoked ribs at ***Country Boys BBQ*** (400 Aplets Way; 509-782-7427; countryboysbbq.com).

In the 1960s ***Leavenworth*** was a worn-out 1920s-style railroad and lum-ber town. Now, with years of revitalization by enthusiastic townsfolk, it is a vibrant Bavarian-style village with a bit of Austria and Switzerland thrown in for good measure. It sits at the edge of the central Washington Cascades in the Icicle River Valley, where the towering mountains look very much like the Alps. The compact village is a good place for walking. Carved window boxes and hanging baskets spill over with bright flowers and greenery; shop signs are handpainted in old Germanic script; building exteriors show gingerbread detailing and rich carving; and tiers of second- and third-floor exterior decks and dormers are also done in the carved and richly appointed Bavarian style.

applets&cotlets

The top-selling concoction of **Liberty Orchards** in Cashmere has been a hit since 1920. Think crisp Washington apples, ripe apricots, and crunchy English walnuts and a secret family recipe. Take a tour of the candy kitchens.

Enjoy strolling and poking into shops like *Die Musik Box* (933 Front St.; 509-548-6152; musicboxshop.com), where you'll find more than 4,000 music boxes and items from around the world, and *Der Sportsmann* (837 Front St.; 509-548-5623; dersportsmann.com) for clothing related to hiking, biking, fishing, climbing, and skiing as well as bike rental and ski rental/repair. For those with a sweet tooth, try *Schocolat* (843 Front St.; 509-548-7274; schocolat.com), making handmade European-style chocolates; or the *Fudge Hut* (933 Front St.; 509-548-0466; fudgehut.com) offering 25 varieties of fudge. Try *Cheesemonger's Shop* (819 Front St.; 509-548-9011; cheesemongersshop.com) for international cheeses, beer, and sausages. Also visit *Alpen Haus Gifts* (807 Front St.; 509-548-7122).

After all this ogling and shopping, you'll be ready to enjoy coffee and a great meal. Your alpine-influenced choices include *Andreas Keller Restaurant* (829 Front St.; 509-548-6000; andreaskellerrestaurant.com), for rotisserie-cooked chicken, German potato salad, sausages, sauerkraut, beer, and wine; *Munchen Haus* (709 Front St.; 509-548-1158; munchenhaus.com), an outdoor Bavarian grill and beer garden with more types of mustard than you'll know what to do with—go to the second level to dine with a mountain view; *King Ludwig's* (921 Front St.; 509-548-6625; kingludwigs.com), famous for pork hocks and simple bench seating; and *Mozart's Restaurant* (829 Front St.; 509-548-0600; mozartsrestaurant.com), offering fine European dining. Tired of Bavaria? Leave it behind when you dine at *Watershed Café* (221 8th St.; 509-888-0214; watershedpnw.com) which serves down-to-earth locavore meals. If you've just come from a day of skiing or hiking and are in the mood for hearty food and suds, try *Blewett Brewing Co.* (911 Commercial St.; 509-888-8809; blewettbrew.com).

There are more than 1,500 rooms available in Leavenworth, including motels, bed-and-breakfasts, condos, campgrounds, and cabins. They can handle thousands of tourists at one time, some arriving by the busload. Visit leavenworth.org for a complete listing. Consider these hospitable inns: The only one with a 24-foot-tall knight in shining armor outside is *Der Ritterhof* (190 US 2; 509-548-5845; derritterhof .com); *Enzian Inn* (590 US 2; 800-223-

christmas traditions

Don't miss **Leavenworth Nut-cracker Museum** (735 Front St.; 509-548-4573; nutcrackermuseum .com), which has one of the largest collections of old nutcrackers in the world and is the only nutcracker museum in the US.

8511; enzianinn.com) offers European-style old-world ambience and feather duvets; and top-notch *Sleeping Lady Resort* (7375 Icicle Rd.; 509-548-6344; sleepinglady.com), where the cabins—and the outdoor hot tubs—are practically art installations set under the mountains in a gorgeous forest. One of our favorites, *Run of the River Inn and Refuge,* is a log cabin–style inn (9308 E. Leavenworth Rd.; 509-548-7171; runoftheriver.com). It has elegant amenities in 6 guest rooms and a lodge with fireplaces, sitting areas, whirlpool tubs, decks overlooking the Icicle River, and heavenly breakfasts in the great room. *Pine River Ranch Bed and Breakfast* (19668 Hwy. 207; 509-763-3959; prranch .com) close to *Lake Wenatchee,* has suites with river-rock fireplaces, whirlpool tubs, and gourmet breakfasts.

Into fine wines? If so, hit the tasting rooms downtown, including *Boudreaux Cellars* (509-548-5858; boudreauxcellars.com), *Hard Row to Hoe* (509-888-8266; hardrow.com), and *Ryan Patrick Wines* (509-888-2236; ryan patrickvineyards.com), before traveling to *Eagle Creek Winery* (10037 Eagle Creek Rd.; 509-548-7668; eaglecreekwinery.com); and *Silvara Cellars* (77 Stage Rd.; 509-548-1000; silvarawine.com), which has a scenic tasting room just west of downtown Leavenworth.

Leavenworth is the city of festivals. January brings Bavarian Ice Fest and Nordic ski events. Springtime blossoms with the *Leavenworth Spring Bird Fest* and traditional *German Maifest.* Choose from the *International Accordion Celebration* and *Leavenworth Wine Walk* both in June, or the children's *Kinderfest* in July, plus numerous productions by *Icicle Creek Center for the Arts* (877-265-6026; icicle.org) and the *Leavenworth Summer Theater* production of *The Sound of Music,* which is outdoors with the Enchantments as a backdrop (509-548-2000; leavenworthsummertheater.org). In the fall, festivals include the *Wenatchee River Salmon Festival, Washington State Autumn Leaf Festival,* and *Oktoberfest.* Thanksgiving weekend

The Wellington Disaster

A half-mile-wide avalanche roared down Windy Mountain near Stevens Pass, moving everything in its path, including two Great Northern trains.

"It seemed as if the world were coming to an end," one railroad worker was quoted.

At 1:42 a.m. on March 1, 1910, it became the worst natural disaster in terms of the greatest number of deaths—96—in Washington State history and one of the worst train disasters in US history.

The two trains were heading for Puget Sound, a combination of several steam and electric engines, passenger cars, sleepers, and boxcars. But they were stopped at the west end of the Cascade Tunnel due to slides and waited near the tiny railroad town of Wellington for six days while a blizzard dumped snow on the tracks and avalanches added more.

The late winter storm had dropped several feet of snow on top of an unstable snowpack, so huge avalanches were likely. Some passengers escaped before the avalanche, over a route called Dead Man's Slide.

The first warning was a crescendo of sounds "that might have been the crashing of 10,000 freight trains," one witness said.

Tons of railroad engines and cars and cabins disappeared down the mountain, some disintegrating, others crushed. Sleeping men and women were taken for a ride and then buried under up to 40 feet of snow; many were dug out alive. The snow turned red.

Bodies of the dead, including 35 passengers, were brought down the west side of the Cascades in toboggan-style sleds and a rope-and-pulley system over the next few months.

Three weeks later, track repair was finished and trains could cross Stevens Pass. But the town of Wellington was so linked to the disaster that residents changed the name to Tye.

Three years later, the Great Northern completed snow sheds over 9 miles of track between Tye and Scenic; later a new tunnel was built. The Iron Goat Trail is now on the old grade.

features the traditional German *Christkindlmarkt,* and December brings three weekends of the award-winning *Lighting Festival.*

The outdoor recreation opportunities are endless in this area, with some of the best whitewater rafting in the state, plus kayaking, canoeing, miles of incredibly scenic hiking trails, rock climbing, and hay wagon horse rides. For additional information about the area, contact the Leavenworth Visitor Information Center at (509) 548-5807 or online at leavenworth.org.

US 2 west up to **Stevens Pass** is spectacular, with colorful fall foliage and scenic views but not nearly as dramatic as it must have been for travelers in the late 19th century, when the first railroad line crossed the Cascade Mountains here. The original route included 12 miles of switchbacks cut into the mountainside that required the train to stop on spur tracks, change the track switch, then reverse up the next leg. Folks now drive the mountainous route with ease.

For another Cascades summertime adventure, detour west across Stevens Pass and walk at least part of the **Iron Goat Trail** (irongoattrail.org), built by volunteers on the old Great Northern railroad bed. From US 2 at milepost 55, 9 miles west of Stevens Pass summit, follow the signs to Martin Creek trailhead and parking area. For great mountain views, waves of blooming wildflowers, and interpretive signs, do the 2.5-mile round-trip hike along the lower grade to the Twin Tunnels and back. The trail is wheelchair accessible. From here continue west on US 2 through the small towns of Skykomish (there's a Forest Service ranger station on the highway), Index, Gold Bar, and Startup toward Snohomish and Everett to the west.

In Everett, Tour the World's Largest Building

If Everett is your destination, put the *Future of Flight Aviation Center* and the *Boeing Tour* on your list. Everett, about 25 miles north of Seattle, is home to the world's largest building by volume, Boeing's 472-million-cubic-foot jet-assembly plant at 8415 Paine Field Blvd. (888-467-4777). It covers 98 acres and has 6 doors each 300 to 350 feet long and 82 feet high. The doors feature the world's largest digital graphic at 100,000 square feet.

You'll feel very small in this space that houses airplanes in various stages of complex testing and manufacturing for customers around the world. The 90-minute tour tickets are a hot item, so reservations are recommended although non-reserved same-day tickets are on sale at 8:30 a.m. until all tickets are gone. Children must be 48 inches (122 cm) tall to join the tour. No personal items, including video and digital cameras, are allowed on the tour.

The excellent Future of Flight Aviation Center and the tour are available from 9 a.m. to 3 p.m. daily except for Thanksgiving, Christmas, and New Year's Day. The 28,000-square-foot aviation center has exhibits, videos, graphics, and interactive stations that involve the whole family. Look up and see the futuristic-looking aircraft overhead and down at the 200-foot-long runway painted on the floor of the gallery that ends in the nose section of a Boeing 727. Digitally design and test your own jet, try out the next generation of in-flight entertainment systems, and touch the high-tech skin of the new Boeing 787 Dreamliner.

Back east of the mountains and heading south from Leavenworth, US 97 takes you through the southeastern section of the Wenatchee National Forest and toward Cle Elum, Roslyn, Thorp, and Ellensburg. The route over Blewett Pass on US 97 is scenic enough, but for a special treat take the narrow winding highway over **Old Blewett Pass.** Except for occasional logging trucks, you're likely to have the road to yourself. It's also a popular route with bicyclists. For an alternate adventure take Liberty Road 2 miles east from US 97 to the town of **Liberty,** the oldest mining town site in Washington State.

The Kittitas Valley pushes into the eastern slope of the Cascade Mountains in the center of the state, and here you'll find the old coal-mining town of **Roslyn,** which has settled back into relative quiet after its starring role in the early 1990s as Cicely, Alaska, on the *Northern Exposure* television series. The entire town is on the National Register of Historic Places. Stop by the **Roslyn Cafe** (509-649-2763; theroslyncafe.com) or **Roots BBQ** (both at 201 W. Pennsylvania Ave.; rootsbbqroslyn.com), with a cute patio and darn good smoked meats. Ask locals to point the way to the town cemetery, which is actually dozens of small abutting cemeteries. People hailing from more than 24 countries were buried here during the town's mining days.

lumpofcoal

Roslyn was so fiercely proud of its mining prowess that it shipped a 22-ton lump of coal to the 1893 Chicago World's Fair as an exhibit.

Nearby, in the small community of **South Cle Elum,** railroad buffs will enjoy a pilgrimage to **Iron Horse Inn Bed and Breakfast** (526 Marie Ave.; 509-674-5939; ironhorseinnbb.com). The renovated railroad workers' bunkhouse offers cozy rooms, and on the grounds 4 comfortable cabooses are additional cozy accommodations, including the 1921 wood-sided Northern Pacific caboose that sleeps 2. Railroad memorabilia at this pleasant inn include tools, switch lights, toy trains, and conductors' uniforms. A major renovation of the 1908 Milwaukee Rail Depot and grounds located behind the inn has opened the 12-acre railyard to the public, including a path through the yard, a cafe, and a museum. For more information, go to milwelectric.org.

Iron Horse Trail State Park on I-90, with a 110-mile section of the **Palouse to Cascades State Park Trail,** runs adjacent to the inn. Ride mountain bikes, enjoy pleasant riverside walks, or try cross-country skiing. In nearby Cle Elum visit the 1914 Craftsman-style **Carpenter House Museum** (302 W. 3rd; 509-674-9766; nkcmuseums.org), open noon to 4 p.m. Fri through Sun. Ask about the **Telephone Museum** (221 E. 1st St.; 509-649-2880). Cle Elum was one of the last towns in the US to use manual switchboards, and this is the oldest complete telephone museum west of the Mississippi. For more information, go to nkc museums.org. For more area history, visit the *Roslyn Historical Museum* (203 W. Pennsylvania Ave.; 509-649-2355; roslynmuseum.com) in nearby Roslyn.

Find good Italian fare at *Mama Vallone's Pasta & Steak House* (302 W. 1st St.; 509-674-5174) located in Cle Elum's small downtown area. For lighter fare, head to local-favorite *Cottage Cafe & Fireside Lounge* (911 E. 1st St.; 509-674-2922; cottagecafecleelum.com) for big breakfasts and homemade pie and *Pioneer Coffee Roasting Company Cafe* (121 Pennsylvania St.; 509-674-3864; pioneercoffeeco.com) for fresh brews.

For a bit of history, turn off I-90 at the Thorp exit (milepost 101), then travel west 3 miles through the village of *Thorp,* past the schools, to the *Thorp Grist Mill.* The mill operated from 1883 until 1946, initially powered by a waterwheel. Local citizens have worked to preserve all 3 stories of the sprawling structure and its 15 antique machines. The mill is open for tours Thurs through Sun from June to Aug and by appointment the rest of the year. Call (509) 964-9640 before you go or visit thorp.org.

The city of *Ellensburg*'s downtown historic district is ideal for strolling. Contact the Ellensburg Visitor Information Center (509-925-2002; myellensburg .com) for a walking-tour guide. You'll discover more than two dozen ornate brick buildings constructed between the 1880s and 1910, most of which have been renovated and now house small businesses and shops. The *Clymer Museum of Art,* in the 1901 Ramsey Building at 416 N. Pearl St. (509-962-6416; clymermuseum.com), highlights the Western wildlife work of artist John Clymer. You'll also see fanciful public art along the streets, including a life-size bronze bull relaxing on a downtown bench located at the Rotary Pavilion.

Welcoming inns in the Ellensburg area include *Canyon River Ranch* (14700 Canyon Rd.; 509-933-2100; canyonriver.net) and *Brew House Boarding* (109 Main St.; 509-968-3388; brewhouseboarding.com) in nearby Kittitas.

Dining in Ellensburg could include the *Dakota Cafe* (417 N. Pearl St.; 509-925-4783; dakotacafe.net) and *Yellow Church Cafe* (111 S. Pearl St.; 509-933-2233; theyellowchurchcafe.com). For pastries, coffee, espresso, and fresh-roasted beans, stop at *D&M Coffee Cafe* (301 N. Pine St.; 509-962-6333; dmcoffee.com), which also has multiple locations in the city. For classic hamburgers with names such as Rumble Seat and Dead Man's Curve and vintage gasoline-pump memorabilia, stop by *Red Horse Diner* (1518 W. University Way; 509-925-1956; redhorsediner.com).

Then plan a brisk walk or bike ride on a section of the Palouse to Cascades State Park Trail (Iron Horse State Park; parks.wa.gov), which follows the former roadbed of the Chicago–Milwaukee–St. Paul-Pacific Railroad two-thirds of the way across the state. From downtown Ellensburg, access the lightly graveled trail on N. Water Street or just off University Way near the Kittitas County Fairgrounds. Canyon Road, the old route between Ellensburg and Yakima or Highway 821, follows the scenic **Yakima River Canyon** for approximately 28 miles. The drive offers outstanding views of the wide valley nestled between sheer basalt cliffs and the river. Raptors and songbirds live in the canyon, as well as herds of bighorn sheep. The river is famous among anglers as a catch-and-release trout stream.

The **Vantage Highway** from Ellensburg east to the Columbia River is a great alternative route that misses the traffic of I-90 and offers views of rich farmlands that give way to rolling sagebrush meadows. The highway passes by the **Quilomene Wildlife Area,** a 45,000-acre preserve popular with hunters. Watch for signs for the **Ginkgo Petrified Forest** and **Wanapum Recreation Area** (509-856-2700; parks.wa.gov) as you descend toward the Columbia River. It has 3 miles of trails highlighting exposed "trees of stone." Fifteen to twenty million years ago this land was all tropical swamps and thick forests. When mudflows and lava from volcanic eruptions covered the area, many logs that had sunk to the bottom of shallow lakes were entombed and eventually turned to stone, after minerals replaced organic materials.

The park also has rock carvings of early peoples dated from 200 to 10,000 years old at the interpretive center (call 509-856-2700 for days and hours). The center features more than 200 petrified wood displays as well as a 12-minute film that tells the petrification story.

Picking up I-90 east, cross the Columbia, turn left, and drive for a few miles and a surprise. Look right and up to see 15 life-size metal horses running free on a desert hilltop. Chewelah sculptor Dave Govedare's **Grandfather Cuts Loose the Ponies** symbolically re-creates the Grandfather Spirit giving the land its first horses. Govedare wants to add a 36-foot diameter metal basket with symbols of sky, land, water, and the human spirit. Park in the rest area. You can scramble up the hill to the horses, but be mindful of the rattlesnakes and keep your children close at hand.

Reverse directions and head south to where you crossed the Columbia but keep going south on the east side of the river, picking up Highway 243 to the **Wanapum Heritage Center,** which is open daily (29086 WA-243; 509-766-3461; wanapum.org). The center offers a detailed description of the people who inhabited the region for thousands of years and explains the impact of European culture on this population. The dam flooded the tribe's historic village site and ended their traditional livelihood of salmon fishing. From here you can return to I-90 and then head south on US 97 to explore Yakima and the Yakima Valley, then continue south to the scenic Columbia River Gorge. Or, you could head east on I-90 toward Spokane and the Palouse region.

Places to Stay in North Central Washington

CHELAN

Chelan House Bed & Breakfast
311 S. 1st St.
(509) 888-4000
chelanhouse.com

Vin du Lac Winery
105 WA-150
(509) 682-2882
chelanwine.com

CLE ELUM

Iron Horse Inn Bed and Breakfast
526 Marie St.
(509) 674-5939
ironhorseinnbb.com

CONCONULLY

Shady Pines Resort
125 W. Fork Rd.
(509) 826-2287
shadypinesresort.com

CONCRETE

Ovenell's Heritage Inn
46276 Concrete-Sauk Valley Rd.
(360) 853-8494
ovenells-inn.com

ELLENSBURG

Canyon River Ranch
14700 Canyon Rd.
(509) 933-2100
canyonriver.net

KITTITAS

Brew House Boarding
109 Main St.
(509) 968-3388
brewhouseboarding.com

INFORMATION CENTERS & OTHER HELPFUL WEBSITES

Cascade Loop Association
(509) 662-3888
cascadeloop.com

Ellensburg
(509) 925-2002
myellensburg.com

Lake Chelan Chamber of Commerce
(509) 682-3503
lakechelan.com

Leavenworth
(509) 548-5807
leavenworth.org

Mount Baker–Snoqualmie National Forest
fs.usda.gov/mbs

North Cascades National Park
810 Hwy. 20, Sedro-Woolley
(360) 854-7200
nps.gov/noca

Okanogan Country
(888) 431-3080
okanogancountry.com
fs.usda.gov/okawen

Outdoor Recreation Information
REI, Seattle
(206) 470-4060

Road Reports
511 or (800) 695-7623 for out-of-state callers
wsdot.wa.gov

Wenatchee Valley
(800) 572-7753
wenatcheevalley.org

Winthrop, Twisp, and Methow Valley
(509) 996-2125
winthropwashington.com

LEAVENWORTH

Der Ritterhof
190 US 2
(509) 548-5845
derritterhof.com

Enzian Inn
590 US 2
(800) 223-8511
enzianinn.com

Icicle River RV Resort
7305 Icicle Rd.
(509) 548-5420
icicleriverrv.com

Pine River Ranch Bed and Breakfast
19668 Hwy. 207
(509) 763-3959
prranch.com

Run of the River Inn and Refuge
9308 E. Leavenworth Rd.
(509) 548-7171
runoftheriver.com

Sleeping Lady Resort
7375 Icicle Rd.
(509) 548-6344
sleepinglady.com

MARBLEMOUNT

Buffalo Run Inn
60117 Hwy. 20
(360) 873-2103
buffalorunrestaurant.com

MAZAMA

Freestone Inn at Wilson Ranch
31 Early Winters Dr.
(509) 996-3906
freestoneinn.com

Mazama Country Inn
15 Country Rd.
(509) 996-2681
mazamacountryinn.com

OROVILLE

Eden Valley Ranch
31 Eden Ln.
(509) 485-4002
edenvalleyranch.net

Sun Cove Resort and Guest Ranch
93 E. Wannacut Ln.
(509) 476-2223
thesuncoveresort.com

PATEROS

Lake Pateros Motor Inn
115 Lake Shore Dr.
(509) 923-2203
lakepaterosmotorinn.com

ROCKPORT

Glacier Peak Resort
58468 Clark Cabin Rd.
(360) 873-2250
glacierpeakresort.com

Ross Lake Resort
503 Diablo St.
(206) 386-4437
rosslakeresort.com

ROSLYN

Huckleberry House Bed & Breakfast
301 W. Pennsylvania Ave.
(509) 649-2900
huckleberryhouse.com

STEHEKIN

North Cascades Lodge at Stehekin
1 Stehekin Valley Rd.
(509) 682-4494
lodgeatstehekin.com

Silver Bay Inn
10 Silver Bay Rd.
(509) 670-0693
silverbayinn.com

Stehekin Valley Ranch
(800) 536-0745
stehekinvalleyranch.com

TONASKET

Bonaparte Lake Resort
615 Bonaparte Lake Rd.
(509) 486-2828
bonapartelakeresort.com

Canaan Guest Ranch
474 Cape LaBelle Rd.
(509) 486-1191
canaanguestranch.com

TWISP

Methow Valley Inn Bed & Breakfast
234 2nd Ave.
(509) 997-2253
methowvalleyinn.com

Riverbend RV Park
19961 Hwy. 20
(800) 686-4498
riverbendrv.com

WATERVILLE

Waterville Historic Hotel
102 E. Park St.
(509) 745-8695
watervillehotel.com

WENATCHEE

Apple Country Bed & Breakfast
524 Okanogan Ave.
(509) 972-3409
applecountryinn.com

La Quinta Inn
1905 N. Wenatchee Ave.
(509) 664-6565
lq.com

Moonlight Motor Lodge
2921 School St.
(509) 663-5157
moonlightmotorlodge.com

WINTHROP

Chewuch Inn Bed & Breakfast
223 White Ave.
(509) 996-3107
chewuchinn.com

River Run Inn & Cabins
27 Rader Rd.
(800) 757-2709
riverrun-inn.com

Sun Mountain Lodge
604 Patterson Lake Rd.
(509) 996-2211
sunmountainlodge.com

Wolf Ridge Resort
412 Wolf Creek Rd.
(509) 996-2828
wolfridgeresort.com

Places to Eat in North Central Washington

CHELAN

Apple Cup Cafe
804 E. Woodin Ave.
(509) 682-5997
applecupcafe.com

Campbell's
104 W. Woodin Ave.
(509) 682-4250 or
(509) 682-2561
campbellsresort.com

Local Myth Pizza
122 S. Emerson
(509) 682-2914
localmythpizza.com

CLE ELUM

Cle Elum Bakery
501 E. 1st St.
(509) 674-2233
cleelumbakery.com

Cottage Cafe & Fireside Lounge
911 E. 1st St.
(509) 674-2922
cottagecafecleelum.com

Mama Vallone's Pasta & Steak House
302 W. 1st St.
(509) 674-5174
mamavallones.com

Pioneer Coffee Roasting Company Cafe
121 Pennsylvania St.
(509) 674-3864
pioneercoffeeco.com

CONCRETE

Annie's Pizza Station
44568 Hwy. 20
(360) 853-7227
anniespizzastation.net

Perks
44586 Hwy. 20
(360) 853-9006

ELLENSBURG

Dakota Cafe
417 N. Pearl St.
(509) 925-4783
dakotacafe.net

D&M Coffee Cafe
301 N. Pine St.
(509) 962-6333
dmcoffee.com

Red Horse Diner
1518 W. University Way
(509) 925-1956
redhorsediner.com

Yellow Church Cafe
111 S. Pearl St.
(509) 933-2233
yellowchurchcafe.com

LEAVENWORTH

Andreas Keller Restaurant
829 Front St.
(509) 548-6000
andreaskellerrestaurant.com

Blewett Brewing Co.
911 Commercial St.
(509) 888-8809
blewettbrew.com

King Ludwig's
921 Front St.
(509) 548-6625
kingludwigs.com

Mozart's Restaurant
829 Front St.
(509) 548-0600
mozartsrestaurant.com

Munchen Haus
709 Front St.
(509) 548-1158
munchenhaus.com

O'Grady's Pantry
Sleeping Lady Mountain Resort
7375 Icicle Rd.
(509) 548-6344
sleepinglady.com

Watershed Café
221 8th St.
(509) 888-0214
watershedpnw.com

MARBLEMOUNT

Buffalo Run Restaurant
60084 Hwy. 20
(360) 873-2461
buffaloruninn.com

Marblemount Diner
60147 Hwy. 20
(360) 873-4503

MAZAMA

Mazama Store
50 Lost River Rd.
(509) 996-2855
themazamastore.com

Sandy Butte Bistro & Bar
31 Early Winters Dr.
(509) 996-3906
freestoneinn.com

OMAK

The Breadline Cafe
102 S. Ash St.
(509) 826-5836
breadlinecafe.com

Magoo's Restaurant
24 N. Main St.
(509) 826-2325

Rancho Chico
22 N. Main St.
(509) 826-4757

OROVILLE

Expressions Espresso
718 Apple Way St.
(509) 476-2970

Hometown Pizza, Pasta
& Bakery
1315 Main St.
(509) 476-2410

ROSLYN

Roots BBQ
201 W. Pennsylvania Ave.
rootsbbqroslyn.com

Roslyn Cafe
201 W. Pennsylvania Ave.
(509) 649-2763
theroslyncafe.com

STEHEKIN

Stehekin Bakery
Stehekin Valley Rd.
(509) 682-7742
stehekinpastry.com

TONASKET

The Kuhler
302 S. Whitcomb Ave.
(509) 486-2996

Rancho Chico
312 Hwy. 97
(509) 486-4030

Shannon's Cafe & Deli
626 S. Whitcomb Ave.
(509) 486-2259

Whistler's Family
Restaurant
616 N. Whitcomb Ave.
(509) 486-2568

TWISP

BJ's Branding Iron
Restaurant & Saloon
123 N. Glover St.
(509) 997-0040

Blue Star Coffee
3 Twisp Airport Rd.
(509) 997-2583
bluestarcoffeeroasters.com

Cinnamon Twisp Bakery
116 N. Glover St.
(509) 997-5030

WENATCHEE

Cottage Inn Steak House
134 Easy St.
(509) 663-4435
cottageinnrestaurant.com

McGlinn's Public House
111 Orondo St.
(509) 663-9073
mcglinns.com

ALSO WORTH SEEING

Lake Chelan area wineries
Chelan
(800) 424-3526
lakechelanwinevalley.com

Olmstead Place State Park
Ellensburg
(509) 925-1943
parks.wa.gov

Wenatchee Valley Museum
Wenatchee
(509) 888-6240
wenatcheewa.gov

Pybus Market
3 N. Worthen St.
(509) 888-3900
pybuspublicmarket.com

Wild Huckleberry
302 S. Mission St.
(509) 663-1013
wildhuck.com

Windmill
1501 N. Wenatchee Ave.
(509) 665-9529
thewindmillrestaurant.com

WINTHROP

Boulder Creek Deli
100 Bridge St.
(509) 996-3990

Old Schoolhouse Brewery
155 Riverside Ave.
(509) 996-3183
oldschoolhousebrewery.com

Rocking Horse Bakery
265 Riverside Ave.
(509) 996-4241
rockinghorsebakery.com

Sheri's Sweet Shoppe
207 Riverside Ave.
(509) 996-3834
sherissweetshoppe.com

South Central Washington

The south-central section of Washington State offers opportunities from apple picking to windsurfing, from two snowcapped mountains each over 8,000 feet high to waterfalls that drop from basalt ledges with one narrow ribbon descending hundreds of feet. On the high plateau above the Yakima River, farmers tend vast orchards of apples, apricots, peaches, and cherries; vintners work hundreds of acres of grapes that will make Pinot Noir, Chardonnay, and Riesling wines. Washington State shares the awesome scenery of the Columbia River Gorge with its southern neighbor, Oregon. Snowy **Mount St. Helens,** now about 8,000 feet high (it was 9,677 feet above sea level prior to the eruption of May 18, 1980), and **Mount Adams,** at 12,276 feet high, guard the Washington side. The watery border extends roughly 300 miles from the eastern end of the gorge at the **Tri-Cities** (Kennewick, Pasco, and Richland) to the Pacific Ocean at the Long Beach Peninsula.

Once the river roared through the gorge, making some sections impassable by canoe or raft. Now dams cross the Columbia, smoothing out the once-swift waters previously navigated by Indian tribes and the first French and American

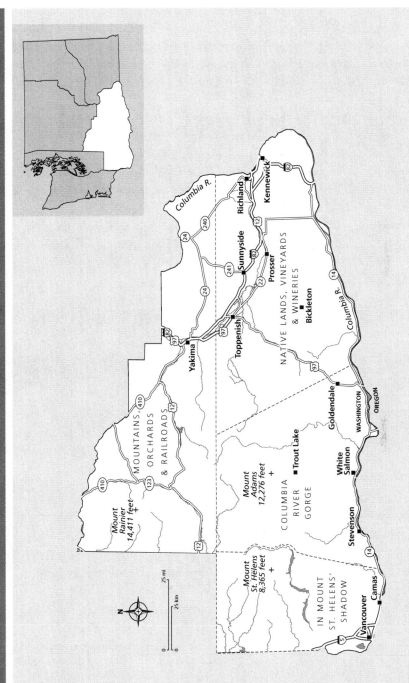

SOUTH CENTRAL WASHINGTON

trappers, British Hudson's Bay Company explorers, US explorers and road surveyors, and the pioneers who traveled west on the Oregon Trail.

One of those early groups of explorers sent by the US government, the *Lewis and Clark Corps of Discovery,* trekked along the north side of the Columbia River in the fall of 1805, reaching the Pacific Ocean around November 20.

Let's start at the 366-acre *Fort Vancouver National Historic Site,* operated by the National Park Service just east of *Vancouver*'s downtown area. Stroll through the informative museum and visitor area at the upper section of the complex, then walk down the grassy lawn or drive to the large parking area, to find the fort and the fully restored *Fort Vancouver Gardens.* In the 1840s grapevines trailed over greenhouses for shade, and the garden yielded such produce as Thomas Laxton peas, English broad beans, and yellow pear tomatoes. The flower garden section contains a walk-through arbor of hop vines, large clumps of scented lavender, old-fashioned climbing roses, and vintage perennials in large beds.

A small admission fee allows entrance to the restored fort inside the re-created stockade walls. Watch living history vignettes in the carpentry shed, blacksmith

SOUTH CENTRAL WASHINGTON'S TOP HITS

Central Washington Agricultural Museum
Union Gap

Columbia Gorge Interpretive Center
Stevenson

Conboy Lake National Wildlife Refuge
Glenwood

Fort Simcoe State Park
White Swan

Fort Vancouver National Historic Site
Vancouver

Goldendale Observatory State Park
Goldendale

Hulda Klager Lilac Gardens
Woodland

Liberty Theatre
Toppenish

Maryhill Museum of Art
Goldendale

Mount St. Helens National Volcanic Monument
Castle Rock

North Front Street Historic District
Yakima

Northern Pacific Railway Museum
Toppenish

Pomeroy House Living History Farm
Yacolt

Sacajawea State Park
Pasco

Yakama Nation Museum and Cultural Center
Toppenish

Lewis & Clark Expedition

Early in the nation's history, President Thomas Jefferson dispatched a corps of men for a discovery expedition (1804–06) to the Pacific Ocean. It is said that Jefferson made the right choice in selecting Meriwether Lewis and William Clark to lead the expedition. Jefferson felt the two men, although different in their personalities, possessed qualities important for exploring uncharted wilderness: youth, intelligence, resourcefulness, courage, and a sense of adventure. Both men were experienced woodsmen and frontiersmen as well as seasoned army officers. The party of nearly four dozen explorers (the exact number is not known) traveled more than 8,000 miles on foot, horseback, and dugout canoe in 2 years, 4 months, and 10 days.

Where it may take today's travelers a day to leisurely drive from the Tri-Cities of Kennewick, Pasco, and Richland to the Pacific Ocean, it took Lewis and Clark one month to cover this leg of their journey. At *Sacajawea State Park,* near Pasco, visit an interpretive center devoted to the expedition and the role of Sacajawea, the Shoshoni Indian woman who served as their guide and interpreter. Interpretive material (along with panoramic views of the gorge and river) can also be seen at *Hat Rock State Park* near Umatilla, Oregon; *Columbia Hills State Park* on Horsethief Lake near The Dalles; the *Columbia Gorge Interpretive Center* near Stevenson; *Beacon Rock State Park,* west of Stevenson; *Lewis and Clark State Park* near Chehalis; and the *Lewis and Clark Interpretive Center* in *Cape Disappointment State Park* near Ilwaco.

shop, baker house, garden, and kitchen; staff and volunteers in period dress offer an authentic look at life in the early 1800s. Both early settlers and members of local tribes often visited the fort to socialize and trade for tobacco, candles, beads, blankets, and cotton cloth as well as vegetables, grains, and other supplies. Dr. John McLoughlin, the fort's chief factor for many years, lived in the large house that stands next to the kitchen. Visitors can tour the house, which contains furnishings and memorabilia from the McLoughlin family's time. Fort Vancouver is located at 612 E. Reserve St.; for information, call (360) 816-6230. Visit the fort and its living history programs Tues through Sat from 9 a.m. to 4 p.m.

You'll notice *Officer's Row,* the stately Victorian-style homes that sit in a tidy line along the boulevard just north of Fort Vancouver. These functioned as housing for military officers during World War II. The lovely houses are now preserved and open to the public during part of the year. Watch the Vancouver Heritage Ambassadors reenact tales from the past, including ghost stories around Halloween, in several of the parlors and on several of the wide verandas. If time allows, call for lunch or dinner reservations at the *The Grant House* (360-906-1101; thegranthouse.us), an 1849 property in the middle of Officer's Row. For more information about the theatrical events and

Ghosts Galore

It is said that ghosts and spirits hang around at times other than Halloween, perhaps to startle and amuse visitors. Folks claim they've heard or seen them in old theaters and hotels, vintage bed-and-breakfast inns, Victorian houses, ghost towns, and other places appropriate for denizens of the otherworld. Here are a few places to look for friendly ghosts on your travels in Washington State:

Snohomish: *Blackman House Museum* (ca. 1878) and also at one of the town's taverns (the ghost's name is Henry)

Spokane: *Monaghan Hall* (ca. 1898) at Gonzaga University

Vancouver: *The Grant House,* Officer's Row National Historic District

Yakima: *Capitol Theatre*

other public events on Officer's Row during the year, call the Fort Vancouver National Trust at (360) 992-1800, or check thehistorictrust.org.

Vintage-airplane buffs can also visit the ***Pearson Air Museum*** (1115 E. 5th St.; 360-816-6232; pearsonairmuseum.org), just east of Fort Vancouver. Located at the 1905 Pearson Field, the oldest continuously operating airfield on the West Coast, the museum is housed in the ***Jack Murdock Aviation Center.*** The center also includes the second oldest wooden hangar in the US, a theater that shows full-length classic aviation-themed films, a hands-on activity center for children, and a vintage airplane-restoration section. It offers a fascinating history that shows aviation up to World War II. The grounds are open from 9 a.m. to 5 p.m. Tues through Sat. There is an admission fee.

Nearby ***Esther Short Park,*** located off Washington Street between 6th and 8th Streets, offers colorful plantings of roses, azaleas, and rhododendrons. At the southeast corner the handsome ***Salmon Run Bell Tower*** displays a historic salmon diorama; its glockenspiel's 36 melodious bells play several times each day. Cafes, delis, and coffee shops are located nearby. In the same neighborhood, there's also the bustling ***Vancouver Farmers' Market*** (605 Esther St.; 360-737-8298; vancouverfarmersmarket.com) on Sat and Sun, Apr through Oct. Also browse up Main Street to find cafes, boutiques, and specialty shops such as ***Ice Cream Renaissance*** (1925 Main St.; 360-694-3892; icecream renaissance.com).

Travel north from Vancouver for about 20 miles to ***Woodland*** to visit the ***Hulda Klager Lilac Gardens*** (115 S. Pekin Rd.; 360-225-8996; lilacgardens .com). Thanks to Hulda's work during most of the 96 years of her life, visitors can enjoy more than 150 hybrid varieties and colors of lilacs and their frothy blooms. Her family settled in this area in 1877, after emigrating from Germany via Wisconsin. She received many honors, including one for her work as a leading lilac hybridizer. To the rear of the Victorian house, volunteers have restored the old woodshed, water tower, picturesque windmill, and carriage house. The house is open selected times in Apr and May, when members of the Hulda Klager Lilac Garden Society don period dresses and greet visitors during the annual open house; lilac starts and plants are for sale. The arboretum is open daily and is wheelchair accessible, but check online for special event dates.

walkthetube

Explore a section of the 13,042-foot lava tube on the south side of Mount St. Helens, one of the longest continuous lava tubes in the world. Known as the **Ape Cave,** it was formed about 2,000 years ago when lava poured into a creek bed and the sides and top cooled quickly, forming a crust while the lava underneath continued to flow away.

The **Cedar Creek Grist Mill National Historic Site** is 9 miles east and north of Woodland (360-225-5832; cedarcreekgristmill.com). Rough-hewn and unpretentious, the mill, which dates from 1876, was for generations the center of local industry and the site of dances, parties, and musical shows. The mill was restored in the early 1980s and is now a working museum, with a water-powered stone flour mill and machine shop. It is open Sat from 1 to 4 p.m. and Sun from 2 to 4 p.m. Admission is free, and you may even be able to take home a small bag of fresh-milled flour; donations are always appreciated.

Continue east toward Amboy, but before reaching the community turn south on Highway 503 through green fields and forests. In about 6 miles turn east on Northeast Rock Creek Road and ignore the road's name changes; just go 4.5 miles to the **Pomeroy House Living History Farm** (20902 NE Lucia Falls Rd., Yacolt; 360-686-3537; pomeroyfarm.org). Call about high teas and other activities at the 1920s homestead. For bedding down within easy driving distances from both Mount Rainier and Mount St. Helens, contact **Cowlitz River Lodge** (13069 US 12; 360-494-4444; whitepasstravel.com/cowlitzriver lodge); **Crest Trail Lodge** (12729 US

eruption

At 8:32 a.m. on Sunday, May 18, 1980, Mount St. Helens exploded in a massive outpouring of lava and ash. The eruption measured 5.1 on the Richter scale and killed 57 people, turned the top 1,200 feet of the mountain's trademark symmetrical peak into ash, and destroyed more than 200 homes, 47 bridges, 185 miles of road, and 250 square miles of forest. Since then, a total of 110,000 acres has been preserved for research, education, and recreation.

Up Close & Personal: Mount St. Helens National Volcanic Monument

The 52-mile drive from I-5 at Castle Rock (exit 49) east on Spirit Lake Highway toward Mount St. Helens offers a number of ogling possibilities, with Johnston Ridge the most spectacular at just 5.5 miles from the crater. Here are a few of the highlights:

Mount St. Helens Visitor Center, milepost 5 on Highway 504 (Washington State Parks)

Charles W. Bingham Forest Learning Center, milepost 33 (Weyerhaeuser)

Hummocks Trail, 2.4-mile loop trail around colorful rock formations deposited during the 1980 eruption, just west of Coldwater Ridge

Johnston Ridge Observation Center, milepost 52 (US Forest Service)

For more information contact Mount St. Helens National Volcanic Monument, Amboy (360-449-7800; fs.fed.us/gpnf/mshnvm) or the Gifford Pinchot National Forest, Vancouver (360-891-5000; fs.usda.gov/giffordpinchot). Ask about Ape Cave, Harmony Interpretive Site, and Windy Ridge, the last with more awesome views of the 1980 volcanic devastation; or the state-parks run Mount St. Helens Visitor Center at Silver Lake, (360) 274-0962.

12; 360-494-4944; whitepasstravel.com/cresttrail); and **Mountain View Lodge** (13163 US 12; 360-494-5555; mtvlodge.com), all in or near **Packwood.** For a rustic stay in a historic atmosphere, try the 1912 **Hotel Packwood,** a national landmark (104 Main St.; 360-494-5431; packwoodwa.com/Hotel Packwood.htm).

Good eats in the Packwood area can be had at the **Blue Spruce Saloon & Diner** on US 12 at Willame St. (360-494-5605). Also check visitranier.com for vacation home rentals and mountain recreation information.

Continuing east on US 12 takes you from Randle to Packwood, then over the high mountain wilderness areas of White Pass, past the fishing resorts along Rimrock Lake, and down the Tieton River Canyon toward Yakima.

Columbia River Gorge

Heading east on Highway 14 from Vancouver, pass the small mill towns of **Camas** and Washougal. Take the highway's business loop to explore the Camas downtown area. Fourth Avenue is a pleasant walking street through the main commercial district. From here the highway climbs to about 1,000 feet up the Columbia Plateau at Cape Horn viewpoint. From the top you'll enjoy an expansive view of the Columbia River Gorge.

After descending back to river level, continue east to 5,100-acre **Beacon Rock State Park** (509-427-8265). **Beacon Rock** is an 848-foot basalt tower, the remains of a volcano core that served as a sign to river travelers dating back to Native Americans and Lewis and Clark (who named it) that they had passed the difficult Cascade Rapids and faced no further obstructions to the Pacific Ocean. For a breathtaking challenge, climb the steep and narrow trail, including a series of stairways with railings, to the top of Beacon Rock for panoramic views of the Columbia River and forested hills on both sides. It's worth the effort.

Just past Beacon Rock and near the town of **North Bonneville,** visit the **Fort Cascades Historic Site,** which includes a 1.5-mile self-guided tour. Along the way you'll see prehistoric Indian petroglyphs, the original site of Fort Cascades (which burned during an attack in 1856), and artifacts from the territorial period, when wagons were needed to portage around the rough river waters.

Water travel is easier now. Lengthy grain and produce barges have replaced canoes and rafts on the Columbia River, passing through a network of dams and locks that begin with the **Bonneville Dam.** Visitors can tour the dam daily from either side of the river (Oregon, 541-374-8820) to see the huge electrical generators and the fish-ladder system that allows salmon and steelhead trout to continue up the river to spawn. Visitors to the Oregon side need a guide to view the generators; in Washington, visitors can see them but need a guide to get closer. On the Oregon side of the river, accessed by the **Bridge of the Gods,** you can also see the locks in action, raising and lowering pleasure boats, fishing boats, and grain barges. The bridge is part of the Pacific Crest Trail.

savesasquatch

If you see a hairy creature between 7 and 10 feet tall and weighing 500 to 800 pounds, don't shoot it, at least if you're in Skamania County, where it's against the law to kill the critter. Violators can be fined $1,000 and face a 5-year jail sentence. But if the Sasquatch is in fact humanoid, the case will proceed as a homicide.

Be sure to visit the **Columbia Gorge Interpretive Center** (990 SW Rock Creek Dr.; 509-427-8211; columbiagorge.org). It's off Highway 14 a couple of miles east of the Bridge of the Gods. This large and excellent glass-walled museum highlights the river's colorful history. Witness the geological and climatic forces that formed the gorge at the Creation Theater's 12-minute multimedia show. Learn about the region's native Indian tribes through oral histories, a Clahclehla trading village, and dip-net fishing displays. Examine the environmental impact of dams on the river. Other highlights include a 37-foot-tall replica of a 19th-century fishwheel, one of many that once harvested millions of pounds of fish each year. The center is open daily (except holidays) from 10 a.m. to 5 p.m. There is a nominal admission fee.

Consider a night at nearby Stevenson's **Skamania Lodge** (509-314-4177; destinationhotels.com/skamania), a large resort and conference center located on a bluff above the interpretive center. The resort offers golf, swimming, tennis, spa treatments, hiking trails on the property, road bikes, guided hikes, and more. The lodge pipes in mineral water for its pools, hot tub, and spa. On the main level at the lodge, find a well-stocked outdoor recreation information center (509-427-2528) and Forest Service staff who provide maps and information. And if you're hot springs hopping, go north to rustic 1892 **Carson Mineral Hot Springs Resort** (372 St. Martin's Springs Rd.; 509-427-8296; carsonhotspringresort.com), open daily. The original 1930s bathhouse is still in use, complete with claw-foot tubs, and the 1901 St. Martin Hotel still stands; more-modern rooms are offered in nearby buildings.

Nearby **Stevenson** is a historic waterfront town and county seat for **Skamania County.** Many of its buildings date to the early 1900s, with new businesses sprouting amid the old. The **River House Art Gallery and Studio** (115 2nd St.; 509-427-5930; riverhouseartgallery.org) features Columbia Gorge images, original watercolors, local pottery, baskets, and pastels.

A number of pleasant eateries dot Stevenson, most of them easy to find along NW 2nd Street (Highway 14). Try **Andrew's Pizza** (310 2nd St.; 509-427-8008; andrewspizzastevenson.com) for New York–style, hand-tossed pizzas. Fresh salads, calzones, and Italian sandwiches top off the main menu.

Visit **Big River Grill** (192 SW 2nd St.; 509-427-4888; thebigrivergrill.com) for Northwest pub fare and microbrews, walls full of memorabilia, and a welcoming atmosphere. **Walking Man Brewing** (240 1st St.; 509-427-5520) offers handcrafted ales and tasty fare such as Caesar salads and clam strips Wed through Sun. In addition to 10 beers on tap, the brewery makes delicious root beer, ginger ale, and cream soda.

sayaprayer

The Columbia Gorge Interpretive Center near Stevenson has a collection of about 4,000 rosaries from around the world, including ones from President John F. Kennedy, conductor Lawrence Welk, and football coach Lou Holtz. The oldest rosary was made in the 18th century.

Gorge Lovers Sneak Over to Oregon

You won't be chided for taking time to visit the Oregon side of the Columbia River, crossing the bridge from White Salmon and Bingen to the bustling small town of Hood River. You could plan a couple of pleasant day trips:

Drive the 35-mile *Hood River County Fruit Loop* into the blooming pear and apple orchards—canopies of white blooms peak around the middle of April. Take in the Hood River Valley Blossom Festival; visit wineries and taste local wines; see arts and crafts exhibits, find delicious baked goods and huge apple pies, sip huckleberry milk shakes; buy hardy perennials and herbs, and visit an alpaca farm and browse its country store. Pick up a Fruit Loop map at the *Hood River Visitor Information Center* (800-366-3530; hoodriverfruitloop.com and hoodriver.org).

For a second day trip and more awesome close-up views of 11,240-foot *Mount Hood* take Highway 35 from Hood River about 40 miles south and west to US 26. Continue about 2 miles west on US 26 to Government Camp and take the 6-mile winding road up to the 1937 *Timberline Lodge* (503-272-3311; timberlinelodge .com) and its ski area at a 6,000-foot elevation. Tour the second-floor lounge area with its towering fireplaces and huge windows that frame snowy Mount Hood, see the dining areas and lodge rooms, and visit the ground-floor exhibit area that details the lodge's construction during WPA days, including a vintage recording of FDR speaking at the dedication ceremony. For informal eats try the Black Iron Grill and Market Cafe in the nearby Wy'East Day Lodge. Retrace your route to Hood River and stay overnight or cross the Columbia River back to the Washington side.

The *Skamania County Chamber of Commerce* in Stevenson (167 NW 2nd St.; 509-427-8911; skamania.org), can provide maps, information about Northwest Forest passes, and other words of wisdom about summer wildflower meadows, hiking trails, and winter cross-country ski areas in the Gifford Pinchot National Forest. Linger overnight in the area by calling *Sandhill Cottages* (932 Hot Springs Ave., Carson; 509-427-3464; sandhillcottages.com).

Farther east along the Columbia is the town of *Bingen,* and just up the hill is *White Salmon.* Until recently these were quiet riverside communities of hardworking old-timers, but they have now become recreation meccas, especially for windsurfers. On spring and summer weekends the beaches along this stretch of the Columbia can be crowded with windsurfing enthusiasts of all ages, and the water is alive with colorful sails. The *Inn of the White Salmon* (172 W. Jewett Blvd.; 509-493-2335; innofthewhitesalmon.com), a boutique hotel and hostel built in 1937, features 17 Craftsman-style rooms and breakfast at 10-Speed Coffee Roasters. Down the street, *Klickitat Pottery Shop* (264 E. Jewett Blvd.; 509-493-4456; klickitatpottery.com), is a fun place to browse and observe an ancient craft in action. The potter often works in a wide-windowed

Catching the Wind

You're adventurous and in excellent physical shape? The ultimate test may be learning to maneuver a windsurfing board to ply the deep waves on a windy day on the mighty Columbia River. Although Washington has good windsurfing on its side of the Columbia, Event Site is one of dozens of surf spots on the south and north sides of the Columbia. To learn more, contact the **Columbia Gorge Windsurfing Association** at 202 Oak St. in Hood River (541-386-9225; gorgewindsurfing.org). Good spots to watch and photograph are the beach at **Port Marina Park** just west of the bridge in Hood River and farther east at **Maryhill State Park,** south of Goldendale on the Washington side. Maryhill also offers picnic shelters, grassy areas, and riverfront campsites.

studio on one side of the shop, creating high-quality stoneware pieces for sale in the shop.

In Bingen try **Everybody's Brewing** (177 E. Jewett Blvd.; 509-637-2774; everybodysbrewing.com) for beer and pub fare, and home cooking at **The Huck Truck** (415 W. Steuben St.; 808-280-0769). There is a lot to see and do in the scenic White Salmon River Valley, which stretches from the Columbia River north to 12,276-foot-high Mount Adams. **Zoller's Outdoor Odysseys** (1248 Hwy. 141, just north of White Salmon; 509-493-2641; zooraft.com) will raft you down the river. It's an exhilarating experience and suitable for families and beginners.

In **Husum,** north of White Salmon on Highway 141, plan to stay overnight in the "shadows" of **Mount Hood** and **Mount Adams** by calling Victorian **Husum Highlands Bed & Breakfast** (509-493-4503; husumhighlands.com), where the cozy rooms come with a hearty farm breakfast.

Consider arranging a horseback ride on gentle steeds at **Northwestern Lake Riding Stables** (1262 Little Buck Creek Rd.; 509-493-4965; nwstables .com) in a valley near White Salmon. There are horses for beginners as well as experienced riders. Children must be age 8 or older. Riding lessons as well as day trips can be arranged.

For lunch or dinner closer to Mount Adams, locals suggest a favorite, the **Logs Family Restaurant** (509-493-1505), located at BZ Corner on Highway 141 about halfway between White Salmon and Trout Lake (mile marker 12). They've been serving up great fried chicken since the early 1930s.

Farther up Highway 141 near the base of Mount Adams, enjoy mountain views from the chalet cabins at **Trout Lake Cozy Cabins** (2291 Hwy. 141; 509-395-2068; troutlakecozycabins.com), 1 mile south of Trout Lake. Each cabin has walls of glass highlighting forested scenery and comes equipped with a kitchenette, a queen-size bed, and a large bathroom. Most have whirlpool tubs, lofts, fireplaces, and TVs; one chalet is wheelchair accessible.

Folks say one of the best places to hunker down for a fresh cup of coffee, a sandwich, a slice of apple pie, and a dose of local gossip is *The Station Cafe* (247 Hwy. 141; 509-395-2211). Look for its huckleberry pancakes in-season. If you travel by recreational vehicle, check with **Elk Meadows RV Park** (78 Trout Lake Creek Rd.; 877-395-2400; elkmeadows rvpark.com). The wooded RV sites come with outrageous views of Mount Adams.

For other cozy places to spend the night close to Trout Lake and snowy Mount Adams, check out several bed-and-breakfasts in the area. At **Kelly's Trout Creek Inn Bed & Breakfast** (25 Mount Adams Rd.; 509-395-2769; kellys bnb.com), innkeepers Kelly and Marilyn Enochs offer travelers a comfortable mix of old-fashioned quilts and rustic decor in 3 cozy guest rooms. During warm weather you can eat outdoors on the deck next to bubbling Trout Lake Creek, where its waters rush over large rocks and low basalt ledges.

treetopview

The world's largest canopy crane was used by scientists to study the ecology of the treetops, until it was mostly dismantled in 2011. But the 70-meter crane tower still stands at the **Wind River Field Station** (509-427-8019; depts.washington.edu/wrccrf), about 10 miles from the Columbia Gorge and north of Carson. Although it's closed to the public, guided field trips can be arranged in advance.

In the Mount Adams area, ancient volcanoes produced numerous lava flows, caves, lava tubes, and other natural structures. Many caves in the area were used by farmers in the days before refrigeration to store butter and cheese until they could be transported to market. These caves make the region popular with serious spelunkers (cave explorers), who approach the caverns with the same sense of challenge and caution that mountain climbers have for major peaks.

The *Ice Caves,* a series of lava tubes, are the easiest of the public caves to explore. Their name refers to columns of ice that develop naturally in the lowest chamber during the winter. A century ago the giant icicles were harvested and sold. The Forest Service has constructed a ladder leading down from the main entrance. A 120-foot tube that slopes southeastward is the most accessible part of the cave. In all there are about 650 feet of passages to explore. Be sure to bring warm clothes, boots, head protection, and dependable lights. Stop at the **Mount Adams Ranger Station** (509-395-3400; fs.fed.us/gpnf), just north of Trout Lake at 2455 Hwy. 141, for more information and directions.

The road east to Glenwood offers killer views of the east slope of Mount Adams (called Pahto by native peoples) as you pass through the rich farmlands and climb hills above the White Salmon River Valley. Watch for the turnoff to **Conboy Lake National Wildlife Refuge** (509-364-3667; fws.gov/conboylake), which takes you to the entrance where you'll find brochures describing this wetland habitat. The **Willard Springs Foot Trail,** a 2-mile loop that runs through timberland with views across the lake bed and includes interpretive signs, is a pleasant way to see carpets of spring wildflowers and learn more about the refuge's wildlife, including porcupines and wood ducks. The refuge is a nesting area for greater sandhill cranes.

Just outside the small community of Glenwood, travelers find the **Mount Adams Lodge** at the Flying L Ranch (25 Flying L Ln.; 509-364-3488; mt-adams .com). The Lloyd family built the house in the mid-1940s, and the Lloyd sons, Darvel and Darryl, further developed the property in the 1970s and 1980s. Current owners Julee Wasserman-Johnson and Tim Johnson have continued to update the facilities, 12 lodge rooms and 3 cabins. Guests enjoy a full breakfast served in the ranch cookhouse. You can also bring your own steaks for a cookout. The area around the ranch is perfect for hiking and biking as well as for winter cross-country skiing and snowshoeing.

Returning to Highway 14 and heading east alongside the Columbia River, consider stopping in the small community of **Lyle** to have dinner at the **Lyle Hotel Restaurant** (100 7th St.; 509-365-5953; thelylehotel.com). The menu changes regularly and is upscale for such an out-of-the-way location, with tasty Northwest fares including smoked salmon and, when available, organic beef. The hotel was built in 1905 to serve travelers when Lyle was a railroad center linking major towns in the region. The boom ended, and most folks moved on. But the hotel remains a nostalgic reminder of earlier times with its 10 small guest rooms featuring early American furnishings, some with sitting areas and views of the Columbia River.

Native Lands, Vineyards & Wineries

Some of the Columbia River Gorge's greatest wonders are now, unfortunately, flooded under the huge reservoirs behind the Bonneville and The Dalles dams. Until 1957 the Oregon side of the Columbia River cascaded over Celilo Falls. Native people had camped and fished this stretch of river for about 15,000 years, making it the longest continually inhabited site in North America. Indians from throughout the region practiced traditional dip-net fishing from pole platforms jutting close to the swirling torrents. The area was also an important gathering place where tribes met to trade goods, enjoy festivities, and conduct peace councils. In 1805 explorer Meriwether Lewis described the Celilo Falls area as a "great emporium . . . where all the neighboring nations assemble." Hundreds of the ancient pictographs (rock paintings) and petroglyphs (rock carvings) that once commemorated this life are now lost beneath the waters of the river, although some of the petroglyphs were relocated to the Horsethief Lake section of Columbia Hills State Park, 10 miles east of Lyle.

She-Who-Watches (Tsagaglalal) is one of the most intriguing depictions still visible. Legend has it that Tsagaglalal, a female chief, told Coyote, the trickster, that she wanted to guide her people to "live well and build good houses" forever. Coyote explained that the time for female chiefs would soon be over, then turned her to stone so she could watch over the river and its people unimpeded into eternity. The original petroglyph can be found amid several others at **Columbia Hills State Park,** which includes the **Horsethief Lake** area (actually an impoundment of the Columbia River). Due to vandalism, however, the only way to see the pictographs and petroglyphs is by a 10 a.m. guided tour on Fri and Sat from the beginning of Apr to the end of Oct. Tours last about 90 minutes and must be booked at least two weeks ahead as they fill up quickly. For information about costs and reservations, call (509) 767-1159.

Fifteen miles east of Horsethief Lake via Highway 14 and near the junction with US 97 is **Maryhill Museum of Art** and a concrete reproduction on a smaller scale of England's **Stonehenge** monument, two legacies of eccentric millionaire road builder Sam Hill. **Maryhill,** an impressive 400-foot-long chateau-like structure, is located at 35 Maryhill Dr. (509-773-3733; maryhill museum.org) and is open 10 a.m. to 5 p.m. daily from Mar 15 through Nov 15; there is an admission fee. It is situated with a fine view of the Columbia River and filled with an eclectic collection that includes Rodin sculptures and watercolors, 19th-century French artwork, Russian icons, regional Indian art, the Queen of Romania's royal memorabilia, and a collection of chess sets. Be sure to see the 1946 collection of French fashion miniatures, **Theatre de la Mode.**

Loïe's, in the museum, serves deli-style lunches and snacks with outdoor seating available overlooking the river. Outside is the museum's sculpture garden. Each year Maryhill hosts an Outdoor Sculptural Invitational open to contemporary sculptors of the Northwest. There's also a permanent collection that can be viewed year-round, for free.

Stonehenge sits on a bluff a few miles from the Maryhill museum. Hill had it built as a memorial to the soldiers of Klickitat County who died in World War I. Hill is buried at the base of the bluff. There is no admission fee to walk among the stones.

The **Maryhill Winery** (509-773-1976; maryhillwinery.com), just west of Maryhill Museum at 9774 Hwy. 14, offers outdoor entertainment and an elegant tasting room with a focus on the winery's premium reds. The intricately carved antique bar fashioned of tiger oak in the early 1900s has a back bar 12 feet high, with mirrors inset along its 12-foot length. It's one of the most-visited tasting rooms in a state that has about 600 wineries. Hours are 10 a.m. to 6 p.m. daily. A patio offers wide-angle views of the gorge. The 4,000-seat amphitheater includes a larger permanent stage and vistas to Mount Hood in Oregon.

Goldendale, 10 miles north via US 97, has been a commercial center for farmers since its beginning. Well-kept homes and an active downtown continue to emanate a friendly, self-sufficient atmosphere. For a historical perspective, visit the **Presby Museum** (411 N. Grant Ave.; 509-773-4303; presbymuseum .com), owned by the Klickitat County Historical Society, in the stately Presby Mansion. Turn-of-the-20th-century dolls left on the antique furniture give the impression that a child has just finished playing in the parlor; the kitchen looks as if someone is cooking dinner; the dining room table is set; and period clothing is laid out in the bedrooms. The museum is open from 10 a.m. to 4 p.m. daily, May to Oct, or by appointment during the off-season. There is a small admission fee.

For an exhilarating look skyward, continue down Broadway Street and turn north on Columbus, past some of Goldendale's fine old homes. Follow signs uphill to **Goldendale Observatory State Park** (1602 Observatory Dr.; 509-773-3141; parks.wa.gov), where amateur astronomers share their enthusiasm for the stars. During the day view the sun using a special telescope, perhaps catching sight of a solar prominence—arcs of light and energy thousands of miles high. At night, the 24.5-inch telescope brings galaxies and nebulae into view. The observatory sits on a 2,100-foot hill and has one of the nation's largest public telescopes, open to sky-watchers since 1973. Its hours are 2 to 5 p.m. and 8 p.m. to midnight Wed through Sun, Apr 1 through Sept 30. The rest of the year, the hours are 2 to 5 p.m. and 7 to 10 p.m. Fri, Sat, and Sun. The park is closed through fall 2019 for upgrades. For more information browse perr.com/gosp.html for the evening star-watching schedule and links to Northwest astronomy clubs, NASA sites, and "This Week's Sky at a Glance." Since you've traveled this far off the beaten path, stop in Goldendale, where Greek Orthodox nuns run **St. John's Gifts & Bakery** (2378 Hwy. 97; 509-773-6650; stjohnmonastery.org).

Now's the time to take a little side trip, at least little by eastern Washington's standards. Drive about 35 miles east on Goldendale-Bickleton Road to the tiny but mildly famous town of **Bickleton,** population under 100. From mid-February to October thousands of mountain bluebirds flock to the area, earning the small town its nickname "Bluebird Capital of the World." About 2,000 small blue-and-white nesting boxes are on posts in yards, farms, and roadsides in a

150-square-mile area around Bickleton, all made by volunteers in what is now a 40-year project for area residents.

As you come into town, look to the right and spot the tall energy-generating windmills on the southern horizon. Bickleton has the state's oldest rodeo, one of the state's oldest taverns *Bluebird Inn Tavern* (509-896-2273), and a treasured 1905 horse carousel. The *Bickleton Market Street Cafe* (509-896-2671) is another food source. You won't have any problem finding them since the main drag is a country block long.

Prosser, located on the high Columbia Plateau about 37 miles northeast of Bickleton on Glade Road and Highway 22, has more to offer than you might expect for a quiet farm town. *Hinzerling Winery* and the *Vintner's Inn* (1520 Sheridan Ave.; 800-727-6702; hinzerling.com) were founded in 1976 by the Wallace family and constitute the oldest family owned and operated winery in the Yakima Valley. Family members share their knowledge of wine production and samples of wines, including sweet dessert wines and dry gewürztraminer. *Pontin Del Roza Winery* (35502 N. Hinzerling Rd.; 509-786-4449; pontindel roza.com) is set in the scenic hill district north of Prosser. You can taste the Pontin family's special Roza Sunset Blush and Pinot Grigio. They've added a spacious tasting room with a double-sided fireplace.

Gourmet cherries, preserves, toppings, and savories are other specialties you'll find near Prosser. The *Chukar Cherry Company* (320 Wine Country Rd.; 800-624-9544; chukar.com) produces chocolate-covered cherries, a pitted, ripe, partly dried cherry dipped in dark chocolate, a royal treat. Visit the gift shop just west of town.

The *Benton County Museum* (1000 Paterson Rd.; 509-786-3842; benton countymuseum.com) is open 11 a.m. to 4 p.m. Wed through Sun. There's a little of everything here including natural history displays, an old-time general

The Bluebird Inn Tavern, ca. 1882, Elevation 3,000 Feet

The tavern has gone through at least 15 owners since it opened in Bickleton in 1882. It used to double as a barbershop, and once was a social club where hats were forbidden. For a long time the place had no telephone, so the women weren't able to call and check up on their card-playing menfolk. Now, the tavern sells candy to kids and serves good food, including a giant Bluebird Burger. Pull up to the small Western-style structure that looks as though it should have several horses tied up out front, just like a John Wayne movie, and head in to shoot a game of pool on the 1903 Brunswick table.

store counter, an 1867 Chickering square grand piano that you may play, and a selection of women's clothing of yesteryear. One of the exhibits contains hand-carved and handpainted wooden automobiles, foot-long replicas of the real thing.

For a bite to eat in Prosser, try **Green Oak Brewing** (1427 Wine Country Rd.; 509-786-4922; whitstranbrewing.com) to sample microbrewed ales with upscale pub favorites, the **Barn Restaurant** (490 Wine Country Rd.; 509-786-1131), or the **El Caporal Mexican Restaurant** (624 6th St.; 509-786-4910).

For a sampling of this rich farming area's home-grown bounty, stop by the **Prosser Farmer's Market** (prosserfarmersmarket.com) next to Prosser City Park (7th Street and Sommers Avenue) for fresh Yakima Valley fruits and vegetables, delectable homemade baked goods, and crafts from local artisans. The market is open from 8 a.m. to noon on Sat, May through Oct.

You can reach the town of **Grandview** by heading northwest from Prosser on Wine Country Road. The **Dykstra House Restaurant** (114 Birch Ave.; 509-882-2082) is in a 1914 building. Dykstra offers delicious meals and desserts with regional wines and ales. Call for dinner reservations.

For a pleasant spot to stay the night in this rich wine country, continue northwest to Sunnyside, the next town on I-82. Call the innkeepers at **Sunnyside Inn Bed and Breakfast** (804 E. Edison Ave.; 509-839-5557; sunnysideinn .com) for accommodations. They offer 13 comfortable guest rooms with private baths in a large 1919 home with all the usual comforts, including restful colors, lovely window treatments, and country accessories. Families are especially welcome here. In the morning a sumptuous country breakfast is served family-style in the large dining area on the main floor.

Hungry in Sunnyside? Try the **Green Olive Cafe** (2926 Covey Ln.; 509-837-9009; greenolivecafe.net). For great ales created in small batches and tasty pub dishes, go to **Snipes Mountain Microbrewery & Restaurant** (905 Yakima Valley Hwy. 12; 509-837-2739; snipesmountain.com).

Before backtracking to the northwest, go east to the cities of Kennewick, Pasco, and Richland, which form the **Tri-Cities.** Located at the confluence of the Columbia, Snake, and Yakima Rivers, the area comes with 300 days of sunshine and seemingly endless recreational possibilities.

The Tri-Cities is the heart of wine country in this corner of the state, with 160 wineries within a 2-hour drive. The region's hot summer days and crisp evening breezes, which naturally stress the vines, combined with the Columbia Valley's volcanic soil, create conditions for making great wines. Visit the state's first barrel-storage caves at **Terra Blanca** (34715 Demoss Rd., Benton City; 509-588-6082; terrablanca.com); the tasting room at **Kiona Vineyards**

Tour Columbia Gorge & Yakima Valley Vineyards & Wineries

Throw a corkscrew into the picnic basket and visit a flotilla of fine vineyards, wineries, and tasting rooms in the fertile regions of the Yakima Valley and Columbia River Valley. Some of the wineries also open by appointment.

Alexandria Nicole Cellars
Prosser
(509) 786-3497
alexandrianicolecellars.com
Open Mon through Sat, 11 a.m. to
5 p.m.; Sun 12 p.m. to 5 p.m.

Barrel Springs Winery
Prosser
(509) 786-3166
barrelspringswinery.com
Open 10 a.m. to 5 p.m. Thurs through
Mon.

Chinook Wines
Prosser
(509) 786-2725
chinookwines.com
Open May through Oct, Sat and Sun,
noon to 5 p.m.

Hedges Family Estate
Benton City
(509) 588-3155
hedgesfamilyestate.com
Open 11 a.m. to 5 p.m. Wed through
Sun, Apr through Nov.

J. Bookwalter Winery
Richland
(509) 627-5000
bookwalterwines.com
Open 11:30 a.m. to 9 p.m. Mon through
Thurs, 11:30 a.m. to 10 p.m. Fri and
Sat, and 10 a.m. to 8 p.m. Sun

For Additional Information and Maps:

Columbia Valley Winery Association
columbiavalleywine.com

Prosser
prosserchamber.org

Tri-Cities
visittri-cities.com

Washington State
winecountrywashington.com

Yakima
visityakima.com

Yakima Valley Wineries
wineyakimavalley.org

Winery (44612 N. Sunset Rd., Benton City; 509-588-6716; kionawine.com), the first winery built on Red Mountain; or the state's first certified organic vineyard and winery at **Badger Mountain Vineyard** (1106 N. Jurupa St.; 509-627-4986; badgermtnvineyard.com).

The area's 12 or so museums and interpretive centers chronicle the region's history, which includes involvement in World War II, Alphabet Houses, Oregon Trail pioneers, early cinematography, railroading, agriculture, Kennewick Man, and more. Visit the exhibits about the 9,200-year-old **Kennewick Man** at the **East Benton County Historical Society Museum** (205 Keewaydin

TOP ANNUAL EVENTS
IN SOUTH CENTRAL WASHINGTON

FEBRUARY

Red Wine and Chocolate Festival
Yakima Valley
President's Day weekend
(800) 258-7270
wineyakimavalley.org

JUNE

Mural-in-a-Day
Toppenish
(800) 863-6375
toppenish.net

SEPTEMBER

The Great Prosser Balloon Rally
Prosser
(800) 408-1517
prosserballoonrally.org

NOVEMBER

Thanksgiving in Wine Country
Yakima Valley, holiday weekend
(800) 258-7270
wineyakimavalley.org

DECEMBER

Annual Lighted Farm Implement
Parade
Sunnyside
(509) 837-5939
lightedfarmparade.com

Dr.; 509-582-7704; ebchs.org); to learn about Hanford's role in the Manhattan Project, World War II, and the end of the Cold War, tour the **Columbia River Exhibition of History, Science and Technology** (95 Lee Blvd., Richland; 509-943-9000; crehst.org).

The **Hanford Reach National Monument** (fws.gov/hanfordreach) is the last free-flowing, nontidal stretch of the Columbia River. An abundance of wildlife can be seen along its 51 miles, including birds, elk, mule deer, coyote, river otter, and other denizens in this natural sanctuary. Explore the Reach on a **Columbia Kayak Adventures** tour (509-947-5901; columbiakayak.com), also in Richland.

For lodging, choose from B&Bs, vacation homes, motels, and hotels. Call the Tri-Cities Visitor & Convention Bureau to learn more (509-735-8486; visittri-cities.com). The reasonably priced **Clover Island Inn Hotel** on Clover Island in the Columbia River has 150 rooms and sweet views of the river (509-586-0541; cloverislandinn.com). Built on the shoreline and connected to the mainland by a causeway, the hotel has its own dock for your boat and bikes for guests (although if the wind is blowing stiffly, you might want to reconsider the bike ride). It's next to the **Cedars Restaurant** (355 N. Clover Island

The Alphabet Houses

A 1943 spin-off of the Manhattan Project was the Hanford Engineer Works near Richland. The 247 Richland residents were evicted, and the town was turned into a bedroom community for a facility on land that was half the size of Rhode Island. The goal was to produce plutonium for the bombs that were dropped on Japan during World War II.

Since speed was necessary, a Spokane architect was given precious little time to create a development plan to house an initial 6,500 people in Richland. Since managers and executives couldn't be expected to live in the same style or size of home as a janitor or an accountant, G. A. Pherson had to design many styles of houses for hierarchical, social, practical, and visual reasons. He labeled each style with a letter.

And so Richland's alphabet houses, also called ABC houses, were built from Pherson's plans at a rate of about 180 buildings a month for a total of 4,732 dwellings placed on streets named after famous engineers or tree species. "A" houses were three-bedroom 2-story duplexes; "D," "F," and "G" were 2-story single-family homes with three or four bedrooms and different exterior designs. There were also dormitories for single men.

One of the housing units, this one with 162 alphabet houses, by and large kept its original appearance and was placed on the National Register of Historic Places in 2005, designated as the Gold Coast Historic District.

Dr.; 509-582-2143; cedarskennewick.com) and close to the Historic Downtown Kennewick District.

Many excellent restaurants offer a wide variety of food choices. From taco wagons to elegant fine dining, specialty coffeehouses to ethnic bakeries, the mix is eclectic. As Washington produces more hops than anywhere else in the US, the area naturally offers a selection of great craft and microbreweries, including *Atomic Ale Brewpub and Eatery* (1015 Lee Blvd., Richland; 509-946-5465; atomicalebrewpub.com), where you can try Atomic Amber, Chinook IPA, or Oppenheimer Oatmeal Stout. Or check out *Ice Harbor Brewing Company* (206 N. Benton St., Kennewick; 509-582-5340; iceharbor.com) and the Rattlesnake Mountain Brewing Company beers served at *Kimo's Sports Bar* (2696 N. Columbia Blvd., Richland; 509-783-5747; kimosrmbc.com). Check out *Drumheller's* in Richland, part of *The Lodge at Columbia Point* (530 Columbia Point Dr.; 509-713-7423; lodgeatcolumbiapoint.com). The restaurant offers waterfront dining and microseasonal cooking with ingredients sourced from within a 50-mile radius.

Pause in the small town of *Granger,* population about 3,300, to visit *Metal and Iron Artistry* (502 Sunnyside Ave.; 509-930-7202; primoartisan

.com). You might catch up with Primo Villalobos, who at age 14 started an apprenticeship with a blacksmith and dreamed about building a 24-foot-tall knight in shining armor. In 1990 his dream came true. Now the knight stands in front of **Der Ritterhof** in Leavenworth. For pizza with views of the local links, stop by **Doc's On the Green** (530 Cherry Hill Rd.; 509-854-2294). Granger, in the heart of the Yakima Valley, logged 100 years of incorporation in 2009. Don't fear the brontosaurus, tyrannosaurus, triceratops, and other dinosaurs as you ride down Highway 223 near Granger, though. In 1958, woolly mammoth tusks and teeth were discovered in a nearby abandoned clay mine. Now steel-wire mesh-and-concrete dinosaurs roam once more.

About 7 miles north of Granger via Highway 22 is **Toppenish,** the small community and capital of the Yakama Indian Nation and dubbed the City of Murals and Museums. Park near the historic railroad depot and enjoy a walking tour of the downtown area and its 74 giant-size murals depicting scenes from early days in the West. From May through Sept, hop on the horse-drawn wagon

One Hundred Years, 1850 to 1950: the Toppenish Murals

Since 1989 folks in the **Toppenish Mural Society** have funded more than 70 gigantic murals painted outdoors on buildings all over Toppenish, from the Western Auto building and the Ray Reid Building to Providence Toppenish Hospital, Pow Wow Emporium, and Old Timers Plaza Park. We are not talking crayon and stick figures here. The historically accurate scenes represent the life and times of the Toppenish area from 1850 to 1950. Folks visit them throughout the year, but on the first Saturday of June you also can watch the Mural-in-a-Day come to life and join the celebration. Stop by the Visitor Welcome Center at 504 S. Elm St. (800-863-6375; toppenish.net); pick up a mural map; and enjoy. Here are a few of the giant-size paintings of bygone days that you'll see:

Hop Museum Murals (#32), a trio of painted archways open to scenes of harvesting hops on two walls of the American Hop Museum

Lou Shattuck (#34), an original booster of the Toppenish Pow Wow Rodeo

Maud Bolin (#27), rodeo rider and early female pilot on the southwest wall of the *Toppenish Review* newspaper building

Rodeo Days (#13), on the west wall of Ferguson's Saddlery

Ruth Parton (#22), cowgirl and trick-rider on the United Telephone Company building

Western Hospitality (#36), bordello ladies of the night on the second-floor windows of the Logan Building

for a narrated tour. Pause for a look at the grand old *Liberty Theatre* at 211 S. Toppenish Ave. Built in 1915, the theater boasted the largest stage at the time between Seattle and Spokane and hosted stars such as Lillian Gish, Raymond Navarro, and even Tex Ritter and his horse.

When it's time to stop for nourishment, locals suggest the authentic fare at *Taqueria Mexicana* (105½ S. Alder St.; 509-865-7116). At *Gibbons Soda Fountain* (113 S. Toppenish Ave.; 509-865-4688), sharing a location with the local pharmacy, order juicy burgers and something cool and tasty at the old-fashioned soda fountain. *Krafts* (111 S. Toppenish Ave.; 888-890-3656; krafts .com), which specializes in colorful Pendleton blankets.

Allow time to visit the country's only museum dedicated to the growing of hops, the *American Hop Museum* (22 S. B St.; 509-865-4677; americanhop museum.org). The museum is open from 10 a.m. to 4 p.m. Wed through Sun, from May through Sept. Look at the splendid murals on the front of the large building, a series of arched windows painted on either side of the entrance. The museum focuses on the hop industry, and the first American hops were planted on Manhattan Island in 1607.

In 1868, the son of a New York hop farmer took the perennial vines westward where the climate was sunnier with fewer mildew issues. The sunny Yakima Valley became a prime area for growing hops, which climb on tall expanses of twine strung in long rows. In the museum are artifacts, memorabilia, and old photographs collected from all over the US, including antique hop presses, tools for cultivating hops, a horse-drawn hop duster, old picking baskets, and an early picking machine. Learn how hop cones are used to flavor and preserve beers and ales, and browse in the gift shop.

The *Northern Pacific Railway Museum* (10 Asotin Ave.; 509-865-1911; nprymuseum.org), in a restored railway depot built in 1911, contains interesting rail and steam artifacts, a completely restored telegraph office, and a gift shop. The third weekend of August folks can attend the *Toppenish Western Art Show* in Railroad Park and return the following weekend for the annual railroad show at the depot museum. Great art, railroad memorabilia, food booths, and live country music along with tours of the museum, engine house, and grounds make for a lively time. If you travel through the area in summer, you can take in the *Toppenish Wild West Parade* on the Fourth of July.

To learn more about Native American culture, visit the well-done *Yakama Nation Museum and Cultural Center* (100 Spilyay Loop, Toppenish; 509-865-2800; yakamamuseum.com). From a distance you'll spot the colorful peaked roof of the center's Winter Lodge, modeled after the ancestral A-shaped homes of the Yakama tribes. Museum exhibits and dioramas show the tribe's history and traditions. A large, angular tule (reed) lodge at the center of the museum presents how extended families lived during the winter. Sweat lodges made from earth, branches, and animal skins illustrate sacred places of physical and spiritual purification. The museum is open daily; there is an admission fee.

At the center's gift shop adjacent to the museum, fine beadwork and other Native American art and cultural items are for sale. The center also maintains an extensive library on First Nations history and culture; it's open Mon through Sat. Twenty-eight miles west of Toppenish is **Fort Simcoe State Park,** a lovely heritage park with large oak trees, a lush green lawn, and a dozen restored and re-created buildings filled with period furnishings. The former military fort is at 5150 Fort Simcoe Rd. (509-874-2372; parks.wa.gov) near the community of White Swan and on a traditional native village site. The ancient **Mool Mool bubbling springs** here have created a shady oasis of reed-filled wetlands surrounded by woods. In summer, you may catch sight of bronze-green and pink Lewis's woodpeckers, which breed in abundance in the Garry oaks. The park, a popular picnic spot for local residents, features plenty of shade trees, running water, and an adventure playground. The historical buildings and interpretive center are open Wed through Sun from 8 a.m. to dusk from Apr through Sept.

The **Toppenish National Wildlife Refuge** is located off Highway 22 southeast of Toppenish (fws.gov/toppenish). The refuge's marshlands and thick riverside forests are excellent places to view the fall and spring migrations of Canada geese, sandpipers, and ducks such as teals, mallards, and gadwalls. There also are bald eagles, prairie falcons, and other wildlife.

Mountains & Railroads

The Rattlesnake Hills AVA is a winery touring region in the hills above the town of **Zillah,** an ideal way to discover the valley's agricultural opulence. To visit Zillah take I-82, exit 52 or 54, or follow the Yakima Valley Highway from Sunnyside through Granger and turn left onto Zillah's 1st Avenue. The Zillah Chamber of Commerce's can be reached at (509) 829-5055; zillahchamber.com. The wineries start in town, so pick up a map from the downtown information office at the corner of 1st Avenue and 5th Street. Along the way you'll enjoy grand views of the lower valley's patchwork quilt of farms, and you'll pass by several wineries.

Of course every winery claims to offer the best product, so it's up to you to determine your favorites. Each has a tasting room where visitors are offered a small sample of the vintages. Employees, and sometimes the owners, are glad to share their knowledge and offer suggestions for the best wine for various occasions. Most tasting rooms also sell nonalcoholic drinks, snacks, and gifts.

Teapot Dome Service Station

Just east of Zillah is an unmistakable landmark, a true vintage roadside attraction just off I-82 exit 54. The 15-foot-tall white teapot structure with its red handle and spout was once a gas station built in 1922. The joke here, which only old-timers or history buffs are likely to catch without explanation, is the name: the Teapot Dome Service Station, a reference to the Wyoming and California oil-lease scandal of the same name, big news in the early twenties; it sent Secretary of the Interior Albert Fall to prison. Zillah residents hope to move the building, on the National Register of Historic Places, to the downtown area and transform it into a visitor center.

If wine tasting has given you an appetite and you forgot the picnic basket, you'll want to eat at *El Porton* (605 Vintage Valley Pkwy.; 509-829-9100; elportonrestaurant.business.site) or *Squeeze Inn Restaurant* (611 1st Ave.; 509-790-7041; squeezeinnzillah.com).

Just south of Yakima is the town of *Union Gap,* the single gap in the line of hills that divides the upper and lower Yakima Valley. Next to the gap is the *Central Washington Agricultural Museum* at 4508 Main St. in Fullbright Park (509-457-8735; centralwaagmuseum.org). The large collection of farm equipment is arranged inside 29 display buildings and also outdoors on spiral terraces around a windmill tower. You'll see horse-drawn plows and mowers, huge old steam tractors, antique threshers, and hop harvesters. A blacksmith shop, furnished log cabin, fruit-packing line equipment, and the Museum Grange Library are also in the 17-acre park. You might even see working horse teams plowing the museum fields or an old steam harvester in use. While you can wander the grounds year-round, the buildings are open Tues through Sat 10 a.m. to 4 p.m., and Sun 1 p.m. to 4 p.m. from Apr until Oct. To get to the museum from Union Gap, follow Main Street south 2 miles and across the US 97 overpass to the Fullbright Park turnoff. If you want to picnic, there are shaded tables on the grounds at Fullbright Park, or for a bite to eat in Union Gap, check out *Old Town Station Restaurant* (2530 Main St.; 509-453-8485; oldtownstationinc.com) and *Jean's Cottage Inn* (3211 Main St.; 509-575-9709; jeanscottageinn.com), which has been a local fixture for its huge steak dinners since 1946. Not to be missed is *Los Hernandez Tamales* (3706 Main St.; 509-457-6003; loshernandeztamales.com) for James Beard Foundation-honored tamales with local vegetables.

The city of *Yakima* offers many activities little-known to outsiders. Walking or bicycling along the 10-mile *Yakima Greenway Trail* (509-453-8280; yakimagreenway.org) is the perfect way to enjoy the Yakima and Naches Rivers from the quiet town of Selah at the north, past several riverfront parks, to the 70-acre *Yakima Area Arboretum* near the south end (509-248-7337; ahtrees .org). The arboretum includes hiking trails, a Japanese garden, and the Jewett Interpretive Center. You can also access the trail and a river landing for launching kayaks and canoes at *Sarg Hubbard Park* off I-82 or off Yakima Avenue onto S. 18th Street.

Railroad themes permeate Yakima. Along the old railroad line through downtown, find renovated N. Front Street and browse its eclectic shops, cafes, and pubs. Check out the *Cowiche Canyon Kitchen and Ice House Bar* (202 E. Yakima Ave.; 509-457-2007; cowichecanyon.com) specializes in modern fare with great cocktails, while *Crafted* (22 N. 1st St.; 509-426-2220; craftedyakima .com) has small plates and late-night eats. On Yakima Avenue between 5th and 6th Streets as well as on 2nd Street, browse a collection of delightful antiques shops.

White House in Yakima (3602 Kern St.; 509-469-2644; whitehousein yakima.com) is in a 1929 farmhouse. It offers tasty breakfast and lunch fare as well as a gift shop and 2 B&B rooms.

In 1889 the *Switzer Opera House* was built at 25 N. Front St. and housed Yakima's first performing arts and vaudeville theater. Now renovated, the building is home to a variety of shops. For great baked goods find *Essencia Artisan Bakery* (4 N. 3rd St.; 509-575-5570).

In 1898 the Lund Building was constructed on the corner of N. Front Street and Yakima Avenue. In those days it housed such colorful establishments as Sam's Cafe, the Alfalfa Saloon, and the Chicago Clothing Company. The early establishments are gone.

The *Capitol Theatre* (19 S. 3rd St.; 509-853-8000; capitoltheatre.org), is another historic structure restored to its 1920s splendor. A resident ghost, Sparky, reportedly decided to stay on after the renovation. The theater is now home to the Yakima Symphony. Music lovers head to the *Seasons Performance Hall,* a onetime church-turned-music-venue at 101 N. Naches Ave. (509-453-1888; theseasonsyakima.com). The nonprofit showcases rising stars and seasoned performers playing jazz, Mexican folk, classical, and world music.

Be sure to plan a stop at the *Yakima Valley Museum* (2105 Tieton Dr.; 509-248-0747; yakimavalleymuseum.org) for a soda, thick milk shakes, and a hot dog ordered at the old-fashioned soda fountain. A bright neon sign greets visitors at the entry to the soda fountain, the floor sports black-and-white square-tiled linoleum, and at the counter folks sit on round stools covered with bright red vinyl. In other sections of the museum you can browse a fine Native American collection, see wagons and carriages (from stagecoach to hearse), and turn the kids loose in the children's interactive center.

Located in a renovated fruit warehouse, ***Glenwood Square*** (5110 Tieton Dr.; 509-966-3580; glenwoodsquare.net) offers old, polished-wood floors and is home to ***Zesta Cucina*** (509-972-2000; zestacucina.com), a local restaurant open daily and offering a variety of Washington wines. The ***Little Soapmaker*** (302 W. Yakima Ave.; 509-972-8504; thelittlesoapmaker.com) in downtown Yakima sells natural handmade soaps and other natural products.

Those who get hungry for fine gourmet Mexican cooking should try the well-known ***Santiago's Restaurant*** (111 E. Yakima Ave.; 509-453-1644; santiagos.biz) at 6 blocks west of the convention center. It's closed on Sun. Or call for dinner reservations at the ***Apple Tree Grill*** at ***Apple Tree Resort***

Smart Elk

This is a tale of unintended consequences. In 1913 a herd of Rocky Mountain elk were introduced into mountains near Yakima to rebuild a nearly extinct herd. The elk thrived, multiplied, and became a costly nuisance to ranchers and orchardists every winter when they migrated to the lowlands for better pickings. In 1939, when 3,000 elk were pitted against irate landowners (shots were fired), the state stepped in and created the Oak Creek Wildlife Area, now 47,200 acres.

About 100 miles of 8-foot-high fence protected landowners, but the elk went hungry because their winter grazing area had been significantly reduced. Elk with their ribs showing created a new class of irate humans—hunters—who objected to prey normally weighing 400 to 900 pounds being reduced to skin and bones from lack of feed. The only solution, other than drastically reducing the herd, was to feed the elk. By 1945 the landowners were happy, the hunters' blood pressures were lowered, and the elk went on the dole, content enough to build their numbers until up to 1,200 can be spotted at one time in the feeding stations.

Let's see, several pounds of hay per elk times the number of elk times the number of feeding days . . . the need for hay made hay farmers happy, too. The annual feeding also attracts about 100,000 visitors, who rarely get the chance to be so close to hundreds of elk, which they do at the main Oak Creek feeding station.

That many visitors needed an interpretive center (call for hours) run by volunteers with videos, exhibits, a kids' corner, and temperatures warmer than those outside. The popular truck tour delights those who take it. Visitors can ride in the trucks that are dropping off the hay, surrounded by hungry elk. The truck experience is by reservation, (509) 653-2390, and first-come, first-served. It's smart to call ahead.

Of course the same rationale led to the reintroduced bighorn sheep getting in line for a winter handout. They're fed mid-morning at the nearby Cleman Mountain feeding station (ask for directions). The elk are fed next to the interpretive center at 1:30 p.m., with January and February driving in the most hay-chompers. A Discover Pass is required to visit (discoverpass.wa.gov).

(8804 Occidental Rd.; 509-966-7140; appletreeresort.com). The chef cooks up delicious apple-wood-smoked prime rib. The best time to go is evening early enough for sunset views of the golf course and surrounding hills. The course's signature hole is number 17, a large apple-shaped island green connected to the fairway by a footbridge "stem" and with an adjacent sand trap shaped like a large leaf.

Consider staying a day or two to further explore this interesting city of railroad memorabilia and this large region of fruit orchards, vineyards, wineries, and tasting rooms. Sleep in a bed-and-breakfast inn in a cherry orchard just west of downtown Yakima. The **Orchard Inn Bed & Breakfast** (1207 Pecks Canyon Rd.; 509-966-1283; orchardinnbb.com) has spacious guest rooms, private bathrooms, and gourmet breakfasts in a casual European atmosphere. Nearby, visit **Washington Fruit Place and Gift Shop at Barrett Orchards** (treeripened.com) for fresh cherries and other juicy fruits of the season in a big red barn located on Pecks Canyon Road. You are also invited to walk an interpretive pathway in the cherry orchard.

Two miles east of Yakima, **Birchfield Manor Country Inn** (2018 Birchfield Rd.; 509-452-1960; birchfieldmanor.com) offers elegant meals and overnight accommodations in a redbrick Victorian-style mansion, complete with crystal chandeliers, a winding staircase, and flower garden. You'll find an abundance of genteel comforts (hot tub, pool, private baths) and a choice of 11 charming, antiques-filled guest rooms in the main house and adjacent cottage. If the notion of a sumptuous 5-course gourmet dinner including decadent desserts sounds appealing, call the Birchfield staff to inquire about reservations Thurs through Sat. US 12 west of Yakima passes through the orchard-filled Naches Valley on its way to 14,411-foot snowy Mount Rainier and the central Cascade Mountains area. Just past the Naches Valley, 2 miles west of the Highway 410 turnoff, is the **Oak Creek Wildlife Area** (509-653-2390; wdfw .wa.gov), a winter feeding station for elk and bighorn sheep in winter and a popular spot for hunting and bird watching. Continuing west, you'll ascend the Tieton River and climb through sagebrush-covered hills and the Gifford Pinchot and Snoqualmie national forests up to **White Pass** at an elevation of 4,500 feet. Along the way see numerous lakes, fishing resorts, and campgrounds. This scenic byway comes with dramatic geological formations and mountain areas covered with Douglas fir, western red cedar, and alpine fir. White Pass has relatively light traffic and long stretches of undeveloped forest, making it a favorite route for bicyclists and a popular destination for all-season outdoor recreation.

To find a good place to eat and sleep that's substantially farther off the beaten path, head northwest from Naches on Highway 410 toward Mount Rainier National Park. You'll reach **Whistlin' Jack Lodge** on the Naches River at

20800 Hwy. 410 (509-658-2433; whistlinjacklodge.com). The restaurant features fresh mountain trout, blueberry cinnamon buns, and Washington's best wines. During summer, enjoy a pleasant lunch outside on the deck. Accommodations include a lodge and streamside cottages with private hot tubs. Call for reservations or winter road conditions.

If you're traveling RV-style, you could check for sites at **Squaw Rock Resort** on the Naches River (15070 Hwy. 410; 509-658-2800). Both the resort and Whistlin' Jack Lodge are less than 40 miles northwest of Yakima and not far from 14,411-foot Mount Rainier. You can access scenic drives and campgrounds on Mount Rainier by crossing over 5,430-foot Chinook Pass. From Naches you could also travel southwest of the mountain on US 12, which winds over 4,500-foot White Pass and down toward Packwood and **Randle.** At Randle inquire at the Cowlitz Valley Ranger Station (360-497-1100) for backroad directions to see sections of trees blown down when Mount St. Helens erupted in May 1980 and again in 2004.

Places to Stay in South Central Washington

KENNEWICK/RICHLAND

Clover Island Inn Hotel
435 Clover Island Dr.
(509) 586-0541
cloverislandinn.com

The Lodge at Columbia Point
530 Columbia Point Dr.
(509) 713-7423
lodgeatcolumbiapoint.com

NACHES

Squaw Rock Resort
15070 Hwy. 410
(509) 658-2800

Whistlin' Jack Lodge
20800 Hwy. 410
(509) 658-2433
whistlinjacklodge.com

PROSSER

Vintner's Inn
1520 Sheridan Ave.
(800) 727-6702
hinzerling.com

STEVENSON/CARSON

Carson Mineral Hot Springs Resort
372 St. Martin's Springs Rd.
(509) 427-8296
carsonhotspringresort.com

Columbia Gorge Riverside Lodge
200 SW Cascade Ave.
(509) 427-5650
cgriversidelodge.com

Sandhill Cottages
932 Hot Springs Ave.
(509) 427-3464
sandhillcottages.com

Skamania Lodge
1131 SW Skamania Lodge Way
(509) 314-4177
destinationhotels.com/skamania

SUNNYSIDE

Sunnyside Inn Bed and Breakfast
804 E. Edison Ave.
(509) 839-5557
sunnysideinn.com

TOPPENISH

Quality Inn & Suites
511 S. Elm St.
(509) 865-5800
qualityinn.com

VISITOR INFORMATION CENTERS

Goldendale
(509) 773-3400
goldendalechamber.org

Hood River
Hood River, OR
(800) 366-3530
hoodriver.org

Kelso Longview Area
(Mount St. Helens)
(360) 423-8400
kelsolongviewchamber.org

Mount Adams and Klickitat County
(509) 493-3630
mtadamschamber.com

Prosser
(800) 408-1517
prosserchamber.org

Skamania County
(509) 427-8911
skamania.org

Toppenish
(800) 863-6375
toppenish.net

Vancouver
(877) 600-0800
visitvancouverusa.com

Washington Road Conditions
511 for locals or (800) 695-7623
wsdot.com/traffic

Yakima Valley
(800) 221-0751
visityakima.com

TOUTLE/PACKWOOD

Cowlitz River Lodge
13069 US 12
(360) 494-4444
whitepasstravel.com/
cowlitzriverlodge

Crest Trail Lodge
12729 US 12
(360) 494-4944
whitepasstravel.com/
cresttrail

Eco Park Resort
14000 Spirit Lake Hwy.
(360) 274-7007
ecoparkresort.com

Hotel Packwood
104 Main St.
(360) 494-5431
packwoodwa.com/Hotel
Packwood.htm

Mountain View Lodge
13163 US 12
(360) 494-5555
mtvlodge.com

**TROUT LAKE/HUSUM/
GLENWOOD**

Elk Meadows RV Park
78 Trout Lake Creek Rd.
(877) 395-2400
elkmeadowsrvpark.com

**Husum Highlands Bed &
Breakfast**
70 Postgren Rd.
(509) 493-4503
husumhighlands.com

**Kelly's Trout Creek Inn
Bed & Breakfast**
25 Mount Adams Rd.
(509) 395-2769
kellysbnb.com

Mount Adams Lodge
25 Flying L Ln.
(509) 364-3488
mt-adams.com

Trout Lake Cozy Cabins
2291 Hwy. 141
(509) 395-2068
troutlakecozycabins.com

VANCOUVER

The Heathman Lodge
7801 NE Greenwood Dr.
(360) 254-3100
heathmanlodge.com

WHITE SALMON

Inn of the White Salmon
172 W. Jewett Blvd.
(509) 493-2335
innofthewhitesalmon.com

YAKIMA

Birchfield Manor Country Inn
2018 Birchfield Rd.
(509) 452-1960
birchfieldmanor.com

Orchard Inn Bed & Breakfast
1207 Pecks Canyon Rd.
(509) 966-1283
orchardinnbb.com

Places to Eat in South Central Washington

BICKLETON

Bickleton Market Street Cafe
106 Market St.
(509) 896-2671

Bluebird Inn Tavern
121 Market St.
(509) 896-2273

BINGEN

Everybody's Brewing
177 E. Jewett Blvd.
(509) 637-2774
everybodysbrewing.com

The Huck Truck
415 W. Steuben St.
(808) 280-0769

GOLDENDALE

St. John's Gifts & Bakery
2378 Hwy. 97
(509) 773-6650
stjohnmonastery.org

GRANDVIEW

Dykstra House Restaurant
114 Birch Ave.
(509) 882-2082

GRANGER

Doc's On the Green
530 Cherry Hill Rd.
(509) 854-2294

KENNEWICK/RICHLAND

Atomic Ale Brewpub and Eatery
1015 Lee Blvd.
(509) 946-5465
atomicalebrewpub.com

Cedars Restaurant
355 N. Clover Island Dr.
(509) 582-2143
cedarskennewick.com

Drumheller's
530 Columbia Point Dr.
(509) 713-7423
lodgeatcolumbiapoint.com

Ice Harbor Brewing Company
206 N. Benton St.
(509) 582-5340
iceharbor.com

ALSO WORTH SEEING

Barrett Orchards
Yakima
(509) 966-1275
treeripened.com

Cave B Estate Winery, Cave B Inn, and Tendril Restaurant
Vantage area
(509) 785-3500 (tasting room)
caveb.com

Gorge Amphitheater
near Vantage
(509) 785-6262
thegorgeonline.com

Mount Hood Railroad
Hood River, OR
(800) 872-4661
mthoodrr.com

Seasons Performance Hall
Yakima
(509) 453-1888
theseasonsyakima.com

Kimo's Sports Bar
2696 N. Columbia Blvd.
(509) 783-5747
kimosrmbc.com

MARYHILL

Loïe's
35 Maryhill Dr.
(509) 773-3733
maryhillmuseum.org

Maryhill Winery
9774 Hwy. 14
(509) 773-1976
maryhillwinery.com

PROSSER

Barn Restaurant
490 Wine Country Rd.
(509) 786-1131

El Caporal Mexican Restaurant
624 6th St.
(509) 786-4910

STEVENSON/CARSON

Andrew's Pizza
310 2nd St.
(509) 427-8008
andrewspizzastevenson
.com

Big River Grill
192 SW 2nd St.
(509) 427-4888
thebigrivergrill.com

Walking Man Brewing
240 1st St.
(509) 427-5520

SUNNYSIDE

Green Olive Cafe
2926 Covey Ln.
(509) 837-9009
greenolivecafe.net

Snipes Mountain Microbrewery & Restaurant
905 Yakima Valley Hwy.
(509) 837-2739
snipesmountain.com

TOPPENISH

Gibbons Soda Fountain
113 S. Toppenish Ave.
(509) 865-4688

Taqueria Mexicana
105½ S. Alder St.
(509) 865-7116

TOUTLE/PACKWOOD

Blue Spruce Saloon & Diner
US 12 at Willame Street
(360) 494-5605

TROUT LAKE/WHITE SALMON/LYLE

Logs Family Restaurant
1258 Hwy. 141
(509) 493-1505

Lyle Hotel Restaurant
100 7th St.
(509) 365-5953
thelylehotel.com

The Station Cafe
247 Hwy. 141
(509) 395-2211

VANCOUVER

Dulin's Cafe
1929 Main St.
(360) 737-9907
dulinscafe.com

The Grant House
Officer's Row
(360) 906-1101
thegranthouse.us

Ice Cream Renaissance
1925 Main St.
(360) 694-3892
icecreamrenaissance.com

YAKIMA/UNION GAP

Apple Tree Grill
8804 Occidental Rd.
(509) 966-7140
appletreeresort.com

Cowiche Canyon Kitchen and Ice House Bar
202 E. Yakima Ave.
(509) 457-2007
cowichecanyon.com

Crafted
22 N. 1st St.
(509) 426-2220
craftedyakima.com

Essencia Artisan Bakery
4 N. 3rd St.
(509) 575-5570
essenciaartisanbakery.com

Jean's Cottage Inn
3211 Main St.
(509) 575-9709
jeanscottageinn.com

Los Hernandez Tamales
3706 Main St.
(509) 457-6003
loshernandeztamales.com

Old Town Station Restaurant
2530 Main St.
Union Gap
(509) 453-8485
oldtownstationinc.com

Santiago's Restaurant
111 E. Yakima Ave.
(509) 453-1644
santiagos.biz

White House in Yakima
3602 Kern St.
(509) 469-2644
whitehouseinyakima.com

Zesta Cucina
5110 Tieton Dr.
(509) 972-2000
zestacucina.com

ZILLAH

El Porton
905 Vintage Valley Pkwy.
(509) 829-9100
elportonrestaurant.business
.site

Squeeze Inn Restaurant
611 1st Ave.
(509) 790-7041
squeezeinnzillah.com

Northeast Washington

Washington's northeast corner is a high desert and farming region of stark contrasts. In a few hours you can travel through steep basalt canyons with the spicy smell of sagebrush, over hills covered with wheat fields and dotted with isolated farmhouses and outbuildings, and through thick pine forests. The region's geological history is dynamic and readily visible in the layered walls of coulees and steep canyons cut deep by ancient glaciers and rivers.

You meet local residents at cafe lunch counters, at small restaurants, or at bistros and brewpubs. They are aware of the seasonal changes and their relationship to the farms, ranches, forests, and rivers upon which so much of the local economy depends. They take pride in their Native American, farmer, rancher, and forestry heritages, which are very much alive.

Northeast Washington also offers a variety of all-season outdoor activities, including hiking, bicycling, fishing, hunting, boating, snowmobiling, ice fishing, and skiing. On the shores of many rivers and lakes, secluded retreats and fishing resorts beckon.

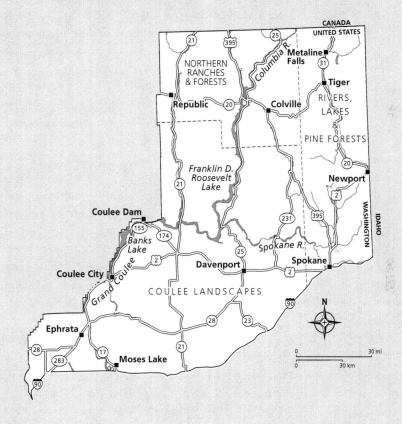

CANADA
UNITED STATES

NORTHERN
RANCHES
& FORESTS

Columbia R.

Metaline
Falls

Tiger

Republic

Colville

RIVERS,
LAKES
&
PINE FORESTS

Franklin D.
Roosevelt
Lake

Newport

Coulee Dam

Banks
Lake

Spokane R.

WASHINGTON

IDAHO

Coulee City

Davenport

Spokane

Grand Coulee

COULEE LANDSCAPES

Ephrata

Moses Lake

N

0   30 mi
0   30 km

Coulee Landscapes

A good place to start your tour of the region is the town of ***Ephrata,*** known primarily for its mint production. From exit 151 on I-90, take Highway 283 northeast through George, or follow Highway 17 northwest from Moses Lake, past enormous circular fields of corn, wheat, potatoes, and legumes kept green by massive central-pivot irrigation systems. This high plain is so wide you can glimpse hills to the north but only a hint of a southern ridge.

Like many northeast Washington counties, Grant County preserves its past. The ***Grant County Historical Museum and Village*** (742 Basin St. NW; 509-754-3334), at the north end of Ephrata, offers more than 30 buildings and shops that showcase the region's past. Walk through carefully re-created print, camera, and blacksmith shops; saloons, a one-room 1910 schoolhouse, homesteads, a 1971 Burlington Northern caboose, laundry, the old *Grant County Journal* building, Saint Rosalima's Church (the first Catholic church in the county), a firehouse with a 1939 fire truck, the original Krupp-Marlin jail, and a collection of the big farm machines that made Grant County a major agricultural producer, all arranged on a 4-acre site. The museum is open Mon to Sat 10 a.m. to 5 p.m. (but closed Wed) and Sun 1 to 4 p.m. For another glimpse of local history, stop by the 1917 ***Grant County Courthouse,*** west of the highway at the corner of 1st NW and C Streets. The courthouse is heated geothermally from a nearby hot spring.

Ritzville, about 45 miles east of Moses Lake at the junction of Highway 395 and I-90, is in the heart of the rolling wheat lands and once may have been the largest wheat-receiving station in the world. A self-guided downtown walking tour is one way to be introduced to the town; printed guides are available at two museums. The large metal sculptures scattered about town represent its history.

About 50 to 60 trains a day roll by the 1910 ***NP Railroad Depot Museum*** (201 W. Railroad Ave.). "That makes this a railroad-lovers paradise. Everything from soup to nuts is shipped through here. It's the main line to Portland," said a volunteer. The women's restroom still has the original tank on the water closet. The depot collection includes a working telegrapher's office, a caboose, and the town's first horse-drawn hearse. Donations are accepted. The ***Frank R. Burroughs Home Museum*** (408 W. Main St.) was the residence of a pioneer physician that has been restored to its original condition with household items from the 1890s to 1920s. The two museums share the same telephone number, (509) 659-1656; both are staffed by volunteers and visitors should call to verify open hours.

Ritzville has limited dining options: check out ***Greenside Cafe*** overlooking the Ritzville Municipal Golf Course (104 E. 10th Ave.; 509-659-9868) or sample the deli and pizza at ***Spike's Deli and Pizza*** (1611 Smitty's Blvd.;

NORTHEAST WASHINGTON'S TOP HITS

Bing Crosby Collection
Gonzaga University
Spokane

Dry Falls Interpretive Center
Coulee City

Fort Spokane
Near Creston

Gehrke Windmill Garden
Grand Coulee

Grand Coulee Dam
Coulee Dam

Keller Ferry

Kettle Falls Historical Center
Kettle Falls

Lake Lenore Caves
Soap Lake

Lake Roosevelt
Kettle Falls

Lincoln County Historical Museum
Davenport

Manito Park Gardens
Spokane

North Pend Oreille Scenic Byway and International Selkirk Loop
Ione

Northwest Museum of Arts and Culture and Historic Campbell House
Spokane

Pend Oreille County Museum
Newport

Sherman Pass Scenic Byway
Sherman Pass

Soap Lake
Soap Lake

Spokane River Centennial Trail
Spokane

Steamboat Rock State Park
Electric City

Stevens County Historical Museum
Colville

Stonerose Interpretive Center
Republic

509-659-0490). Another option out of Moses Lake is to follow Highway 17 north to **Soap Lake.** Cherished by local tribes and early settlers for its healing properties, Soap Lake continues to draw people seeking physical rejuvenation. Twenty-three minerals, with sodium and bicarbonate being the most common, give the water its soapy texture.

Soap Lake's popularity is nothing like its heyday at the turn of the 20th century, but the crowds still come. Experience the water's effects with daily soaks at one of the town's two beaches or in baths piped from mineral waters deep in the lake to several of the motels. East Beach, located near the highway and motels, is the most popular with tourists. West Beach, separated by a small, rocky peninsula, is preferred by local residents.

If you'd like to linger a day or two, ask about accommodations at **Notaras Lodge** (236 E. Main Ave.; 509-246-0462; soaplakeresort.com/notaras-lodge).

Choose from 15 different rooms in 4 large log structures that offer outside entrances and small sitting decks. Each room has handcrafted log walls, a comfortable sitting area, and a small kitchenette (3 rooms have full kitchens). All rooms are decorated with Western and antique memorabilia. Or check out the *Inn at Soap Lake* (226 Main Ave. E; 509-246-0462; soaplakeresort.com/inn-soap-lake) with its fascinating stone walls and history as a stable and smithy turned hotel in 1915.

Lakeside Bistro (14 Canna St.; 509-246-1217), just across the street from Notaras Lodge, is a local favorite for burgers, wraps, and salads.

Soap Lake is the southernmost of the Grand Coulee's chain of mineral-rich lakes. The *Grand Coulee* was formed by glacial action that cut through layers of thick volcanic basalt. Highway 17, from Soap Lake to *Coulee City,* provides a scenic route through the lower end of the coulee. You'll follow secluded lake beds, cut deep into reddish-brown cliffs, their shorelines often crusted white with minerals. Lake Lenore has public access, with several spots to launch a boat or to stop and watch the waterfowl in lakeside wetlands.

Off the highway opposite Lake Lenore is the turnoff to the *Lake Lenore Caves,* 8 miles north of Soap Lake. A gravel road takes you to the trailhead for a 1.5-mile hike through sagebrush and up the cliff sides to the ancient caves. There, like ancient hunter-gatherers, you can find shelter from the heat in these cool, rocky overhangs—but watch for snakes that cool off in the shade. See graceful cliff swallows, listen to crickets, hear the dry scrub rustling in the breeze, and absorb the stark beauty of the wide coulee landscape. Contact Sun Lakes–Dry Falls State Park at (509) 632-5583 or the Dry Falls Visitor Center at (509) 632-5214 (parks.wa.gov) for information on the area. Between Alkali and Blue Lakes, you may catch sight of the *Caribou Cattle Trail.* A sign marks the point where the trail crosses the road. Originally a native path, the 800-mile trail was used in the late 19th century as a supply route by miners and Blue Lake homesteaders. A few miles north on Blue Lake, *Coulee Lodge Resort* (33017 Park Lake Rd. NE; 509-632-5565; couleelodgeresort.com) offers 6 cabins, 8 well-equipped mobile homes, and campsites. Rent a 14-foot aluminum boat to chase trout or ride the paddleboat to slowly take in the scenery. The site includes a nice swimming beach. The resort is located 15 miles north of Soap Lake.

Nearby, off Highway 17, *Sun Lakes–Dry Falls State Park* (509-632-5583; parks.wa.gov) offers camping, boating, golf, mountain biking, and wildlife viewing. The *Dry Falls Visitor Center* (509-632-5214), open daily Apr through Oct near Coulee City at the south end of *Banks Lake,* offers spectacular views of what was once a gigantic waterfall—possibly the largest that has ever existed on Earth. It is now a dry cliff 400 feet high and 3.5 miles wide. Exhibits explain the geological forces that created this massive precipice and why it is now without water. Learn of the lush environment that covered this area 20 million years ago and how the largest basaltic lava flows on Earth, up to a mile thick, eventually engulfed 200,000 square miles of the Pacific Northwest. Powerful forces buckled and warped the cooled lava plateau, followed by glaciation and massive flooding, creating the dramatic landscape before you.

US 2 and Highway 17 intersect at fittingly named Junction Lake, then US 2 crosses the Dry Falls Dam at the south end of Banks Lake. Turn right off US 2 at Coulee City to explore this windblown Western town, originally a watering hole along the Caribou Trail that is now dominated by huge grain elevators. If you happen into Coulee City on Tuesday or Saturday between 10 a.m. and 3 p.m., you can learn about art and local history from members of the ***Highlighters Art Club,*** who meet at 504 W. Main St. (509-632-5373), tucked next to Couleegans, a tavern. The gallery, in a building constructed in 1905, features art produced by members, such as oil paintings, wood carvings, and dried-flower arrangements.

If you continue east, US 2 passes through a series of small farm towns at about 10-mile intervals. ***Wilbur,*** at the junction of US 2 and Highway 21, is worth a stop. The town's main park, located south of Main Street, is a shady oasis of mature trees and green lawns. The town displays its history at the ***Big Bend Historical Society Museum*** (wilburwa.com; 509-647-5821), housed in a 1915-era Lutheran church 1 block north of Main Street on Wilbur's west side. The museum is open Sat 2 to 4 p.m. June through Aug, as well as during Wild Goose Bill Days, named for the town's infamous founder and held the third weekend in May. The museum's collection from the late 1800s and early 1900s includes old farm machinery and an extensive photography collection. It represents the towns of Wilbur, Creston, and Almira.

Wilbur has but one thoroughfare, Main Street, and the eateries there include ***Billy Burger*** (you're unlikely to miss the cartoon sign on a tall post), ***Doxie's Drive-In,*** and the ***Alibi Tavern.*** "You really can't get lost in Wilbur," points out a longtime resident. You could also drive 8 miles east to ***Creston*** and try the ***Corner Cafe*** on Watson Street, the main thoroughfare. You can't get lost in Creston, either.

For another taste of Washington's varied topography, head north from Wilbur on Highway 21 past trees and farms in distant clumps like islands in a sea of grain before the road winds abruptly down through layered coulee cliffs to the Columbia River and the Lake Roosevelt National Recreation Area. If you're traveling RV-style, plan to spend at least one night at ***Keller Ferry*** at the splendid ***River Rue RV Campground*** (509-647-2647; riverrue.com). Folks will find full hookups, clean restrooms, and a full-service deli here.

Two companies rent houseboats on the lake: *Lake Roosevelt Adventures* (800-816-2431; lakerooseveltadventures.com) at Seven Bays Marina, and the *Lake Roosevelt Houseboat Vacations* (800-635-7585; lakeroosevelt .com). The boats are 35 to 64 feet in length, and the larger crafts can sleep up to 13 people. For information and current rates, contact the companies directly. This is a popular Coulee Country vacation option; reservations are accepted well in advance. You could also bring your own canoe or kayak to reach isolated campsites along Lake Roosevelt's pristine shoreline. Lake Roosevelt and the *Lake Roosevelt National Recreation Area* extend 151 miles north from Grand Coulee Dam to the scenic Colville National Forest (fs.usda.gov/colville) and to the US–Canadian border into British Columbia. The lake offers 630 miles of shoreline and year-round fishing for kokanee, walleye, large- and smallmouth bass, rainbow trout, perch, crappie, and sturgeon. Head north on Highway 25 into the northern section of the recreation area that borders the Colville National Forest to find some of the most scenic lakeside campgrounds. For information and maps, contact the National Park Service headquarters for the Lake Roosevelt National Recreation Area (509-633-9441; nps.gov/laro) in the town of Coulee Dam or the district park service office and visitor center in Kettle Falls (509-738-2300).

The *Keller Ferry* offers a free 10-minute crossing with runs every 15 minutes between 6 a.m. and midnight. We're talking a very small ferry here; yours may be the only car on the small deck, which can hold up to 12 cars. The river is often so placid you can see the dry sage-covered cliffs and hills reflected in the water. From the landing on the north side, you can turn left on Swawilla Basin Road to Grand Coulee Dam or continue north on scenic Highway 21 up the Sanpoil River to the old mining town of Republic.

thegehrke windmills

Erected in North Dam Park overlooking Banks Lake and near the city of Grand Coulee, more than 650 windmills have been built by local resident Emil Gehrke. He fashioned the folk art treasures from old cast-off iron parts and painted them in bright colors. Take a camera for good shots of you and the kids and the fanciful windmills.

The 20-mile Swawilla Basin Road west toward Grand Coulee Dam is a hilly one, surrounded by ponderosa pine, wild roses, purple lupine, and woolly mullein, with occasional old barns and glacial erratic along the way. *Grand Coulee Dam* is located 3 miles north of the junction of Highways 155 and 174.

Stop by the Grand Coulee Dam Interpretive Center (509-633-9265; grandcouleedam.org) across the bridge to learn the story of one of the world's largest concrete structures, celebrated in Woody Guthrie's famous song "Roll on, Columbia," and the largest component of the Pacific Northwest's extensive hydroelectric system. Exhibits explain the dam's history and engineering. Inquire about tours. The 40-minute laser light show of animated graphics projected on the dam's spillway runs every night Memorial Day weekend through Sept.

Or enjoy the extensive **Community Trail** that connects all four towns (West and East Coulee Dam, Grand Coulee, and Electric City) and offers exercise and spectacular views. The **Down River Trail,** a 6.5-mile hiking, biking, wheelchair-accessible path, follows the Columbia River north from the dam. With gentle grades and landscaped rest stops, these trails offer relaxing strolls.

For an overnight option that offers expansive views of Grand Coulee Dam, including its grand evening laser light show, call **Columbia River Inn** (10 Lincoln Ave., in Coulee Dam; 800-633-6421; columbiariverinn.com). For information on other lodging, contact the Grand Coulee Dam Area Chamber of Commerce (grandcouleedam.org).

Highway 155 follows the eastern shore of Banks Lake back to Coulee City. It is preferable to drive south on this road so that you can easily pull over at viewpoints and appreciate the awesome geology and the varied wildlife.

Grand Coulee Dam

One of the most popular tourist attractions in Washington and one of the most impressive feats of engineering in the country, the Grand Coulee Dam attracts superlatives, comparisons, and illustrative examples to convey its sheer magnitude. Here are a few:

- The dam is the largest concrete dam in North America with enough concrete to build a standard 6-foot-wide sidewalk around the world at the equator. Twice.

- The dam is 500 feet wide at its base, 5,223 feet long, and stands 550 feet above bedrock—5 feet shorter than the Washington Monument.

- It is the country's largest hydroelectric producer and the world's third-largest, generating 6,494,000 kilowatts in a single instant—more power than a million locomotives.

- Each of the six conventional pumps in Grand Coulee's Pump-Generator Plant is powered by a 65,000-horsepower motor that can pump 1,605 cubic feet of water per second, or 720,374 gallons per minute. In addition, six pump-generators, each having a 67,500- or 70,000-horsepower rating, can pump 1,948 cubic feet of water per second. One of these 12 units can fill the water needs of a city the size of Chicago.

Steamboat Rock, a former island in an ancient riverbed, rises like a solidified wave from the lake's north end. Picturesque *Northrup Canyon Trail* begins at the end of a half-mile road across the highway from the rest stop near Steamboat Rock's north end. This moderately difficult trail stretches from a sheltered canyon, through pine forests, and up a steep path to Northrup Lake atop the gorge. You'll see signs of pioneers having preceded you and perhaps spot eagles soaring overhead.

Steamboat Rock State Park (509-633-1304; parks.wa.gov) offers campsites with full hookups and day-use facilities on the shore of Banks Lake just south of Grand Coulee and Electric City. Reservations are recommended because this is one of the state's more popular campgrounds (888-226-7688; parks.wa.gov/reservations). A hiking trail to the summit of the butte offers excellent views. Bring water for everyone in your group, and wear good walking shoes. Keep your distance from the edge of the cliff since basalt breaks easily; rattlesnakes in the area aren't considered particularly aggressive or lethal but a bite is still painful and dangerous. On scenic Banks Lake near Electric City, find beach and picnic areas, year-round fishing, immaculate grounds, cozy cabins, large villas, and RV spaces with hookups at *Sunbanks Lake Resort* (509-633-3786; sunbanksresort.com).

The town of *Creston,* east of Wilbur on US 2, begins and ends in wheat fields near the crest of the Columbia Plateau. Take the left fork 2 miles east of Creston to follow the Miles Creston Road to *Seven Bays* and *Fort Spokane.* The route zigzags through a narrow, wooded valley back to rolling wheat fields before it descends into pine forests near Lake Roosevelt and the Lake Roosevelt National Recreation Area.

You can also visit and camp at nearby Lake Roosevelt National Recreation Area's (509-633-3830; nps.gov/laro) *Fort Spokane* and *Fort Spokane Campground* (509-754-7800). The campground has 67 sites, all under the national reservation system (877-444-6777; recreation.gov). Built in 1880 after the wars against Native Americans ceased, Fort Spokane was designed to maintain a truce between settlers and seminomadic tribes. Park volunteers and staff show what life was like back then through living-history programs, call the park for dates and hours. The visitor center is located in the former guardhouse, one of the original fort buildings. An interpretive trail leads through the grounds, and the camping and RV sites are rimmed by forest-covered hills.

Continue north on scenic Highway 25 to *Kettle Falls,* about 40 miles south of the Canadian border, to reach the scenic *Colville National Forest* area (509-738-7700; fs.usda.gov/colville) and the far north section of Lake Roosevelt. Houseboat vacations are a strong draw in the northern lake area. Contact *Lake Roosevelt Houseboat Vacations* in Kettle Falls (800-635-7585; lakeroosevelt

The Colville Confederated Tribes

Named for an Englishman and Hudson's Bay Company governor who was in the rum and molasses business and who never set foot in America, the Colville Confederated Tribes is made up of 12 different bands: Chelan, Entiat, Arrow Lakes, Nez Percé (from Northeast Oregon), Methow, Moses-Columbia, Nespelem, Palus, Sanpoil, Colville, Okanogan, and Wenatchi. Prior to the 1820s these separate nomadic bands fished, hunted, and traded furs and goods with each other in the area of Kettle Falls before European settlers and business interests established the Fort Colville trading post. From 1820, a Hudson's Bay Company trading post was established at Kettle Falls. The Indians traded the lush pelts and hides of beaver, brown and black bear, grizzly, muskrat, fisher, fox, lynx, martin, mink, otter, raccoon, wolverine, badger, and wolf at the post.

St. Paul's Mission near Kettle Falls includes the original site of Fort Colville and a rustic log missionary church. In 1872 the Colville Indian Reservation was formed; today it contains about 1.4 million acres. Travelers are invited to visit the tribal headquarters located near Nespelem about 17 miles north of Grand Coulee Dam. Here you can learn about the enterprises owned and operated by the tribes, including a timber and wood products operation; three stores; a fish hatchery that provides fish for the lakes and streams in the region; and a casino. To enjoy fishing on the reservation, contact the *Tribal Fish and Wildlife Department* in Nespelem (509-634-2110). For a historical look, visit the *Colville Tribal Museum* (512 Mead Way; 509-633-0751), which is open daily 8:30 a.m. to 5 p.m. Call ahead to arrange a tour.

.com) to explore the world of luxurious 62- and 64-foot-long houseboats, many of which have hot tubs on the top deck. The houseboats accommodate up to 13 people and contain full kitchen facilities, baths, common areas, sleeping areas, and outside and topside decks. Bring your own bedding, bath linens, food, and beverages. Cruise the upper section of the lake and pull into a secluded cove and enjoy. Houseboats are rented by the week, midweek, or weekends.

From Highway 25 you can head south, away from the Lake Roosevelt National Recreation Area, and plunge back into rolling grain country on the way to *Davenport.* This large agricultural town 33 miles west of Spokane is vibrant with farm life, sitting as it does in Lincoln County, which claims to be the second largest wheat-producing county in the world.

The *Davenport City Park,* south of the highway, surrounds a natural spring where huge cottonwoods have grown for centuries. The sweet water made this an important campsite for native tribes and, in the late 19th century, for settlers and miners traveling along the White Bluffs Road. It is a pleasant spot for a picnic, with playground equipment, tables, and shade.

Nearby, at 7th and Merriem, is the **Lincoln County Historical Museum and Visitor Information Center** (509-725-6711), chock-full of items and images collected over the past century, including a general store and a blacksmith shop. The museum is open Tues through Sat from 10 a.m. to 4 p.m., May 1 to Sept 30, and by appointment the rest of the year. Davenport has motels, or consider the **Morgan Street B&B** (1001 Morgan St.; 509-725-2079), a multi-roof home built in 1896.

The rolling landscape continues east along US 2. At the town of Reardan, continue to Spokane or turn north toward Colville on Highway 231 for a scenic 70-mile drive up Spring Creek Canyon. Along this road is a scattering of old farms, many of which still use windmills to pump water for irrigation. By the time you reach the Spokane River at Long Lake Dam, the wheat fields and farms have given way to ponderosa pine forests and meadows.

Continue on Highway 231 as the road curves west through Springdale. Nine miles north at the town of Valley, turn left on a 3-mile spur road to reach **Waitts Lake,** a spring-fed lake surrounded by wetlands and pine forests. Farms and fields dot its western shore, summer cabins and resorts hug the northeast shore, and public fishing spots offer recreation at the south end. The resorts are informal, catering to local families as well as visitors. **Silver Beach Resort** (3323 Waitts Lake Rd., Valley; 509-937-2811; silverbeachresort.net) is open Apr 15 through Oct 15 and offers travelers 6 cabins, a campground, a general store, boat rentals, swimming and picnic sites, and a pleasant restaurant with a patio overlooking the lake.

Rivers, Lakes & Pine Forests

Spokane, the largest city in the inland Northwest, started along the Spokane River near an ancient Indian campsite where members of the Spokanee tribe gathered for centuries to fish at the rapids. Although Spokane has grown into a major urban center, it retains much of its frontier identity. You'll see plenty of cowboy hats and pickup trucks even in downtown, and you don't have to go far past the city's suburban developments to find ranches and farms.

The Spokane River is still a dominant feature in the city. The **Spokane River Centennial Trail,** which follows the river, offers an ideal path for walking, bicycling, running, or skating (spokanecentennialtrail.org). The Washington portion of the Centennial Trail runs 37 miles—22 from the Idaho border to Spokane's **Riverfront Park** in the center of downtown, where you can see the churning rapids where the tribe fished for salmon. Nearby you'll find espresso and hot dog stands as well as many pleasant eateries.

The recently renovated **Northwest Museum of Arts and Culture** and 1898 **Campbell House,** located in the city's historic Browne's Addition (2316 W. 1st Ave.; 509-456-3931; northwestmuseum.org), display the region's Native American and pioneer past and current culture. The 30-room English Tudor-revival mansion showcases the opulent lifestyle of one of the region's mining barons. The museum is open 10 a.m. to 5 p.m. Tues through Sun, and there are midday tours of the Campbell House. Call ahead to confirm the times.

Consider staying at the **E.J. Roberts Mansion** (1923 W. 1st Ave.; 509-456-8839; ejrobertsmansion.com), which involves sharing an 1889 Queen Anne–style mansion that has been restored with the Roberts descendants' memorabilia, china, gowns, pictures, and other items for the public to view on tour. It has been featured in *Victorian Homes* magazine and on HGTV's *If Walls Could Talk.*

At the **Marianna Stoltz House Bed & Breakfast** (427 E. Indiana Ave.; 509-483-4316; mariannastoltzhouse.com), in a shaded residential neighborhood, innkeeper Phyllis Maguire will offer visitors 4 comfortable guest rooms on the second floor of her large, 1908 Craftsman-style home. The living room, dining room, and parlor come with leaded-glass windows, high ceilings, and fine woodwork of polished fir. Antique light fixtures and fringed lampshades mix well with the other period furnishings. The inn is just 5 blocks from **Gonzaga University** (502 E. Boone Ave.), where the **Bing Crosby Collection,** or the Crosbyana Room (gonzaga.edu), located in Crosby Student Center and open to the public, is filled with photographs, letters, musical memorabilia, and even an Oscar from the crooner's life. Crosby lived in Spokane as a boy.

In the early 1900s **Corbin Park,** then the regional fairgrounds, housed a half-mile racing track, and the Gentlemen's Riding Club was soon established nearby. Harness racing was a popular sport, with many prominent gentlemen of Spokane and their ladies attending regularly. Enjoy the park and its shady walking paths that pass by many vintage homes built in the early 1900s.

honorthyfather

Father's Day was "invented" in Spokane in 1910 by Sonora Smart Dodd. She wanted a special day to honor her father, William Smart, a Civil War veteran who had raised her and her five brothers after his wife's early death. The new Downtown Spokane historic walk brochure pinpoints the church where Sonora Smart Dodd heard the sermon that inspired her to create Father's Day. She contacted the local YMCA and the Spokane Ministerial Association, who persuaded the city government to set aside the third Sunday in June to "honor thy father." Father's Day was signed into national law by President Richard Nixon in 1972.

Good eateries abound in the Spokane area. In the downtown and near Riverfront Park check out the **Onion** (302 W. Riverside; 509-747-3852; theonion .biz) for pastas, pizzas, chicken, gourmet salads, and a variety of hamburgers; **Rock City Italian Grill** (808 W. Main; 509-455-4400; rockcitygrill.com) inside River Park Square for serious Italian food lovers; and **Steam Plant Grill and Brew Pub** (159 S. Lincoln St.; 509-777-3900; steamplantspokane.com) in historic Steam Plant Square Near Manito Park. **Lindaman's Gourmet Bistro** (1235 S. Grand Blvd.; 509-838-3000; lindamans.com) shouldn't be missed for freshly made entrees, great salads and sandwiches, and tempting desserts (if possible take a picnic along to the park).

Whether or not you're staying the night at the grand **Davenport Hotel** downtown (10 S. Post St.; 509-455-8888; davenporthotelcollection.com), try the restaurant on the ground floor. **Table 13** (333 W. Spokane Falls Blvd.; 509-598-4300) bills itself as a whiskey bar with small plates and a great wine selection. Nearby, **Zona Blanca** (154 S. Madison St.; 509-443-5427; limefishsalt.com) serves up great Baja cuisine, like ceviche and tacos. Artisan bread, pastries, and other baked goods are top notch at **The Grain Shed** (1026 E. Newark Ave.; 509-241-3853; thegrainshed.coop).

Craft beverages are gaining ground in the Inland Northwest, thanks in part to places like **Liberty Ciderworks** (164 S. Washington St.; 509-321-1893; libertycider.com); **Hierophant Meadery** (16602 N. Day Mt. Spokane Rd.; 509-294-0134; hierophantmeadery.com); and **Bellweather Brewing** (2019 N. Monroe St.; 509-328-0428; bellweatherbrewing.net).

To get acquainted with the natural history of the area, go hiking at **Dishman Hills Natural Area** (509-477-4730; dhnaa.org), a 530-acre sanctuary just outside Spokane with an easy trail system with short walks under 1 mile in the southeast hills. Check out additional outings in the Spokane area through the **Inland Northwest Trails Coalition** (inlandnorthwesttrails.org) for information on mountain biking, hiking, and road biking. Take a walk in the splendid **John A. Finch Arboretum** (3404 W. Woodland Blvd.; 509-624-4832), part of Spokane City Parks, with its stands of rhododendrons, azaleas, and lilacs. About two-thirds of a mile-long, the natural area covers 65 acres along the banks of Garden Springs Creek west of downtown Spokane.

One of the best outdoor experiences is to visit **Manito Park Gardens,** South Grand at 18th Avenue (509-625-6200; manitopark.org), surrounded by historic homes and offering an extensively diverse horticultural display. Start your tour at Rose Hill, situated on a slope that overlooks the other garden sections. Formal beds of about 1,500 roses represent more than 150 varieties. Walk down to the Joel E. Ferris Perennial Garden, a 3-acre oasis of lawns and large perennial beds. Next visit the splendid 3-acre Duncan Garden, just opposite Gaiser Conservatory, which houses collections of begonias, fuchsias, and tropical plantings in a European Renaissance style. Follow a meandering path beyond the Lilac Garden to find the secluded *Nishinomiya Tsutakawa Japanese Garden.* The graceful curved bridge over the reflecting pond, called a ceremony bridge, is borrowed from the Asian tradition. A small waterfall flows from the rising sun toward the setting sun; the three vertical stones in the central pond suggest cranes or ships at sea.

Another Spokane garden is the *Moore-Turner Historical Garden* adjacent to the *Corbin Art Center* (509-625-6677) in *Pioneer Park* at 7th and Stevens Streets. Restored to their 1911 lushness, the gardens offer examples of private residential landscapes that were adapted to the country garden look of the Arts & Crafts style. For more information on area activities, contact the Spokane Area Visitor Information Center at 201 W. Main Ave. (888-776-5263; visitspokane.com).

Before heading north from Spokane, gas up and fill your picnic cooler. Take US 2 north or first detour onto US 395 and visit the *Fire Lookout*

TOP ANNUAL EVENTS
IN NORTHEAST WASHINGTON

MAY

Laser Light Show on the Grand Coulee Dam
Through Sept
(800) 268-5332
grandcouleedam.org

Lilac Festival
Spokane
(509) 535-4554
spokanelilacfestival.org

JUNE

Colville Panorama Rodeo
Colville
(509) 684-5973
colvillepanoramarodeo.com

Curlew Barrel Derby
Curlew
(509) 779-4742
curlewcivicclub.org

JULY

Pioneer Days
Davenport
(509) 725-6711
davenportpioneerdays.org

AUGUST

Pend Oreille Poker Paddle
Newport
(509) 447-5812
newportareachamber.com

DECEMBER

Holiday Lights
Grand Coulee area
(800) 268-5332
grandcouleedam.org

Museum, 123 W. Westview, 7 miles north of downtown Spokane. It's open only by appointment (509-466-9171; firelookouts.com) Mar to Nov. Inspect a replica of the type of lookout used to house volunteers in the high mountain areas during summer and fall fire seasons. Continue north to the community of *Deer Park* to visit the *North Spokane Farm Museum* (509-466-2744; north spokanefarmmuseum.com), which has a collection of vintage farm machinery and household items dating from the 1850s to the 1950s, mostly in the 5,000-square-foot Red Shed. It's open Apr 1 through Oct 15, 9 a.m. to 4 p.m. daily, and otherwise by appointment.

From Deer Park head east a few miles to US 2 and north on this route through lush farmlands to the gentle Pend Oreille (pond-er-RAY) River Valley. On the banks of the Pend Oreille River is the town of *Newport,* about 60 miles south of the Canadian border, and its Idaho neighbor, Oldtown. As you enter Newport from the southwest, you'll see Centennial Plaza to your right with its huge steam-engine wheel. The *Pend Oreille County Museum* (509-447-5388; pocmuseum.org) is in the 1908 brick I&WN Railroad depot, but there are outbuildings that create a 2-block-long "village" with a settler's cabin, three log cabins, and a one-room schoolhouse. It is open daily from 10 a.m. to 4 p.m. May through mid-Oct. Located nearby, is *Owen's Grocery & Deli* (337 S. Washington St.; 509-447-3525), a great spot for snacks, espresso, and a cool treat at the old-fashioned soda fountain.

The *Newport-Oldtown Visitor Center* (509-447-5812; newportareachamber.com) is right behind the 16-foot Big Wheel that powered the Diamond Match Lumber Mill. It is open 10 a.m. to 4 p.m. weekdays and 10 a.m. to 2 p.m. on summer Sat. Newport's *Centennial Plaza* has a 3-level drinking fountain "serving man, beast, and dog" since 1911. Across the street is Newport's oldest building, *Kelly's Bar & Grill* (324 W. 4th St.; 509-447-3267), a watering hole for miners, loggers, settlers, railway workers, visitors, and townsfolk since 1894. The tavern's impressive lead-glass bar was shipped around Cape Horn to San Francisco and then carried by wagon train to Newport.

Lodging options include motels as well as the *Walden House Inn* (631 N. Warren Ave.; 509-447-5771; thewaldenhouse.com) and the luxurious *Inn at the Lake* (581 S. Shore Diamond Lake Rd.; 509-447-5772; innatthelake.com). The Italian-style villa, built in 1993, offers water views, and the largest suite has a four-poster king-size bed and a whirlpool tub.

You can travel northwest on either side of the Pend Oreille River, but Le Clerc Road on the east bank is quieter and more scenic. Two and a half miles north from the Newport/Oldtown bridge, visit an ancient Indian campsite at *Pioneer Park.* Recent archaeological studies have uncovered artifacts, earth ovens, and house pits that indicate use by the Kalispel Tribe for at least 800 years and by prehistoric hunter-gatherers for possibly 2,000 to 4,000 years. The park offers forested camping, picnic spots, and views of herons and waterfowl in nearby wetlands and on river islands. As you continue north, watch for osprey that catch fish by diving into the water. They build large nests on river pilings and snags.

A few miles north of the Usk bridge (named by a Welsh immigrant after his hometown) on Le Clerc Road, keep an eye out for a herd of buffalo in pastures by the river on the **Kalispel Indian Reservation,** the smallest reservation in Washington. The Kalispel people once numbered more than a thousand; now in the hundreds, the tribe has consolidated its small holdings and developed community buildings, a bison herd raised for meat, and an aluminum plant in Cusick.

At the **Manresa Grotto** on the Kalispel Reservation, a tribal holy site located a few miles north and on the east side of the river near Usk, take a short climb up a winding pathway and through boulders to the dome-shaped grotto, theoretically formed by the waves of an ancient glacial lake. Rows of flat stone pews sit before an altar of mortared rock, a site of religious ceremonies for more than a century. The view is enchanting—the peaceful river valley surrounded by forested hills, all framed by the gray stone arch of the grotto entrance. The grotto's name was provided by a missionary priest who named it after a famous Spanish cave.

Le Clerc Road ends across the bridge from the town of **Ione,** once the site of the most successful lumber mill in northeast Washington. From the Old Railroad Depot, built in 1909, take in breathtaking scenery on the historic **North Pend Oreille Lion's Club Train Ride** from Ione to Metaline Falls and back. Ninety-minute rides through forests, two tunnels, and over the Box Canyon trestle high above the Pend Oreille River are scheduled during selected summer and fall weekends. Call (844) 724-5743 (lionstrainrides.com) for information and reservations, which are a good idea due to the limited schedule.

For more scenery, continue northeast on Sullivan Lake Road on the east side of the Pend Oreille River. **Sullivan Lake,** created by a dam in 1910 to run the cement plant at Metaline Falls, is situated at the foot of snowcapped peaks. There are forested campsites at Noisy Creek at the lake's south end and near Colville National Forest's Sullivan Lake Ranger District office at 12641 Sullivan Lake Rd. (509-446-7500) at the north end. The 4.2-mile **Lakeshore Trail** connects the two campgrounds and offers great views, especially during autumn, as well as lakeshore access. The **Mill Pond Historic Site,** 2 miles northwest of Sullivan Lake, includes a barrier-free interpretive trail from the western edge of Mill Pond, a small lake created in 1910. The path follows a wooden flume that once ran between Sullivan Lake and Metaline Falls.

Continue west on Sullivan Lake Road to reach **Metaline Falls,** a small town nestled on the east bank of the Pend Oreille River that has attracted a lively artist community that has been voted one of the "100 Best Small Art Towns in America." The town's block-long main street (5th Avenue) ends at the city park and visitor center, a brightly painted railway car above terraced flower beds. To the left of the park is the old **Washington Hotel** (225 E. 5th Ave.). Built in 1910, the hotel was the centerpiece of a bustling turn-of-the-20th-century mining town. "It was never an elegant hotel. It was a working man's hotel," said owner Lee McGowan, Metaline Falls artist and former mayor. Nearby, you can meet the locals over breakfast, lunch, or dinner at **Cathy's Cafe** (221 E. 5th Ave.; 509-446-2447).

The building that is now a performing arts center, the **Cutter Theater** (302 Park St.; 509-446-4108; cuttertheatre.com) was constructed early in the century as a school and named for talented Spokane architect Kirtland Cutter. Browse the permanent history and traveling art exhibits. A mile away is the town of Metaline, started during a gold strike and named for the many metals found in the area.

For a spectacular view, follow Highway 31 north about 12 miles, then turn left on the 2-mile access road to **Boundary Vista House** with a platform suspended directly over the Boundary Dam for the best views of the dam, roaring river, and valley. Cross back over the river west of Metaline Falls and take the Boundary Road turnoff to Boundary Dam and Gardner Cave. Along the way, try to spot beaver dams in the wetlands next to this scenic woodland road.

Boundary Road divides after about 10 miles. Take the left fork to reach the 1,055-foot-long **Gardner Cave** at Crawford State Park (May through Sept: 509-446-4065; other times: 509-238-4258). The cave's limestone walls were formed from the bodies of ancient sea creatures that settled into ooze on the floor of an ancient ocean 500 million years ago. Groundwater seepage cut away the stone over the past 70 million years, creating the passage with its fantastic stalagmites and stalactites. Visitors must be accompanied by a ranger to enter the cave. Thirty-minute tours are conducted Thurs through Mon from Memorial Day through Labor Day. The cave is always cool (40 degrees) and lighted, but bring a flashlight as well; cameras with flashes are okay.

Northern Ranches & Forests

Three miles south of Ione, Highway 20 turns west from the riverbank and heads over the Selkirk Mountains. As you drive through the small community of **Tiger,** stop at the **Tiger Historical Center/Museum** (509-442-4656). The original store and post office were constructed in 1912 and served the community until 1975, when the post office was moved to Cusick. The Tiger Store was restored in 1999 and converted to a visitor center, museum, and gateway to the *North Pend Oreille Scenic Byway* and *International Selkirk Loop* (selkirkloop.org). It also has a gift shop carrying creations of local artists. The center is open 10 a.m. to 5 p.m. Thurs to Mon from Memorial Day through Sept and the first three weekends in October. They have a 24-hour restroom.

The road climbs and descends through evergreen forests and past a chain of glacial lakes cradled between the peaks. Among the biggest trees are Douglas fir, spruce, grand fir, and tamarack (aka mountain larch), all giant conifers. The aspen, birch, and tamarack turn vibrant colors of yellow, orange, and lime green in late September and October. The highway follows the Little Pend Oreille River through the Colville National Forest and past the *Little Pend Oreille National Wildlife Refuge* (fws.gov/littlependoreille). Leo, Thomas, Gillette, and Twin Lakes have campsites, reservable through the national system (877-444-6777; reserveamerica.com). The *Springboard Trail* from Gillette Campground offers an easy 2.4-mile loop with interpretive highlights on the area's history and ecology as well as a platform with a view of the lakes.

The pine forest begins to thin as you move west on Highway 20 and descend into the pastoral Colville River Valley. *Colville* is a large, bustling town at the junction of Highway 20 and US 395. In town follow signs from the highway (5th Street) leading 2 blocks uphill on Wynne Street to reach the *Keller Heritage Center* and *Stevens County Historical Museum* (509-684-5968; stevenscountyhistoricalsociety.org). The museum is open 10 a.m. to 4 p.m. Mon through Thurs, and 1 to 4 p.m. Fri through Sun from May to Sept. Call for an appointment in the off-season. A short trail leads up from the museum to the *Graves Mountain Fire Lookout,* moved from its original location to the top of a small hill. Enjoy a panoramic view of the valley, town, and mountains. The 1910 *Keller House Museum* tells the area's story in chronological order from geological, Native American, and European perspectives.

If you've worked up an appetite during your travels, several pleasant restaurants are in Colville. Try *Ronnie D's Drive-In* (505 N. Lincoln; 509-684-2642; ronnieds.com) for good burgers and ice cream.

For another adventure, drive about 45 miles north of Colville into the *Colville National Forest,* past Aladdin, Spirit, Northport, and Deep Lake, bringing you within 7 miles of the Canadian border surrounded by classic scenery and hiking opportunities.

The original site of *Kettle Falls,* northwest of Colville, is believed to be one of the oldest continuously occupied spots in the Northwest. As long as 9,000 years ago, an ancient people fished the steep falls. Over the centuries

Indians established permanent communities near the falls that existed until European settlement eroded traditional lifestyles. The falls and historic sites are now submerged under Lake Roosevelt. During the early spring drawdown in March or April, remnants of flooded islands and historic towns like Old Marcus (located about 5 miles north on Highway 25) are revealed.

You can learn more about the "People of the Falls" at the impressive *Kettle Falls Historical Center* (1188 St. Paul's Mission Rd.; 509-738-6964) on a spur road north of Highway 20 and 3 miles west of Kettle Falls, just before the bridge over Lake Roosevelt. The center features murals and models for each season that tell the ancient story of tribal life near the falls.

Family owned farms and fruit orchards in the area offer berries, cherries, apricots, peaches, pears, apples, nectarines, and plums in season from June through Sept. Look for signs along nearby Peachcrest Road. Contact Kettle Falls Area Chamber of Commerce (509-738-2300; kfchamber.org) for an orchard directory and map of fruit-picking spots.

The annual *Garlic Faire* at *China Bend Winery,* about 28 miles north of Kettle Falls (3751 Vineyard Way; 800-700-6123; chinabend.com), occurs each August. From roasted garlic and garlic corn to garlic soup and pizza, garlic lovers indulge in a festive day of tasting and buying garlic products. The winery produces delicious table and dessert wines that don't contain sulfites. China Bend also offers a bed-and-breakfast for one party at a time.

If you are traveling in winter when Lake Roosevelt is at its fullest, the best bald eagle viewing area is along Highway 25. Take the turnoff south before Kettle Falls Bridge and head toward the Gifford ferry. The concentration of eagles reaches a peak in mid-February, when they're perched on top of gnarled snags and rocky outcroppings while on the lookout for fish.

Take the toll-free state ferry to *Inchelium.* For a quiet retreat on Twin Lakes try *Log Cabin Resort* (509-722-3543; hartmanslogcabin.com) for cozy cabins and a homey family-style restaurant. After crossing the Kettle River Range and intersecting with Highway 21, head north along the picturesque Sanpoil River for about 30 miles to the community of Republic. You can also reach *Republic* from Kettle Falls by continuing west on Highway 20, the *Sherman Pass Scenic Byway,* winding up and over 5,575-foot Sherman Pass. The larches along this route are especially vibrant come autumn.

If you've ever hankered for wide-open spaces, Western hospitality, and delicious family-style meals, try a dude ranch, in this case the 1,600-acre *K-Diamond-K Guest Ranch* (15661 Hwy. 21 S.; 509-775-3511; kdiamondk .com), 5 minutes south of Republic. A new 16-room guest lodge opened in 2007 that's suited to families and retreat-seekers. Activities include horseback riding, mountain biking, fishing, wildlife watching, stargazing, hunting, winter snowmobiling, cross-country skiing, archery, trap shooting, and, in season, riding along on a cattle drive.

A loop around **Curlew Lake** to the north of Republic makes a pleasant bike ride or drive. The nearly 5-mile-long lake, named after the bird, is surrounded by mountains and rolling hills. **Curlew Lake State Park** (509-775-3592; parks .wa.gov) offers a swimming area, boat launches, and campsites. Several small resorts are scattered along the lakeshore. **Fisherman's Cove Resort,** 11 miles north of Republic (15 Fisherman's Cove Rd.; 509-775-3641; fishermanscove.us) welcomes families and offers rustic cabins in a quiet, lakeside setting. **Tiffany's Resort** (58 Tiffany Rd.; 509-775-3152; tiffanysresort.com) on the opposite shore has been in business since 1939 and has comparable amenities.

The Kettle River History Club's **Car and Truck Museum** (17812 Hwy. 21; 509-779-4648) between the towns of Malo and **Curlew.** This is an old-car aficionado's dream: dozens of carefully preserved and restored cars, including vintage Model T Fords, Buicks, actor Walter Brennan's 1928 Phaeton, the only 1917 Chevrolet Royal Mail Roadster still running, and one of the only three 1920 Howard Cooper fire trucks ever made, all in operating condition. The museum is open from 11 a.m. to 5 p.m. Sat and Sun, from June 28 through Labor Day.

When is a ghost town not a ghost town? When it's Curlew, nestled between dry hills on the east bank of the Kettle River with a population of about 1,600. A popular website lists Curlew and 97 other Washington communities as ghost towns, although many of those designations fly in the face of any number of dictionaries' definitions. Maybe they're semi–ghost towns.

But back to the living . . . Follow signs to the right off Highway 21 into town. Curlew's main street, lined with dark-wood buildings with Western false fronts, overlooks the river through tall cottonwoods. Enter the time warp of the 1903 **Ansorge Hotel Museum** at the corner of River Street and Railroad Avenue (509-779-4742). It's a relic with clothes left in the bureau drawers and rope ladders on the second floor windows; guests are dissuaded from going into furnished rooms. A main town hub is the **Second Time Around Country Store,** (509-779-4808, which also serves as the phone number for the Ferry County Chamber of Commerce. There's good information at the community website of ferrycounty.com.

Tradition says that moonshiners used to drop off barrels of illegal whiskey into the Kettle River in British Columbia and let them float across the border past customs officials. They'd be reclaimed when they reached Curlew. Since 1950 (with the exception of a few years in the 1970s), residents and visitors have placed their bets on the first Sunday in June during **Barrel Derby Days.** A barrel of water is dropped off the Midway Bridge near Ferry, Washington, and the bets reflect what time and day people think the barrel will arrive in front of the Second Time Around store. Proceeds support Curlew's civic hall, built in the 1930s.

The tiny *Tugboats Espresso, Deli, and Grill* (18085 N. Hwy. 21; 509-779-4444) is one of the town's limited dining options.

On your way back south on Highway 21 toward Republic, take the W. Curlew Lake Road turnoff (west) at Curlew Lake's north end for a less-traveled route along the western shore. Klondike Road veers right about a mile south of the lake and then descends past pine trees and houses hugging the steep hillside into Republic.

Clark Avenue, the town's main street, was named for Republic Gold Mining and Milling Company president "Patsy" Clark. While most buildings' false fronts are recent additions to boost the town's already rustic feel, the ca. 1904 *Republic Drug Store* (6 N. Clark Ave.; 509-775-3351) boasts an original storefront with hand-cranked awnings and pressed tin ceiling.

To participate in a paleontology treasure hunt, follow 6th Avenue west to the *Stonerose Interpretive Center* (15 N. Kean St.; 509-775-2295; stone rosefossil.org). The curator and assistants can introduce you to the fascinating world of 50 million years ago, when an ancient lake covered the future site of Republic. Fossil-hunting tours are permitted when the center is open (call for hours). Bring along a hammer and chisel, or rent some there, to use at the dig site north of town. The fossils you discover will be identified for you to take home, or, if you are lucky enough to find a new or rare species, you will be applauded as a paleontology hero, and your fossil will be kept for further study.

For tasty eats in the Republic area, try *Esther's Mexican Restaurant* (90 N. Clark St.; 509-775-2088) for super burritos, shredded beef taco salads, and homebaked pies. For local ales and homemade sodas (but no food), grab a seat in the town's old firehall that's now *Republic Brewing Company* (26 Clark Ave.; 509-775-2700; republicbrew.com). The space is a lively community gathering spot.

Places to Stay in Northeast Washington

COLVILLE/KETTLE FALLS

Beaver Lodge Resort
2430 Hwy. 20 E
(509) 684-5657
beaverlodgeresort.org

China Bend Winery
3751 Vineyard Way
(509) 732-6123
chinabend.com

Lazy Bee Wilderness Retreat
3651 Deep Lake Boundary Rd.
(509) 732-8917

COULEE CITY

Coulee Lodge Resort
33017 Park Lake Rd. NE
(509) 632-5565
couleelodgeresort.com

COULEE DAM

Columbia River Inn
10 Lincoln St.
(800) 633-6421
columbiariverinn.com

ELECTRIC CITY

Sky Deck Motel
138 Miller Ave.
(509) 633-0290
skydeckmotel.com

Sunbanks Lake Resort
S. Hwy. 155
(509) 633-3786
sunbanksresort.com

INCHELIUM

Hartman's Log Cabin Resort
S. Twin Lake
(509) 722-3543
hartmanslogcabin.com

LAKE ROOSEVELT HOUSEBOATS

Lake Roosevelt Adventures
(800) 816-2431
lakerooseveltadventures.com

Lake Roosevelt Houseboat Vacations
(800) 635-7585
lakeroosevelt.com

NEWPORT

Inn at the Lake
581 S. Shore Diamond Lake Rd.
(509) 447-5772
innatthelake.com

INFORMATION CENTERS
& OTHER HELPFUL WEBSITES

Colville
(509) 684-5973
colville.com

Grand Coulee Dam Area
(509) 633-3074 (chamber)
grandcouleedam.org

Kettle Falls Area
(509) 738-2300
kettle-falls.com

Newport Area
(509) 447-5812
newportoldtownchamber.org

Republic Area
(509) 775-3387
republicchamber.org

Spokane Area
(800) 662-0084
visitspokane.com

Walden House Inn
631 N. Warren Ave.
(509) 447-5771
thewaldenhouse.com

REPUBLIC/CURLEW

Fisherman's Cove Resort
15 Fisherman's Cove Rd.
(509) 775-3641
fishermanscove.us

K-Diamond-K Guest Ranch
15661 Hwy. 21 South
(509) 775-3511
kdiamondk.com

Northern Inn
852 S. Clark St.
(509) 775-1068
northern-inn.com

Tiffany's Resort
58 Tiffany Rd.
(509) 775-3152
tiffanysresort.com

Wolfgang's Riverview Inn
2 Valhalla Ln.
(509) 280-3904
wolfgangsriverviewinn.com

SOAP LAKE

Inn at Soap Lake
226 Main Ave. E
(509) 246-0462
soaplakeresort.com/
inn-soap-lake

Notaras Lodge
236 E. Main Ave.
(509) 246-0462
soaplakeresort.com/
notaras-lodge

SPOKANE

Davenport Hotel
10 S. Post St.
(509) 455-8888
davenporthotelcollection
.com

Marianna Stoltz House Bed & Breakfast
427 E. Indiana Ave.
(509) 483-4316
mariannastoltzhouse.com

Red Lion River Inn
700 N. Division
(509) 326-5577
redlion.com

VALLEY

Silver Beach Resort
3323 Waitts Lake Rd.
(509) 937-2811
silverbeachresort.net

Places to Eat in Northeast Washington

COLVILLE/NORTHPORT

Ronnie D's Drive-In
505 N. Lincoln St.
(509) 684-2642
ronnieds.com

COULEE CITY

Banks Lake Brew & Bistro
9701 US-2
(509) 632-5611

DAVENPORT

Edna's Drive In
302 Morgan St.
(509) 725-1071

Tribune Smokehouse
502 Morgan St.
(509) 725-8509
tribunesmokehouse.com

METALINE FALLS

Cathy's Cafe
221 E. 5th Ave.
(509) 446-2447

NEWPORT

Owen's Grocery & Deli
337 Washington St.
(509) 447-3525

REPUBLIC/CURLEW

Esther's Mexican Restaurant
90 N. Clark St.
(509) 775-2088

Republic Brewing Company
26 Clark Ave.
(509) 775-2700
republicbrew.com

Tugboats Espresso, Deli, and Grill
18085 N. Hwy. 21
(509) 779-4444

RITZVILLE

Greenside Cafe
104 E. 10th Ave.
(509) 659-9868

Spike's Deli and Pizza
1611 Smitty's Blvd.
(509) 659-0490

SOAP LAKE

Lakeside Bistro
14 Canna St.
(509) 246-1217

SPOKANE

The Grain Shed
1026 E. Newark Ave.
(509) 241-3853
thegrainshed.coop

Lindaman's Gourmet
Bistro
1235 S. Grand Blvd.
(509) 838-3000
lindamans.com

Onion
302 W. Riverside
(509) 747-3852
theonion.biz

Rock City Italian Grill
808 W. Main St.
(509) 455-4400
rockcitygrill.com

The Shop Coffeehouse
924 S. Perry St.
(509) 534-1647

Steam Plant Grill and
Brew Pub
159 S. Lincoln St.
(509) 777-3900
steamplantspokane.com

Table 13
333 W. Spokane Falls Blvd.
(509) 598-4300

Zona Blanca
154 S. Madison St.
(509) 443-5427
limefishsalt.com

VALLEY

Silver Beach Resort
Restaurant
3323 Waitts Lake Rd.
(509) 937-2811
silverbeachresort.net

WILBUR

Alibi Tavern
4 SW Main St.
(509) 647-2649

Billy Burger
804 NE Main St.
(509) 647-5651

Doxie's Drive-In
523 NW Main St.
(509) 647-5544

Southeast Washington

Southeast Washington is a region of rolling hills and wide blue skies. Much of the terrain is covered with fields of dry-land (unirrigated) wheat that casts a blanket of waving, textured green, then brown. The best way to explore this area is to get off the major highways and drive or bicycle along miles of farm roads that connect small communities. Walking, bicycling, or sitting in a grassy park or meadow, you often will hear the melodious trill of a western meadowlark, catch sight of a soaring hawk, and smell the soil warmed in the sun.

Few corners of this fertile region have been left untouched by human enterprise, although the seasonal crops still depend on natural cycles of snow, rain, and sun. Tens of thousands of acres burst with new green shoots following spring rains or undulate with tall golden grains in the late summer sun. The lives of farm and ranch families are integrated with their land and the seasons. In early spring, huge 8-wheel-drive tractors comb the terrain for planting, pulling 20-foot-wide plows that raise spires of dust. In late summer, giant combines harvest wheat, lentils, barley, and peas. Farmhouses and big old barns nestle in valleys surrounded by tall shade trees planted by previous generations.

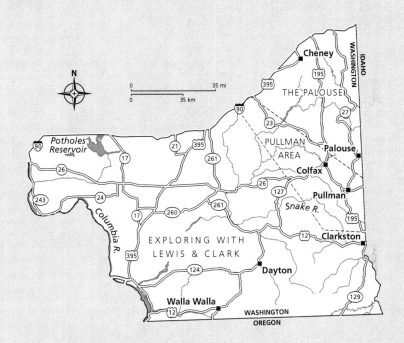

SOUTHEAST WASHINGTON'S TOP HITS

Appaloosa Museum & Heritage Center
Moscow, ID

The Bank Left Gallery and Green Frog Cafe
Palouse

Bishop's U-Pick Orchard
Garfield

Dayton Historic Depot
Dayton

Ferdinand's Ice Cream Shoppe
Washington State University
Pullman

Fort Walla Walla Museum Complex
Walla Walla

Heritage Square
Walla Walla

Palouse Falls
Starbuck

Perkins House
Pullman

Roy Chatters Newspaper and Printing Museum
Palouse

Steptoe Butte
Colfax

Turnbull National Wildlife Refuge
Cheney

Weinhard Hotel
Dayton

Whitman Mission National Historic Site
Walla Walla

The quiet towns of this region, devoted to serving hardworking farm families, also welcome travelers. Walk any main street to see old brick buildings that once housed banks, stores, and fraternal organizations, many now in the process of being renovated for new enterprises such as coffeehouses, bakeries, cafes, and tasting rooms for the many new wineries in the region. Tall grain elevators stand like sentinels next to rail depots. Many abandoned depots have been, or are in the process of being, preserved and are coming to life again as local museums and vibrant community art centers.

Stop at the local cafe (many small towns have only one), where for the price of a cup of coffee and a piece of homemade pie you might hear stories of local history and gossip from fellow patrons eager to swap tales.

The Palouse

Palouse is derived from the French word *pelouse,* meaning "green lawn," an appropriate name for one of the most fertile grain-growing regions in the world. The Appaloosa, a breed of horses distinguished by its spotted coat and gentle disposition, is a descendant of early horses used by the native people of the Palouse.

Although most of this region is now farmed, there are still areas where the original Palouse environment is preserved. Chief of these is the ***Turnbull National Wildlife Refuge*** (S. 26010 Smith Rd.; 509-235-4723; fws.gov/turnbull) south of Spokane near ***Cheney.*** The 16,000-acre refuge includes lakes and marshes that attract a wide variety of wildlife including elk, deer, coyotes, beaver, and muskrat. More than 208 kinds of ducks, geese, and other migratory birds cruise in for rest stops along the ***Pacific Flyway.***

Generations before pioneers arrived, the Spokane tribe cherished this natural garden for its abundant roots and herbs, such as blue camas, wild onion, and kinnickinnick. Early farmers tried to drain these marsh areas but found that the resulting soil was poor. Rescued from development in the 1920s, the area was set aside as a wildlife preserve in 1937. Now visitors to Turnbull can bicycle, walk, or drive on a 5-mile gravel loop auto-tour road to experience the area's original beauty. Signs along the ***Pine Lake Loop Trail*** help acquaint you with the area's background and natural history. A wooden boardwalk over shallow ***Black Horse Lake*** allows close-up viewing.

Heading south from Cheney and the wildlife refuge on Rock Lake Road, watch the landscape change from rocky pine-covered meadows to rolling wheat farms. The terrain changes again around Rock Lake, a quiet expanse of water surrounded by basalt outcroppings. This area, near the Palouse River, was the home of Chief Kamiaken of the Yakama Indian Nation. Along the lake's southeast shore is the ***Milwaukee Road Corridor,*** a railroad line from Chicago to Seattle until 1980 but converted to a public trail. This 100-mile-long trail system, known as the Palouse to Cascades State Park Trail (parks.wa.gov), stretches from Cedar Falls near North Bend on the fringes of Seattle's suburbia east across the Cascade Mountains and to the Columbia River. The popular trail is used by hikers, bicyclists, equestrians, and even wagon trains, and there are many access points.

Appaloosa Horse Museum

For history surrounding the Palouse's namesake horse, head east from Pullman on Highway 270 to the **Appaloosa Museum & Heritage Center** (2720 W. Pullman Rd., Moscow; 208-882-5578, press five; appaloosamuseum.org). Straddling the state line but technically in Moscow, ID, the museum explores the Nez Percé, excellent breeders of horses whose spotted horses became known as Appaloosas. Exhibits include Native American artifacts, the Appaloosa's roots, saddles, Western art, and Western tack and clothing. During the summer, you can see Appaloosas in their fenced pasture. The museum is open 11 a.m. to 3 p.m. Mon through Sat.

After traveling through the rolling hills of the Palouse, head for panoramic views from two towering buttes. *Kamiak Butte County Park,* named for Chief Kamiaken, is a 3,641-foot-tall "island" of pine, fir, and larch surrounded by wheat fields. The butte is 5 miles southwest of the town of Palouse near the Idaho border. The 3.5-mile *Pine Ridge Trail* through the forest takes you on a self-guided nature walk to the top of the butte and back.

The park has 7 campsites, with campfire pits and cooking grills. Picnic tables and 4 shelters with electricity, water, and barbecue make this a great spot for an impromptu outdoor feast. There is also an amphitheater for summer evening programs on local and natural history presented by volunteers. For information contact Whitman County Parks in *Colfax,* (509) 397-6238.

Steptoe Butte, 15 miles north of Colfax, is, at 3,612 feet, one of the highest points in the region and a National Natural Landmark. Drive the road that spirals three times around the butte to the top to enjoy panoramic views of the Palouse's rolling fields and low hills as well as the distant Blue and Bitterroot Mountains. At the base you'll find a pleasant picnic area in an old apple orchard planted by one of the area's early homesteaders. In the 1880s another entrepreneur operated a roadhouse at the bottom of the butte and a hotel at the top, which burned down in 1911.

Oakesdale, a few miles north of Steptoe Butte, is home to *Barron's Flour Mill,* a huge timber-frame structure, which was built in Illinois in 1890 and then moved piece by piece to Oakesdale in 1907, and which still contains the original milling and sifting equipment. The mill was used to produce flour until 1939 and continued as a grain cleaning and storage facility until 1960. You can stop to take a gander at the historic structure by parking off Highway 27 as you leave Oakesdale heading north.

Travel northeast on Highway 27 from Oakesdale to reach the village of *Tekoa,* population 808. Or, travel south on the country highway to *Garfield* (population 611). Garfield's *Riverside Retreat and Inn* offers a homey place to spend a night or two (124 W. Main St.; 208-301-8014; riversideretreat andinn.com).

whataworm

If you happen to find a 3-foot-long pinkish-white wiggler, please don't bait your hook. It could be the rare (but not officially endangered) giant **Palouse earthworm.** They were thought to be confined to what was left of the native prairie's deep soils until 2008, when one was found in the wooded slope above Leavenworth. While the worm has rarely been seen in the last 30 years, four specimens were unearthed in three sightings during 2012.

Bishop's U-Pick Orchard (509-635-1276; bishop-orchard.com), in Garfield at 8th and Adams Streets offers a wealth of apples from September through the end of October. People come from miles around to make fresh juice on Steven Bishop's handmade oak cider presses, patterned after the ones his great-grandfather used when he homesteaded in Garfield. Bring a picnic lunch and make it a real outing.

South of Garfield is the town of *Palouse,* once a bustling commercial center supplying gold-mining and logging camps in Idaho. Despite its size (population 1,045), it has three vehicle bridges and a footbridge across the Palouse River. The town's main street is lined with splendid old brick buildings, many now in the process of being renovated. Palouse's historic district on Main Street is listed on the National Register of Historic Places. One old storefront now houses *Roy Chatters Newspaper and Printing Museum,* a half-block east of Division Street/Almota Road, at 110 E. Main St. In some guide books it's called the Boomerang Museum, probably because the paper founded in the 1882 was called the *Boomerang.* The museum features newspapers from the area as well as an impressive collection of old presses and other printing equipment dating from the late 1800s. It's open 10 a.m. to 1 p.m. on Sat; or call Janet Barstow at (509) 878-1742 for an appointment. Stop in at 110 S. Bridge St. in the 1889 Bank Building in Palouse that houses the *Bank Left Gallery* (509-878-8425; bankleftgallery.com) and a tea-and-chocolate shop behind a colorful front. For a bite, try the *Palouse Caboose Bar and Grill* (110 N. Beach St.; 509-878-1704).

Bagels, Lentils, or Split Pea Soup, Anyone?

Wheat, lentils, and peas are major crops grown in the Palouse region. After harvest they are barged about 200 miles down the Snake River from the Clarkston-Lewiston area to Pasco, passing through the scenic 2,000-foot-deep Snake River Canyon and negotiating through locks at Lower Granite Dam, Little Goose Dam, Lower Monumental Dam, and Ice Harbor Dam. At Pasco the large barges, pushed by fat tugboats and each carrying the equivalent of 134 truckloads, enter the wide Columbia River and travel another 200 miles downriver, passing McNary, John Day, The Dalles, and Bonneville dams and by Maryhill, Hood River, Cascade Locks, Washougal, and Camas and detouring onto the Willamette River at Portland-Vancouver. Here the wheat, lentils, and peas are loaded onto huge transport ships at the Port of Portland. These vessels travel another 100 miles downriver on the Columbia River to Astoria and then out onto the Pacific Ocean for journeys to ports far and wide.

Browse at **Open Eye Antiques** (119 E. Main St.; 509-878-1210) for retro and country antiques and collectibles and **Linda's Whimseys** (100 W. Main St.; 509-878-1678) for a splendid selection of Victorian gift items. Then pop into nearby **Dot's Vintage Funk** (130 E. Main St.; 509-595-4459) in the 1888 St. Elmo's Hotel. **Note:** The best days to visit small towns in the Palouse area are Wed through Sat, when most establishments are open.

Pullman

Pullman is the Palouse region's largest city and a bustling mixture of agricultural businesses and student life. **Washington State University** (WSU, affectionately called Wazzu) is this city's Center of the Galaxy. Founded in 1890, WSU emphasizes agricultural sciences. The main number for the university is 509-335-3564. Or contact the Pullman Visitor Information Center (800-365-6948; pullmanchamber.com) for the current sports schedules and information about lodgings, tours of the scenic campus and its historic buildings, and a campus map.

WSU has a splendid **Museum of Anthropology** (509-335-3441; archaeology .wsu.edu) featuring displays on human evolution and the development of language and culture—and on the Northwest's mysterious Sasquatch. The museum is open 9 a.m. to 4 p.m. weekdays during the academic year. Art lovers can enjoy the University's **Museum of Art** (509-335-1910; museum.wsu .edu). The gallery has changing exhibitions featuring past and contemporary international, regional, and student artists working in painting, sculpture, photography, and architecture. The gallery is open 10 a.m. to 4 p.m. Tues through Sat.

Walk of Fame

Although WSU students are often ribbed (particularly by University of Washington students) about attending a small school focused more on agricultural than more (supposedly) cerebral occupations, the Cougars can point to the downtown Pullman Walk of Fame to show the bright minds of their graduates, including Phil (Class of '33) and Neva ('34) Abelson. He helped develop the first nuclear submarine and was longtime editor of *Science* magazine; she codeveloped the Rh blood test that saved the lives of countless babies. Others who have risen to the top of their professions include CBS radio and TV broadcaster Edward R. Murrow ('30), TV sports commentator Keith Jackson ('54), "The Far Side" cartoonist Gary Larson ('72), and Orville Vogel ('39), a wheat breeder whose findings sparked the Green Revolution.

After you've worked up an appetite from museum touring, stop at *Ferdinand's Ice Cream Shoppe* (509-335-2141), a campus ice-cream parlor named after the friendly, flower-sniffing bull from the Disney short *Ferdinand the Bull.* On the walls are quotations by author Munro Leaf and illustrations by Robert Lawson from the classic book about Ferdinand, which has been beloved by generations of children. Ferdinand's sells WSU Creamery's own Cougar brand of high-quality dairy products (such as the award-winning Cougar Cheese), produced on campus.

Although it's a busy college town servicing Washington State University and its thousands of Cougar fans, Pullman offers a variety of pleasant reasons for lingering in your travels to the far southeast corner of the state. Take an invigorating walk in a splendid city park or along a rails-to-trails pathway, stroll in a lovely garden, play a round of golf, put together an impromptu picnic, or stop at a friendly cafe. Another very popular stop at the university is the *Bear Center,* the only research facility in the world that's home to adult grizzly bears.

Reaney Park at 609 Reaney Way is home of the *Reaney Park Summer Concert Series* (509-338-3227) and the *National Lentil Festival* in August. Find outdoor pools, a gazebo, playground area, picnic tables, and barbecue area.

Lawson Gardens, located at Derby Street near Dilke Street, offers 13 acres of formal gardens including a reflecting pool, gazebo, seasonal annuals and perennials, and splendid rose gardens. The *Bill Chipman Palouse Trail,* reclaimed from a former railroad bed near the Pullman-Moscow Highway (Highway 270), offers 8 miles of bicycle- and pedestrian-friendly trails between Pullman and Moscow, Idaho, the home of the University of Idaho.

In downtown Pullman you can find a jolt of java at *Cafe Moro* (100A E. Main St. (509-330-6722), and *Daily Grind Downtown Coffee House* (230 E. Main St.; 509-334-3380). *Caution:* If the notion of enduring pep rallies, marching bands, and being trampled by some 40,000 WSU Cougar sports fans doesn't appeal, plan your trips to the Pullman area on weekends sans football. Also best to avoid Dad's Weekend and Mom's Weekend. Check pullmanchamber .com (800-365-6948) and football-weekends.wsu.edu for current schedules and information.

One option after leaving Pullman is to head northwest on Highway 195 about 15 miles to *Colfax.* The highway runs right through town so keep a lookout on the right for Colfax's most unusual attraction, the 65-foot-tall *Codger Pole,* possibly the world's tallest chainsaw carving and, if not, probably the world's tallest chainsaw carving of faces, or if not that, certainly the world's tallest chainsaw carving of football players. The pole commemorates a grudge

TOP ANNUAL EVENTS
IN SOUTHEAST WASHINGTON

APRIL

Asotin County Fair
Asotin
(509) 243-4101
asotincountyfairandrodeo.org

Dogwood Festival
Lewis-Clark Valley, throughout Apr
(208) 792-2447
lcsc.edu/dogwood

MAY

Dayton Days
Dayton, Memorial Day weekend
(800) 882-6299

JUNE

Slippery Gulch Celebration
Tekoa
(509) 284-3861
slipperygulch.com

JULY

Sweet Onion Festival
Walla Walla
(509) 525-0850
wwvchamber.com
sweetonions.org

AUGUST

National Lentil Festival
Pullman
(800) 365-6948
lentilfest.com

OCTOBER

Autumn Harvest Hullabaloo & Arts and Antiques Fair
Colfax
(509) 397-3712
colfaxhulla.com

Balloon Stampede
Walla Walla
(877) 998-4748
wallawallaballoonstampede.com

Dayton on Tour and Historic Homes Tour
Dayton
(800) 882-6299
historicdayton.com

match in 1988 played between former football players (then in their late 60s) of Colfax and St. John. The Colfax team of elders attained the victory that was snatched from it 50 years earlier. The bundle of five cedar logs has the likeness of 51 players with a generic Old Codger standing on the top.

The Whitman County seat sits along the banks of the Palouse River. Stop to see the splendid Victorian **Perkins House** (623 N. Perkins St.), built by city founder James Perkins, who made his fortune with the region's first sawmill, in 1886. The oldest standing house in Whitman County is listed on the National Register of Historic Places and was once the center of Colfax's society. It is open for tours 10 a.m. to 2 p.m. Mon through Sat, though the staff recommend calling to verify hours, as they're subject to change. An old-fashioned ice-cream social is held at the mansion the last Sunday in June. For current information contact the Colfax Visitor Information Center at (509) 397-3712.

Meet the local folks at *Top Notch Cafe* (210 N. Main St.; 509-397-4569), or just head for a good night's sleep at the *Potting Shed Guesthouse* (911 S. East St.; 509-397-2014; thepottingshedguesthouse.com). On the property of a historic home, this retreat has been a stable, a playhouse, an office, and a mother-in-law residence until it was completely remodeled, complete with flat-panel TV, kitchen, and laundry.

To bed down in the ponderosa pine and farm country near Colfax, call the Gilchrest family at *Union Creek Guest Ranch* (2501 Upper Union Flat Rd.; 509-397-3292) located a few miles southwest via US 195. Guests are welcomed to this 2,200-acre ranch nestled in the hills. The working farm and cattle ranch offers horseback riding and hayrides as well as hunting and fishing opportunities and stalls for your horses. Penny Gilchrest serves a hearty country breakfast of bacon, ham, eggs, and hash browns along with fresh fruit, juices, homemade cinnamon rolls, and, often, her delicious apple crisp tortillas.

Miracle on the Palouse

It could be called a miracle, a deteriorating 1935 dairy barn used until 1953 that was brought back to life by a volunteer-run nonprofit with grants and donations after Steve and Junette Dahmen donated the Uniontown property. The town of 300 residents pulled together and volunteers donated more than 5,200 hours.

Fifty years of pigeon droppings were taken out of the loft; a beam-and-cable system pulled the tilting barn into plumb; an interior support structure was built; and amenities, including an elevator and the hot-water radiant-heat system in the ground floor's concrete slab, were added. Much credit goes to Jennifer Anthony of Fearless Engineering of Missoula, a specialist in log and timber-frame construction.

After giving the barn new physical life, the spirit was added with working artists in 10 small studios as well as a name: *Artisans at the Dahmen Barn* (419 N. Park Way; 509-229-3414; artisanbarn.org). They use their spaces to show their creations; each works there 8 hours a week (Thurs through Sun). An excellent gift shop sells work on consignment from nearly 100 regional artists. The Hayloft Hall is used for dances, exhibits, classes, and concerts.

You won't miss the barn because of the eye-catching wheel fence. Steve Dahmen had a folk-art gate-building project and friends started donating wheels, including those from various machines and an antique baby buggy. Eventually more than 1,000 wheels of up to 60 inches in diameter created the landmark fence line off the main road. The Adopt-a-Wheel program raises money that helps maintain the barn and fence. Select a wheel or have one chosen for you for $25 to $100, based on size.

Another option is to leave Pullman and head south on US 195 toward **Uniontown.** A splendid option in Uniontown is the **Churchyard Inn Bed & Breakfast** (206 Saint Boniface St.; 509-229-3200; churchyardinn.com). Guests find comfy bed-and-breakfast accommodations in the 1905 European Flemish-style parish-turned-convent. The house and its interior were completely renovated in 1995, including the fine hand-detailed woodwork, moldings, doors of red fir, the impressive staircases, 7 bedrooms, and several balconies. The inn is located next to the 1904 **Saint Boniface Catholic Church,** which has an interior beauty worth your time.

Since 1948 the men of Uniontown have made sausage from a secret recipe for the annual **Sausage Feed** on the first Sunday in March.

About 25 minutes southwest of Pullman is the delightful little **Wawawai County Park** with campsites and a small bay on the Snake River. The phrase "wa-wa-wai" means "council grounds" in the native language; three "wa" together essentially means "talk-talk-talk" together. The boat landing on Lower Granite Lake, part of the Snake, is home to the Washington State University crew teams and boathouse; you might catch them training on the water.

From there, follow the road that hugs the Snake all the way to Clarkston.

Exploring with Lewis & Clark

South of Pullman at the confluence of the Snake and Clearwater Rivers, the twin cities of **Clarkston** and, across the Snake River, **Lewiston, Idaho,** have become the embarking point for adventures at Hells Gate State Park, the Nez Percé Reservation, and boat or raft trips through Hells Canyon National Recreation Area, the deepest river gorge in North America. Contact the Lewis Clark Valley Visitor Information Center at 502 Bridge St., Clarkston (509-758-7712; lcvalleychamber.org) or the Hells Canyon Visitor Bureau at 504 Bridge St. (877-774-7248) for information on river trips, bike and walking paths, and lodgings.

Captain William Clark, Meriwether Lewis, and their original Corps of Discovery camped from September 26 to October 7, 1805 at **Canoe Camp,** where the Nez Percé show them how to build wooden canoes. Their camp is about 5 miles west of Orofino, Idaho. Visit the **Lewis and Clark Expedition Timeline,** etched and painted in the pavement at Hells Canyon Resort Marina, 1560 Port Dr. The nearly block-long timeline illustrates key events from the Corps of Discovery's journey across the western half of the US, including canoeing down sections of the nearby Snake River and the Columbia River on their way to the Pacific Ocean. US 12 from Lewiston and Clarkston, west toward **Pomeroy** and **Dayton,** roughly parallels the party's return journey in 1806.

After all this busy history-browsing you may be ready for some vittles. Find tasty homemade pie and cool libations at the old-fashioned soda fountain at **Wasem's Drugstore** (800 6th St.; 509-758-2565; wasems.com); and for water-side dining with great views, call **Rooster's Landing** on the Snake River (1010 Port Way; 509-751-0155; roosterslanding.com).

Heading west on US 12, you may want to stop and explore Pomeroy. Park 1 block over on Columbia Street, where you'll see colorful flower beds planted down the center of the street where the train tracks once ran. Browse along Main Street and poke into inviting shops such as the **Victorian Rose** (741 Main St.; 509-843-1989) with its fine collectibles. Admire the 16-foot-high

From Flour Mill to Bugs Bunny Cartoons

One of the bonuses to traveling off the beaten path is the number and quality of surprises that pop up out in the country. Do you remember the XXX Flour seen in some of the early Bugs Bunny cartoons? That brand was produced in the 1878 **Pataha Flour Mill** in Pomeroy and was the first patented flour, known across the nation for its high protein content. High in gluten, it was often used to make macaroni.

Also known as the Houser Mill, it closed in 1943 when the owners were unable to meet federal regulations. They walked away and left all the milling equipment behind. Jon VanVogt bought the mill in 1998 and, after clearing some of the interior and painting the exterior, opened the building to the public in August 1998 with a Hometown Revival of gospel music.

Most important, the previous owners left the milling equipment. Start in the basement to see the coal-burning furnace and a 6-foot bull wheel and wide leather belts. The first floor has grinders used to process 100,000 bushels of wheat each year, or 80 barrels of flour a day. Now there's also a restaurant.

Bran, used for animal feed, was sacked on the second floor, which still has various milling machines as well as a special events space. The third floor houses a plane sifter, with wooden augers suspended by wooden dowels, and a fan separator, in which the wheat went first. All the floors have huge timbers from the nearby Blue Mountains and tongue-and-groove floors and siding.

At Pataha, there are surprises within surprises. In one small room check out Delbert Niebel's branding iron collection that includes the brands Duck Foot, Goose Egg, Hoof & Nail, One Pipe, and Rocking A. Another room, one of five cribs for wheat, has a large train garden, all lit up. Another room has Neil Keatts's collection of more than 400 antique cameras, including a No. 4 Folding Pocket Kodak Model A 4x5 from about 1915.

The **Pataha Flour Mill & Museum** is at 50 Hutchens Hill Rd., Pomeroy (509-843-3799). Renovation work continues; the restaurant is open for lunch Wed through Sat and dinner on Sat.

ceilings in the 1900 building that houses *Meyers Hardware* (796 Main St.; 509-843-3721) and its eclectic collection of hardware items, gifts, and the Bean Counter espresso bar.

Check out the 1913 *Seeley Building* at 67 7th St., which housed an early vaudeville theater; the historic *Hotel Revere,* recently renovated by Beverly and John Gordon, owners of *Castlemoyle Books* (509-843-5009; castlemoyle .com); and *Garfield County Museum* (708 Columbia St.; 509-843-3925; historic pomeroy.com/museum).

You can also bed down in Pomeroy in a comfy style by checking on guest rooms at *Maggie's Garden B&B* (714 Arlington St.; 509-843-2495; maggies gardenbandb.com). If you're traveling RV-style and want hookups, contact the *Last Resort Store & Blue Mountains KOA* (2005 Tucannon Rd.; 509-843-1556; thelastresortrv.com), about 13 miles southwest of Pomeroy in the *Umatilla National Forest.* The Pomeroy Ranger Station (71 W. Main St.; 509-843-1891) can supply information about camping, hiking, and fishing (including fly fishing) along the Tucannon River.

The town of *Dayton* is another well-preserved historic community. When Lewis and Clark explored the region on their return trip in 1806, what is now Dayton's main street served as a racetrack for American Indian tribes who camped in the area. Although this land was first homesteaded by cattle ranchers in 1859, grain farming took over within a few years. Dayton was also a stage-coach stop between Walla Walla and Lewiston. Logs from the Blue Mountains traveled down to the town mill by an 18-mile flume.

Its one claim to fame for about 70 years was the world's largest asparagus cannery, run by Seneca Foods, which moved its operations to Peru after the 2005 season. For a couple of decades, a farmer would fertilize the huge shape of the iconic *Jolly Green Giant* high on a hillside. The giant got greener and more visible as the season progressed. In the early 1990s, locals decided on a more permanent approach that used white patio blocks along the 300-foot-tall, 40-foot-wide outline, which can be seen about a mile west of Dayton.

To see the 1881 *Dayton Historic Depot* (509-382-2026; daytonhistoric depot.org), the oldest surviving railway station in the state, turn west from Main Street onto Commercial. Call for hours or check with daytonhistoricdepot .org. For information about self-guided historic walking tours and lively local events, contact the Dayton Visitor Information Center at (509) 382-4825 or go to historicdayton.com. Dayton's 1887 Columbia County Courthouse, across from the depot, is the oldest operating courthouse in the state.

The *Purple House B&B* (415 E. Clay St.; 509-382-3159; the-purple-house-bb.business.site), built in 1882 by a pioneer physician and philanthropist, is one of Dayton's finest homes with 4 guest rooms, a guest library, and

Patit Creek Campsite: Camping Lewis and Clark Style

On May 2, 1806, the Lewis and Clark Corps of Discovery camped near Dayton for one night on their return trip home. Eighty life-size metal silhouette sculptures produced and arranged on the site by Dayton artists and community members show the entire party setting up camp. The silhouettes include horses, cooking gear, and even Clark's dog, Seaman. To reach the site, turn off US 12 just northeast of downtown Dayton and onto Patit Road.

a lovely parlor. Just for fun stop by **Dingle's of Dayton** (179 E. Main St.; 509-382-2581). In this old-fashioned general store, you'll find everything from nuts and bolts, nails and screws, and plumbing supplies to teddy bears, coloring books, crystal glassware, and fishing rods. "If you can't find it at Dingle's, you don't need it," is the store motto.

If exploring makes you thirsty, stop at the **Elk Drug Store** (176 E. Main St.) to order milk shakes and sodas from an old-fashioned soda fountain. Step back in time in grand style at the 1890 **Weinhard Hotel** (235 E. Main St.; 509-382-4032; weinhard.com), restored in a Victorian motif with 14-foot-high ceilings, elaborate antiques, and a rooftop garden. All 15 rooms have private baths and antique furniture. Enjoy fine Italian specialties at **Weinhard Cafe** (258 E. Main St.; 509-382-1681; weinhardcafe.com). The cafe is open Wed through Sat for lunch and dinner. For healthy comfort food, locals love **Manila Bay Café** (700 Artisan Way, Ste. B; 509-593-0486; manilabaycafe.squarespace.com). Another local favorite, **Skye Book & Brew** (148 E. Main St.; 509-382-4677; skyebookandbrew.com) offers good reads along with microbrews, espresso, and casual fare.

About 15 miles northeast from Dayton, towering wind turbines generate electricity near the tiny hamlet of Turner. Puget Sound Energy offers **Wind Tours** of the Hopkins Ridge Wind Facility. Call the Dayton office, (509) 382-2043.

Dayton is the access point for the Blue Mountains in the Umatilla National Forest, which includes the **Wenaha-Tucannon Wilderness,** an area of steep basalt ridges, talus slopes, and tablelands accessible only by backcountry trails. Wildlife includes Rocky Mountain elk, white-tailed and mule deer, bighorn sheep, black bear, cougar, and coyote. For information, call the Pomeroy Ranger Station at (509) 843-1891.

Palouse Falls State Park, 37 miles north of Dayton, offers a glimpse of what some river canyons in the area looked like before they were dammed. The spectacular falls tumble 198 feet over basalt-column cliffs, surrounded by grass- and sage-covered hills. This 105-acre park offers only 10 primitive campsites. To the south, the **Walla Walla Valley** is known primarily for fertile fields of grain, but since the late 1980s the valley has also hosted more than 100 wineries and large vineyards with grapes that will produce Merlot, Cabernet Sauvignon, and Syrah each year. For lists and maps of tasting rooms, check with the Walla Walla Area Visitor Information Center (26 E. Main St.; 877-998-4748; wallawalla.org) or the **Walla Walla Valley Wine Alliance** (509-526-3117; wallawallawine.com). Collect self-guided tour maps for the nostalgic downtown area and helpful information about the bustling arts scene in this farm and college town. The **Walla Walla Foundry** (405 Woodland Ave.; 509-522-2114; wallawallafoundry.com) specializes in bronze but also produces works in gold, silver, and aluminum. You can visit more than 20 eclectic art galleries and also see 28 historic homes, buildings, and places in the area.

Downtown, after browsing the art galleries, gift shops, historic buildings, and antiques shops along Main Street, join the locals and relax in **Heritage Square** in the heart of town. On one side of the square is a mural of 19th-century downtown Walla Walla. On the opposite wall is the 1902 Odd Fellows building facade. The park also has playground equipment, a picnic area, and restrooms. For a pleasant all-day breakfast or lunch on a sunny day, find an outdoor table under the striped awnings at **Olive Marketplace and Cafe** (21 E. Main St.; 509-526-0200; olivemarketplaceandcafe.com), which also offers a take-out deli, freshly baked pastries, and regional wines. Locals suggest **Colville Street Patisserie** (40 S. Colville St.; 509-301-7289; colvillestreetpatisserie.com) for desserts, wines, and espresso. There's great Italian dining at **Passatempo Taverna** (215 W. Main St.; 509-876-8822; passatempowallawalla.com), which sports a patio and a great local wine list, plus excellent cocktails. **Saffron Mediterranean Kitchen** (330 W. Main St.; 509-525-2112; saffronmediterranean kitchen.com) has polished plates and funky décor. **Public House 124** (124 E. Main St.; 509-876-4511; publichouse124.com) is a local favorite for globally inspired happy hour bites, beer, craft cocktails, and patio seating.

Trust us on this one: Some of the best food in this entire region is being served out of a gas station in Walla Walla. **Andrae's Kitchen** (706 W. Rose St.; 509-572-0728; andraeskitchen.com) is a counter-service restaurant inside a Cenex Gas Station. Also operating as a food truck, the meals here are memorable, with flavorful executions and creative takes on hamburgers, hot dogs, sandwiches, and breakfast foods.

Walla Walla is home to several inviting bed-and-breakfast inns and guest ranches. The 1909 Craftsman-style **Green Gables Inn** (922 Bonsella St.; 509-876-4373; greengablesinn.com), once a residence for nurses, has 5 guest rooms, elegant and comfortable havens with private baths. Or call the **Inn at Blackberry Creek** (1126 Pleasant St.; 509-522-5233; innatblackberrycreek

.com), a 1906 Victorian farmhouse offering travelers 3 guest rooms, a private garden suite, and tasty breakfasts. Other options include staying at the upscale and more modern *Areus* (1903 Smith Rd.; 509-200-9931; areusyoga.com), just outside of town. Stay at a stunningly restored turn-of-the-century farmhouse surrounded by gorgeous gardens and wheat fields at *The Inn at Abeja,* a bed and breakfast with an estate winemaking operation.

wallawalla sweets

About 60 growers produce 39 million pounds of the jumbo-size sweet onions. They're sweeter because of a 6 to 15 percent sugar content, well above the 3 to 5 percent sugar content of regular onions.

Walla Walla has many good dining options. A local favorite is *Clarette's Restaurant* (15 S. Touchet St.; 509-529-3430) for all-American-style fare and all-day breakfast; try *Big House Brewpub* (11 S. Palouse St.; 509-522-2440; bighousebrewpub.com) for pub food and regional ales.

Southwest of town is the splendid *Fort Walla Walla Museum Complex* (755 Myra Rd.; 509-525-7703; fwwm.org) on the grounds of Fort Walla Walla Park. The museum complex includes a re-created pioneer village with more than 20 historic log buildings filled with antique items; and five large museum buildings with additional displays. The historical complex is open daily 10 a.m. to 5 p.m., Apr through late Dec, and 10 a.m. to 4 p.m. Mon through Fri from Jan to Mar. There is an admission.

exploringthe blues

The *Blue Mountains* run from their northern point in Washington's southeastern corner to a southern tip in northeastern Oregon. The Umatilla National Forest is in the Blues. Umatilla is a Native American word for "water rippling over sand."

Be sure to visit the *Whitman Mission National Historic Site* 7 miles west of town (509-529-2761; nps.gov/whmi). It commemorates the Waiilatpu Mission, established by Marcus and Narcissa Whitman in the early 1800s. The visitor center displays and an interpretive trail on the grounds describe the history of the mission and bring to life activities in the Walla Walla Valley between 1836 and 1847, when waves of settlers stopped here on their arduous trek along the Oregon Trail. For a panoramic view of the grounds, walk through the small grove of trees, past the tepee, and up the path to the nearby hilltop monument. The visitor center is open daily 9 a.m. to 4 p.m. in summer and 9 a.m. to 4 p.m. Wed through Sun in winter. It's closed entirely in Dec and Jan.

Places to Stay in Southeast Washington

CLARKSTON

Best Western Rivertree Inn
1257 Bridge St.
(509) 758-9551
bestwestern.com

COLFAX

Potting Shed Guesthouse
911 S. East St.
(509) 397-2014
thepottingshedguesthouse
.com

Union Creek Guest Ranch
2501 Upper Union Flat Rd.
(509) 397-3292

DAYTON

Purple House B&B
415 E. Clay St.
(509) 382-3159
the-purple-house-bb
.business.site

Weinhard Hotel
235 E. Main St.
(509) 382-4032
weinhard.com

PALOUSE

Riverside Retreat and Inn
124 W. Main St.
(208) 301-8014
riversideretreatandinn.com

POMEROY

Last Resort Store & Blue Mountains KOA
2005 Tucannon Rd.
(509) 843-1556
thelastresortrv.com

Maggie's Garden B&B
714 Arlington St.
(509) 843-2495
maggiesgardenbandb.com

PULLMAN

Quality Inn Paradise Creek
1400 SE Bishop Blvd.
(509) 332-0500
qualityinn.com

UNIONTOWN

Churchyard Inn Bed & Breakfast
206 Saint Boniface St.
(509) 229-3200
churchyardinn.com

WALLA WALLA

Areus
1903 Smith Rd.
(509) 200-9931
areusyoga.com

Green Gables Inn
922 Bonsella St.
(509) 876-4373
greengablesinn.com

The Inn at Abeja
2014 Mill Creek Rd.
(509) 522-1234
abeja.net

Inn at Blackberry Creek
1126 Pleasant St.
(509) 522-5233
innatblackberrycreek.com

Places to Eat in Southeast Washington

CLARKSTON/LEWISTON

Rooster's Landing
1010 Port Way
(509) 751-0155
roosterslanding.com

Wasem's Drugstore
800 6th St.
(509) 758-2565
wasems.com

COLFAX

Top Notch Cafe
210 N. Main St.
(509) 397-4569

DAYTON

Manila Bay Café
700 Artisan Way, Ste. B
(509) 593-0486
manilabaycafe.squarespace
.com

Skye Book & Brew
148 E. Main St.
(509) 382-4677
skyebookandbrew.com

Weinhard's Cafe
258 E. Main St.
(509) 382-1681
weinhardcafe.com

PALOUSE

Palouse Caboose Bar and Grill
110 N. Beach St.
(509) 878-1704

INFORMATION CENTERS
& OTHER HELPFUL WEBSITES

Clarkston
(800) 933-2128
clarkstonchamber.org

Colfax
(509) 397-3712
visitcolfax.com

Dayton
(509) 382-4825
historicdayton.com

Pullman
(800) 365-6948
pullmanchamber.com

Walla Walla
(877) 998-4748
wallawalla.org

Walla Walla Valley
(509) 525-0850
wwvchamber.com

Washington Road Conditions
511 for locals or (800) 695-7623
wsdot.com/traffic

PULLMAN

Cafe Moro
100A E. Main St.
(509) 330-6722

Daily Grind Downtown Coffee House
230 Main St.
(509) 334-3380

Ferdinand's Ice Cream Shoppe
Food Quality Building
WSU Campus
(509) 335-2141

TEKOA

The Feeding Station
205 N. Crosby
(509) 284-3141

WALLA WALLA

Andrae's Kitchen
706 W. Rose St.
(509) 572-0728
andraeskitchen.com

Big House Brewpub
11 S. Palouse St.
(509) 522-2440
millcreek-brewpub.com

Clarette's Restaurant
15 S. Touchet St.
(509) 529-3430

Colville Street Patisserie
40 S. Colville St.
(509) 301-7289
colvillestreetpatisserie.com

Olive Marketplace and Cafe
21 E. Main St.
(509) 526-0200
olivemarketplaceandcafe.com

Passatempo Taverna
215 W. Main St.
(509) 876-8822
passatempowallawalla.com

Public House 124
124 E. Main St.
(509) 876-4511
publichouse124.com

Saffron Mediterranean Kitchen
330 W. Main St.
(509) 525-2112
saffronmediterraneankitchen.com

Stone Soup Cafe
105 E. Alder St.
(509) 525-5008
stonesoupcafe.net

Useful Resources

Government Agency Resources

Bicycle Program
Washington State Department of Transportation
Olympia
(360) 705-7277 Bicycle Hotline
wsdot.wa.gov/bike
Ask for the state bicycle map.

National Park Service, US Forest Service Outdoor Recreation Information Center
REI, 222 Yale Ave. North
Seattle
(206) 470-4060
nps.gov and fs.fed.us/recreation
Information on camping, hiking, and trail conditions for western Washington's national
parks and national forests.

North Cascades National Park Service Complex
810 Hwy. 20
Sedro-Woolley
nps.gov/noca and fs.usda.gov/mbs
The complex, about 5 miles east of I-5, is open daily 8 a.m. to 4 p.m. from Memorial
Day weekend through Sept 30 and Mon through Fri (same hours) during the rest of
the year. For information about North Cascades National Park, Ross Lake, and Lake
Chelan, call (360) 854-7200. For information about Mount Baker and Mount Baker
Ranger District call (360) 856-5700. For information about backcountry hiking, call the
Wilderness Information Center in Marblemount at (360) 854-7245. Call (360) 854-2599
for the North Cascades Institute and ask about a catalog of year-round seminars on
the state's natural and cultural history. Farther east on Highway 20 and 14 miles east of
Marblemount, the North Cascades Visitor Center in Newhalem (206-386-4495) is open
daily at 9 a.m. from early May to early Sept.

US–Canadian Border Crossing
(703) 526-4200
cbp.gov

Washington Department of Fish and Wildlife
Olympia
(360) 902-2200
wdfw.wa.gov

Washington State Department of Natural Resources
1111 Washington St. Southeast
PO Box 47000
Olympia, 98504
(360) 902-1000
dnr.wa.gov
DNR manages more than 143 primitive recreation sites with more than 1,100 miles of hiking trails, 4WD roads, and limited backcountry facilities.

Washington State Ferries
Pier 52
801 Alaskan Way
Seattle
For schedule information call (206) 464-6400 in Seattle or in-state only
(888) 808-7977
wsdot.wa.gov/ferries

Washington State Parks
1111 Israel Rd. Southwest
Olympia, 98504
(360) 902-8844
parks.wa.gov
Information on state parks and campgrounds.

Washington Tourism Information
Call (800) 544-1800 and request a *Washington State Visitors' Guide*
experiencewa.com

Other Resources

BIRDS & BIRDING

Audubon Washington: wa.audubon.org (Ask about *The Great Washington State Birding Trail* map.)

Seattle Audubon Society online guide: birdweb.org

Washington Ornithological Society: wos.org

PRINTED MATERIALS

Art Guide Northwest
(206) 367-6831
artguidenw.com
The guide lists all galleries, museums, and antiques shops west of the Cascades.

Exploring Washington's Past: A Road Guide to History
Ruth Kirk and Carmela Alexander
University of Washington Press
This comprehensive handbook describes local history for much of Washington, including fascinating stories and insights about many of the places described in *Washington Off the Beaten Path.*

Washington State Atlas & Gazetteer
This Delorme atlas provides topographical maps covering all of Washington State at approximately half an inch to the mile, making it ideal for exploring back roads.

OUTINGS

Sierra Club, Washington State Chapter
Seattle
For outings and events check
cascade.sierraclub.org.

Sound Experience
Port Townsend
(360) 379-0438
soundexp.org
A nonprofit educational organization specializing in environmental, marine science, and sailing programs for youths and adults aboard the 133-foot-long 1913 tall ship *Adventuress.*

Washington Trails Association
(206) 625-1367
wta.org
WTA is the state's most active volunteer trails-maintenance organization with an excellent website that includes trip notes from hikers in the field.

Washington Water Trails Association
Seattle
(206) 545-9161
wwta.org
Promotes preservation of marine shorelines and the creation of the Cascadia Marine Trail, a network of sites accessible to kayaks and canoes throughout Puget Sound.

Index